Responding to School Violence

Social Problems, Social Constructions

Joel Best and Scott R. Harris, series editors

Responding to
School Violence

Confronting the
Columbine Effect

edited by

Glenn W. Muschert, Stuart Henry,
Nicole L. Bracy, and Anthony A. Peguero

LYNNE
RIENNER
PUBLISHERS

BOULDER
LONDON

KH

Published in the United States of America in 2014 by
Lynne Rienner Publishers, Inc.
1800 30th Street, Boulder, Colorado 80301
www.rienner.com

and in the United Kingdom by
Lynne Rienner Publishers, Inc.
3 Henrietta Street, Covent Garden, London WC2E 8LU

Library of Congress Cataloging-in-Publication Data
 Responding to school violence : confronting the Columbine effect / [edited by]
Glenn W. Muschert, Stuart Henry, Nicole L. Bracy, and Anthony A. Peguero.
 Includes bibliographical references and index.
 ISBN 978-1-58826-907-2 (hc: alk. paper)
 1. School violence—United States—Prevention. 2. Schools—United States—
Safety measures. I. Muschert, Glenn W.
 LB3013.32.R47 2013
 371.7'82—dc23   2013005177

British Cataloguing in Publication Data
A Cataloguing in Publication record for this book
is available from the British Library.

Printed and bound in the United States of America

The paper used in this publication meets the requirements
of the American National Standard for Permanence of
Paper for Printed Library Materials Z39.48-1992.

5 4 3 2 1

10/20/14

Contents

v

Tables and Figures

Tables

Figures

Preface

This book is about the formation of public policy, in this case school antiviolence policy, based on the social construction of a problem through distorted media images and fear of risk. The "Columbine Effect" refers to the way that a series of events symbolized in a tragic massacre can become the exemplar for a set of policies that have both questionable effects on the problem and negative and far-ranging effects on those subjected to such policies.

The book emerged from a scholarly discussion among the editors (sociologists who study crime and deviance), which paralleled discourse taking place in a number of disciplines, including sociology, criminology, education, and cultural studies. The points of departure for that discussion were two articles: First, Glenn Muschert and Anthony Peguero's 2010 "The Columbine Effect and School Anti-Violence Policy" argued that fear generated by Columbine-style school attacks often motivated the institution of irrational school policies to combat violence. Second, Stuart Henry's 2009 "School Violence Beyond Columbine: A Complex Problem in Need of an Interdisciplinary Analysis" discussed the broad nature of school violence and the existence of a wide range of causes (and thus solutions) that lie at various levels of social organization, including the individual, group, organizational/institutional, community/neighborhood, and social/cultural levels. The integration of the ideas contained in these two articles provided a basis for this book. Each of the contributors was asked to consider the Muschert and Peguero (2010) and Henry (2009) articles and then add their own interpretations and perspectives to the discussion.

The outcome presented here is a complex argument, and of course we are not the first to consider such issues. Indeed there are developing literatures in the social sciences that address both the social construction of the school violence problem and school antiviolence policies (see Herda-Rapp 2003; Killingbeck 2001; Williams 2005). Our unique contribution here is an analysis of the interrelated issues of the social construction of school violence as a social problem and the policy responses intended to reduce or control violence in North American schools. In connecting these two intimately related elements of the school violence issue, we present in a single volume three important aspects: (1) the constructionist work on school violence, (2) policy analysis of school antiviolence policies, and (3) a forward-looking and prescriptive view of how social scientists and policy analysts can effectively understand and respond to varying forms of violence in schools.

1

The Columbine Effect

Glenn W. Muschert, Stuart Henry,
Nicole L. Bracy, and Anthony A. Peguero

Numerous school shootings or threats for intended school shootings
that have shocked and frightened the entire nation have been featured
in the media both before and after the massacre in Littleton, Colorado.
We have been bombarded with media images of dangerous white, suburban, affluent youths and notions that schools are far more violent
places than ever. This is not necessarily the case, but now those in
power are paying attention to these images, and they are motivated to
do something about the problem. (Williams 2005, p. 3)

For well over a decade, the 1999 shootings at Columbine High
School have framed how we perceive and respond to continued
occurrences of school-related violence. This phenomenon has
resulted in a social, cultural, political, and media image that schools
are dangerous places for youths, in spite of the reality that such incidences are rare and that the rate of school violence has decreased
since the mid-1990s (DeVoe et al. 2005; Dinkes et al. 2006).[1] Indeed
schools are statistically one of the safest places for youths, with only
1 percent of youths ages 12–18 reporting violent victimization, and
less than .5 percent reporting serious violent victimization in 2009
(Robers, Zhang, and Truman 2012). Nonetheless, the discourse about,
and responses to, school violence have been ardent and alarming. The
social problem of school violence, especially extreme violence such
as rampage shootings, remains a source of fear, and risk tolerance for
these events is extremely low. The general anxiety about the risk of
school shootings, when coupled with the consensus about their intol-
erability, has been a catalyst to the development of wide-scale policy
responses for managing this and related social problems that are

based more on fear than fact, and more on reaction to images than on sound judgment based on evidence.

In the same year as the Columbine shootings, the social theorist Beck (1999; see also Giddens 1999) posited the global emergence of a "risk society," one in which our technological and social systems are out of control, and where people are future-directed and increasingly preoccupied with controlling or limiting risk for human or technical events that are the "normal" outgrowth of complex social systems. While traditional conceptions of such fears derived from moral panics connected to groups that were demonized as "folk devils," this new conception viewed terrible events, such as school violence, as deriving from systematic complexity. From this point of view, the risk and danger are seen as inevitable and the only possible societal response is to either reduce the risk of such events or to deal with them more effectively, more rapidly, and more demonstrably when they do occur.

Because the 1999 Columbine school shooting is an arguable impetus for the social, cultural, political, and media belief that schools are dangerous places for youths, Muschert and Peguero (2010; Cloud 1999) adopted the term the "Columbine Effect," which refers to the way public fear of school rampage shootings has changed how we think about school violence and has affected the types of policies implemented in pursuit of school safety. The fundamental premise is that the Columbine shootings remain a potent (yet inaccurate) image of violence in contemporary American schools. The Columbine Effect phenomenon includes media portrayal and public perception of school violence as ubiquitous, parents' fear over the safety of their children in schools and demands for security, and school administrators' response to parents' demands via the institution of antiviolence policies and practices. Whether these policies are necessary, appropriate, or effective is contested by many scholars (e.g., Kupchik 2010; Lyons and Drew 2006), by some practitioners (Beckham 2009), and by authors of the chapters in this volume. Often, such policies address only a narrow range of the multiple interrelated causes behind school violence, and emerging research suggests they may have unintended negative consequences for students, schools, and communities.

Clearly, school violence was a concern well before the 1999 shootings at Columbine High School in Colorado; however, the Columbine shootings helped to crystallize the issue. Columbine sparked broad social concerns regarding school violence and subsequent scrutiny of school antiviolence policies. Typically this discourse assumed two debatable facts: first, that the levels of school violence were unacceptably high and rising, and second, that current antiviolence policies were insufficient, ineffective, or nonexistent. Despite the rarity of rampage attacks on schools, the fear generated by school shootings has widely influenced antiviolence policies in urban schools, suburban schools, and even rural schools.

The perception of the problem of school violence is related to the perception of, and tolerance for, the risk of violence and victimization in schools. While school shootings are undoubtedly horrific tragedies and grave in their consequences, they are extremely rare and they occupy the extreme end of the continuum of school violence. Shocking events like Columbine and the 2012 Sandy Hook shootings exert disproportionate leverage on the discussion (and subsequent control responses) about school violence, and many policies instituted may be irrational in their applications to preventing more common (and often less severe) forms of violence in schools.

Henry (2009) also argues that antiviolence policies tend to look at school violence in fragmented ways, which reflects a disciplinary analysis of social problems. Such explanations about the causes of school violence tend to be at the individual or micro-level of analysis, such as theories of rational choice and routine activities, psychological and developmental explanations about why school-age children become violent, and social control theory about the lack of attachment and involvement by youths in conventional culture. Therefore, the consequential policies implemented to deal with the problem of school violence have focused on controlling access to schools, better detection, preemptive intervention, closer supervision, zero-tolerance, and peer mediation. These school antiviolence policies, Henry argues, are too narrow, and they fail to consider the multiple causal components of this complex problem, which include the interrelated role of teachers, school administrators, educational practices and effective pedagogy, school district policy, cultural framing, gendered educational expectations, and the changing state of family and community relations in a postmodern society. In short, they fail to deal with the wider cultural and structural context of the school.

However, instead of simply critiquing the existing policies for failure to address the scope of school violence, this volume examines school antiviolence policy in the context of the totality and complexity of the problem, seeking to relate specific policies to different levels and dimensions of the problem. Rather than taking policies in isolation or as alternatives, this book argues that effective prevention policy requires the multiple, cumulative causes of school violence to be simultaneously addressed through a comprehensive web of policies. We do so to provide readers with more than critique, by working to connect the discursive and policy aspects of this field with more practical and applied aspects. Thus we conclude the volume with statements about policies or approaches that might prove to be among the most progressive and effective measures available today. It is our hope that the various audiences who might read this volume (among them scholars of all types, school administrators, teachers, concerned parents, journalists, and security personnel) might become more knowledgeable about what seems to work to mitigate the challenges of school security without causing damage to one or more of the levels of social organization that undergird the educational process.

In summary, the core arguments of this book are that since the Columbine shootings, the development of school antiviolence policy: (1) has been based on fear driven by extreme, low-probability events, such as school rampage shootings; (2) may have unintended negative effects in (a) damaging the school learning environment, (b) undermining relationships among students and teachers, and/or (c) exacerbating the problems of violence that they are intended to alleviate; and (3) distracts from the development of a comprehensive, multilevel approach to deal with the multifaceted causes of the problem. We propose moving beyond Columbine Effect policy.

The Organization of the Book

This volume proceeds in three parts: the first examines the role of fear and the so-called Columbine Effect, the second examines contemporary antiviolence policies in schools, and the third concentrates on alternative responses to school violence. The first part builds directly on the foundation laid by Muschert and Peguero in their article on the Columbine Effect (2010).

Part 1: Contexts

The first part, on contexts, lays a foundation for understanding current anxieties about school violence in their historical and cultural contexts, and for situating the discussion within broader academic discussions about youth violence and reactions to threats to school security, including both rampage-style attacks and other, more mundane forms of misbehavior.

In Chapter 2, "Fear of School Violence in the Post-Columbine Era," Glenn W. Muschert and Eric Madfis provide a constructionist starting point for the volume by exploring the role of risk and risk tolerance in contemporary society. The chapter explores the historical development of anxiety about violence in schools, the influence of highly publicized school crimes such as school shootings, and this tendency within the wider discourses of fear and risk. The chapter concludes by exploring what might be seen as rational, feasible alternatives to such a discourse.

In Chapter 3, "Negotiation of Care and Control in School Safety," Curtis A. Brewer and Jane Clark Lindle discuss how the Columbine Effect was the forced reinterpretation of the commonsense notion that safety is an essential requirement for learning. However, when relationships in schools are disrupted, learning ceases. Responses to disruptions actually perpetrate uncertainty and increase perceptions about lack of safety. In this chapter, the authors discuss how school personnel continually balance their duty to provide a low-risk environment with their professional ethic of care. School personnel experience stress from policies and hierarchies that mandate control of schooling with simultaneous professional demands for nurturing relationships. Through a discussion of the common dilemmas faced in schools and the application of our framework, they argue for school administrators to embrace their dual obligations of safety and concern in the midst of daily conflicts. In sum, Brewer and Lindle argue that school leaders must become adept at "walking the line" in recognition of their role in negotiating these dual obligations across multiple social levels.

In Chapter 4, "The Dynamics of School Discipline in a Neoliberal Era," Aaron Kupchik and Thomas J. Catlaw discuss why schools have acted so similarly in their efforts to promote safety, despite evidence that their efforts may have little effect or even backfire. Reducing students' democratic participation in schools through authoritarian discipline was one solution among many available in response to the moral panic over school violence, but it is by far the most common one. Though a Columbine Effect certainly has been important, the tragedy at Columbine did not ensure policy action in the particular form that we have seen. As Kupchik and Catlaw argue, contemporary school security and punishment practices are informed by, and implemented against, the backdrop of longer-term general trends in US governance and policymaking. These broader governance trends, referred to as "neoliberalism," constitute the interpretive context within which schools and policy makers make sense of events such

as Columbine and assess the menu of practically available and politically appropriate responses.

Part 2: Contemporary Policies

The chapters in the second part, "Contemporary Policies," demonstrate how the public's fear of school violence has influenced school
policy changes, most notably changes to school discipline and security. This second part draws on the multilevel theory of school violence developed by Henry (2009) to argue not only that these policies
are directed at a narrow range of causes and therefore insufficient,
but also that they often produce negative, unintended consequences.
Although each of the chapters varies in its precise focus, they all
examine aspects of school discipline in contemporary society, and all
point out that there are many unintended negative consequences to
how security is conducted in schools.

Lynn A. Addington opens the part with an overview of discipline
in the aftermath of Columbine in Chapter 5, "Surveillance and Security Approaches Across Public School Levels." In particular she
focuses on policies and practices that involve using visible security
measures in public schools as a preventive strategy. Using a nationally representative sample of public elementary, middle, and high
schools in the United States, Addington highlights the rapid increase
in the use of visible security measures in the decade since Columbine: notably, the use of security officers, surveillance cameras, and
metal detectors across all school levels. This chapter also identifies
differences in schools that employ security officers, surveillance
cameras, and metal detectors.

In Chapter 6, "Zero-Tolerance Policies," Aviva M. Rich-Shea
and James Alan Fox discuss how the zero-tolerance approach to
school discipline arose with the federal requirement for automatic
suspensions and expulsions of students caught bringing a firearm to
school. Mass school shootings in suburban communities reinforced
the pressure for all school administrators to institute a tough disciplinary policy. However, research evaluating the effectiveness of zero-
tolerance has failed to uncover measurable improvements in school
safety. In fact, these policies have been found to breed a hostile
school climate and a decline in academic achievement in the face of
increased school exclusions. The Community Oriented Policing Services (COPS) program provided federal funding to accelerate the
placement of armed police called School Resource Officers (SROs)

in public middle and high schools. While their duties vary from school to school, their fundamental responsibility is to "prevent another Columbine," with training focused on neutralizing an active shooter. Various researchers have noted that the confluence of zero-tolerance and SROs produces a punitive school climate and forms the bedrock of the school-to-prison pipeline. The authors use Black's theory of law as a theoretical framework and their own research as evidence to show that the more fully an administration embraces a zero-tolerance approach, the more likely the school is both to have an SRO and to use the SRO to institute more formal methods of social control. Thus, the SRO operates as a tool in the toolkit of formal social control utilized disproportionately by authoritarian school administrators.

In Chapter 7, "Safe Schools Initiatives and the Shifting Climate of Trust," Valerie Steeves and Gary T. Marx use ethnography to examine the impact of formal school antiviolence policies and related behaviors in two Canadian schools in the years following the Columbine High School shootings. Steeves and Marx build on Henry's (2009) insight that school violence is the result of a complex set of influences that operate at the institutional and individual levels. In particular, they argue that the policies enacted in response to Columbine to reduce individual acts of violence have reshaped the social relationships between administrators, teachers, and students, and inadvertently created a school climate that undermines students' trust in the ability of school administrators to respond to violent incidents. The chapter provides two added dimensions to the volume, first, a detailed description of antiviolence policies, and second, a view of the Columbine Effect in Canada.

Chapter 8, "Racial Implication of School Discipline and Climate," by Kelly Welch and Allison Ann Payne, discusses how harsh disciplinary practices are applied unequally in response to student violations, and the fact that black students are more likely than white students to be subjected to relatively strict treatment and harsh punishment. They argue that, coupled with the fear of school-based violence that characterizes the Columbine Effect, criminal stereotypes of black youths may exacerbate that impulse to intensify school discipline, particularly for minorities. This is a trend that mirrors patterns in the US penal system: criminal justice institutions have not only become increasingly punitive, despite two decades of decreasing crime rates, but have also produced a dramatic racial disparity in who is punished in the criminal justice system relative to representations in the larger national population. The authors discuss the possibility of how to restore racial equity within school institutions.

Concluding Part 2, Chapter 9, "Violence Prevention and Intervention," by Jun Sung Hong, Dorothy L. Espelage, Christopher J. Ferguson, and Paula Allen-Meares, assesses school antiviolence programs and policies that were enacted in the aftermath of the Columbine High School shootings in 1999 within the context of Bronfenbrenner's (1976, 1979) ecological systems theory. The authors argue that effective school violence prevention and intervention programs and policies require multidisciplinary and integrative approaches. Building on the works of several researchers, they examine recent school and youth violence programs and policies within the context of the ecological systems levels: micro-, meso-, exo-, and macro-systems. The authors then discuss alternative ways to best better address school violence and enhance school safety in US schools.

Part 3: Alternatives

The chapters in the third part, "Alternatives," examine different approaches to the risks of school violence, which rely on a comprehensive view of school antiviolence policy based on a causal analysis of the problem. In this part, the contributing authors discuss the kinds of policies that a comprehensive, multilevel analysis of school violence suggest will be effective for reducing school violence and promoting positive outcomes for students, teachers, and communities. It is in this final part that the volume fully integrates a discussion of the environment of fear in contemporary schools, the policy problem and its failures, a cause-based analysis of the problem, and the potential for a new direction in school antiviolence policy. Here we offer a point of departure for future development in school antiviolence policies.

Jeffrey R. Sprague, Daniel W. Close, and Hill M. Walker address the topic of school violence from the perspective of a social-ecological framework in Chapter 10, "Encouraging Positive Behavior." This theoretical formulation offers traction in defining and cataloging risks to school safety as well as in conceptualizing intervention approaches to reducing such risks. In particular, they describe a well-established, effective, and broadly accepted social-ecological intervention, called School-Wide Positive Behavioral Intervention and Supports (SWPBIS). In addition to improving school safety, SWPBIS can also lead to improvements in school climate, a positive schooling ecology, and enhanced academic achievement. Evidence for the efficacy of SWPBIS is discussed along with its key components and details of its implementation.

In Chapter 11, "Ecological, Peacemaking, and Feminist Considerations," Daniel Hillyard and M. Joan McDermott discuss how "get tough," retributive, and fear-driven school antiviolence policies are related to broad social structures and cultural values concerning crime, and how alternatives to getting tough seek to transform those structures and values. Hillyard and McDermott link the punishment response to social inequality and discuss how both peacemaking and feminist perspectives seek to change "get tough" systems based on domination of some groups by others. The authors also discuss the punishment response in terms of its societal and individual consequences, and highlight the significance of transformation of the individual, as well as social transformation, to both feminism and transformative justice perspectives. The authors root their analysis in literatures on the criminalization of deviance and overcriminalization (the limits of the criminal sanctioning).

Finally, in Chapter 12, "Diagnosing and Preventing School Shootings," Douglas Kellner argues that episodes of mass violence like the shootings at Virginia Tech, Columbine High School, Chardon High School in Ohio, and Oikos University in Oakland are complex historical events and require a multiperspectivist vision. Addressing the causes of problems like domestic terrorism, school shootings, and societal violence involves a range of apparently disparate and wider social and cultural phenomena, such as a critique of male socialization and construction of ultramasculine male identities, the prevalence of gun culture and (para)militarism, and a media culture that promotes violence and retribution while circulating and sensationalizing media spectacle and a culture of celebrity. Kellner presents a critical diagnostic of the key macro-level reasons for school shootings and suggests ways to reorient educational systems to alleviate some of the underlying causes.

Overall, the following eleven chapters in this book provide an interwoven critique of the limits of public policy formation in the context of contemporary social problems. The authors highlight the process, which is distorted by images of fear and the consequences for schools, students, and their communities, as well as for the educational process, of the failure to take a more measured approach to policy formation. They also offer a way forward toward a comprehensive approach to the development of school antiviolence policy that goes beyond the Columbine Effect and addresses the interconnected and multifaceted nature of the problem.

Note

1. Although between the years 2003 and 2006, the number of deaths from violence in school increased, it has been falling ever since, and in 2009 it was at its lowest since 1999–2000 (Robers, Zhang, and Truman 2012).

Part 1
Contexts

2

Fear of School Violence in the Post-Columbine Era

Glenn W. Muschert and Eric Madfis

In recent decades, school antiviolence policies and other forms of discipline seem, in part, driven by fear of extreme violence, such as multiple-victim rampage-type attacks with guns and explosives. Although the consequences of such attacks are grave, thankfully they are extremely rare. Despite the low probability of such events, they exert a disproportionately strong leverage on our conceptions of school violence and misbehavior, and therefore may skew the focus of school disciplinary practices away from more common, less severe forms of rule transgression. At the same time, school discipline, particularly in its more punitive forms, seems to have expanded greatly, especially in police presence in schools, zero-tolerance policies, mandatory punishments, and use of school exclusion. The contemporary regime of school discipline is characterized by a one-size-fits-all approach, as it takes remarkably similar forms in widely divergent school contexts, regardless of whether schools have high levels of student misbehavior (see Kupchik 2010).

Just as law enforcement and anti-terror squads refer to our contemporary climate as the post-9/11 era, some practitioners of school discipline refer to the post-Columbine era in schools (Madfis 2012). Americans have long been aware that some schools (especially those in urban, disorganized areas) experience higher levels of violence and other misbehavior (and therefore are in need of intensive security). However, they were often able to disassociate from the phenomenon by discursively relegating such threats to different locales, ones that putatively were subject to such threats due to the presence of a variety of factors, such as a prevalence of racial and ethnic minorities, high rates of poverty, exposure to the urban underclass, or a culture of violence. In terms of the problem awareness of school violence, the 1999 Columbine shootings changed that, as white, middle-class Americans (those traditionally more protected from exposure to risks) were no longer able to disassociate from the potential threat posed by cases of extreme violence. Generally, this spawned a great deal of anxiety, and despite Columbine's status as an infamously tragic case of school violence, the term *Columbine* has taken on a life of its own. Thus, in reference to discipline and security in schools, we hear such statements as *pulling a Columbine* (meaning that someone undertakes a Columbine-style rampage attack), journalists refer to more recent rampage attacks on high schools as *another Columbine* that takes place in the *Columbine style* (meaning all subsequent attacks rhetorically refer back to Columbine), and we hear about the *pre-Columbine* and *post-Columbine* eras (meaning that Columbine changed things so much that we now have to think about school crime and safety in entirely new ways; see Kupchik and Bracy 2009). Indeed, as it is typically used, the term *Columbine* is a "keyword for a complex set of emotions surrounding youths, fear, risk, and delinquency in 21st Century America" (Muschert 2007a, p. 365).

The term *Columbine Effect* is used to describe the leveraging of anxiety about youth social problems in the expansion of school discipline, particularly punitive measures aimed at preventing extreme forms of violence (Muschert and Peguero 2010). The spirit of this chapter, if not the volume as a whole, is the exploration of the Columbine Effect as the cause of a disjuncture and underlying irrationality in the ways in which schools go about achieving safety. Despite the seeming rationality of punitive disciplinary measures in schools, social scientists often argue that such processes (at best) ignore the underlying causes of many forms of rule transgression in schools, and (at worst) may exacerbate the very causes they are designed to address. This irrationality is often based on misconceptions about what causes (as well as what prevents) school misbehavior, and is driven by ill-founded anxiety about rare, though extremely horrible, events.

Studying how a problem is understood, regardless of whether that understanding is verified with scientific evidence, is a crucial part of understanding any social problem. For each perceived social problem there is a solution, which is, indeed, implied in the problem frame itself. Sociologists of social problems have noted the importance of understanding problem frames, as they define what a problem is about, as well as what a problem is not about. Such frames can be read in a number of ways, via following the logic of social policies backward to their source in problem frames, or via studying the varieties of public discourse that occur during problem definition. The discussion that ensued following the Columbine event is of particular import as this event continues to influence contemporary practices of school discipline, as Columbine exerts a great symbolic leverage (perhaps more than its rightful share) on the understanding of school violence as a problem and on disciplinary efforts to prevent or respond to school misbehavior. Such occurrences are known as problem-defining events (Lawrence 2001), which means that the frames applied to these landmark incidents become a subsequent form of shorthand in future discussion of the problem, and are applied to events or problems that are similar enough to be interpreted under a comparable rubric.

   In this chapter, we discuss the evolution of youth violence and its control over the past few decades. In this, we take a longer view of the issue, examining the development of the problem of school misbehavior and the risks posed by the youthful transgression of rules. We then examine risk tolerance in schools, which has become notably low. In society in general, we have become risk intolerant, and perhaps especially so in schools, where we have observed great calls for risk assessment. Where risks are unacceptable, we observe the rapid deployment of efforts to control risks to school safety, often in the form of punitive measures (although not exclusively so). We then conclude by revisiting the role of risk tolerance in schools, placing the tendency in its proper context, and by suggesting some rational, feasible discursive alternatives to the present anxiety-driven conception of school discipline.

A Recent Cultural History of Youth Violence

The Columbine case is an infamous incident of school violence; however, it is not the only or even the first such horrible case to have occurred in US history, nor should it be considered as an entirely idiosyncratic case. Rather, it is more appropriate to consider Columbine as occupying an extreme end of the continuum of school violence, one connected with all other cases of school violence, most of them both more common and less severe than school rampages. While we do not wish to overstate the cultural relevancy of Columbine by making it stand out as a unique case, we nonetheless consider Columbine and similar attacks important because they exert a larger leverage on the discourse of school violence than do other, more common cases. In this section, we situate Columbine in its historical context so that we can identify it as a case emerging from its proper discursive field, and so that we can identify how it punctuated the broader, decades-long discourse on school violence.

The 1990s, when the phenomenon emerged as an ascendant social problem, was an interesting decade for youth violence. Certainly the 1990s were not the first time that youth violence was perceived as problematic—consider the urban youths who were the subject of much attention during the Progressive Era of the late nineteenth and early twentieth centuries, or the oppositional youth culture of the 1950s, as iconized by James Dean or Marlon Brando. In the 1980s, public anxiety focused on out-of-control urban youths who were associated with criminal youth gangs. However, in the 1990s, the problem was rediscovered with renewed vigor (see Spencer 2011 for a detailed analysis), and fears about youth violence reach a feverish pitch when media accounts portrayed horrible phenomena such as groups of "wilding" youths prowling the streets of urban areas and engaging in violence for the pleasure of it (Derber 1996; Welch, Price, and Yankey 2002) and extremely high rates of violence in some major US cities (see, e.g., Colomy and Greiner 2000). These reports were corroborated by official statistics on crime published by the US government, which indicated that 1994 was the year in which the arrest rate for juvenile violent index crimes (i.e., homicide, aggravated assault, robbery, and rape) peaked. By the mid-1990s, the US public discourse focused strongly on youth violence as a social problem; however, the variety of youth violence of concern was of a particular type: centered in urban areas, carried out by racial or ethnic minorities, and understood as an outgrowth of these youths' exposure to the criminogenic environment of the urban underclasses.

In response to public outcry and anxiety about the risks of youth violence, policymakers and those in the juvenile justice system intensified a punitive turn that had begun a decade or two earlier, enacting more punitive measures to crack down specifically on youth violence. Among these were easier transfer of youth offenders to adult court (sometimes mandatory transfer for some crimes), expanding the types of penalties that juvenile courts could apply to violent offenders, and reducing the ability of juvenile courts to shield young offenders from receiving adult criminal records or sentences.

Such punitive measures emerged from the tendency to think of the worst examples as typical of the problem as a whole—as is the case when school rampages symbolize school violence in general. In the mid-1990s, the worst youth violent offenders were purported to be particularly bad seeds among violent urban youths, known as the juvenile superpredators (Kappeler and Potter 2005; Spencer 2011, ch. 2). Such youths behaved apparently without remorse, acted out in violent ways without hesitation, and were considered to be beyond rehabilitation. What is more, the maturation of this crop of super-predators signaled an impending crisis for crime in America, as these youths were expected to mature into career criminals of the super-predator type (Dilulio 1995; Fox 1996). Though the emergence of these ideal criminals was erroneously predicted as a coming crisis for urban areas and those who police them, as far as most Americans were concerned, it was possible to feel unaffected by this variety of youth violence. Within the next five years, that was to change radically.

By the end of the 1990s, the generalized concept of youth violence expanded to include suburban school shooters, largely as a result of media attention to a series of high-profile school-shooting events in places such as Frontier Middle School in Washington, Bethel Regional High School in Alaska, Pearl High School in Mississippi, Health High School in Kentucky, Westside Middle School in Arkansas, and Thurston High School in Oregon. In the school shootings that took place from 1996 to 1998, the media framing was largely localized or regionalized; however, in 1999 the Columbine shootings brought the discourse of school shootings to a national level (Muschert 2009; Muschert and Carr 2006). As an apparent widespread national phenomenon, it was no longer possible for "mainstream America" (i.e., the white suburban middle class) to disregard the threat of extreme school violence, meaning that such events were no longer unfortunate events that happened in some distant blighted urban area. As reported repeatedly in the news, school shootings "could happen anywhere," and therefore such a threat demanded a response. Consistent with the prevailing punitive attitude relating to crime and delinquency that had begun in the decades before Columbine, the policy responses instituted after Columbine generally entailed "getting tough" on those who misbehave in schools. However, Columbine seems to have been a catalyst to punitive policy, one that intensified the already punitively oriented regime of school security.

Ironically, the predictions made earlier in the decade about the threats posed by a crop of violent youth superpredators did not pan out. Rather than observing an increased rate of juvenile offenses driven by a core of urban youth offenders, the rate of juvenile offense and victimization (particularly in violent crimes) declined precipitously from 1994 onward (Butts 2000). If youths were becoming less violent in general, schools were becoming safer as well, for students and teachers alike. Indeed, the percentage of teachers who had been threatened or physically attacked by their students similarly declined (Fox and Burstein 2010). This background knowledge was lost on many Americans, who consumed a wave of school rampage coverage that greatly exaggerated their prevalence and potential risk (Aitken 2001; Burns and Crawford 1999; Cornell 2006). In fact, the events at Columbine High School amounted to the most followed story for the entire year of 1999 (Pew Research Center 1999), and indeed the case has been heavily discussed for many subsequent years (see Kupchik and Bracy 2009). As a result, fear of schoolyard killers became rather commonplace throughout the United States (Gallup 1999; Kiefer 2005; Newport 2006), and the discourse regarding the prevalence, significance, and amelioration of school violence as a social problem changed drastically.

An important aspect of this evolving discourse regarding school violence is that fears about youth violence rhetorically moved away from urban youths as a focus of concern, and began to center on the suburban school shooter as a new brand youth superpredator. This transition seems to be punctuated aptly in the media's portrayal of the Columbine shooters: Dylan Klebold and Eric Harris. As Spencer (2005) points out, youthful offenders often create ambiguity, because we want to exact retribution (especially when they do horrible things), but we also simultaneously have a tendency to view youth as a factor that mitigates moral responsibility for wrongdoing. This was especially the case in the Columbine shootings in 1999 (see Spencer and Muschert 2009 for details). For example, the May 3, 1999, cover of *Time* featured large pictures of both shooters, smiling and jejune, beneath the caption, "The Monsters Next Door." Bordering the top and left sides of the cover were smaller photos of the thirteen fatally wounded victims from the attack (twelve students and one teacher). The visuals of the cover suggest a doublecasting of the shooters, a cognitive position that reveals moral ambiguity regarding the shooter's culpability (see Cerulo 1998). On the one hand, they had recently carried out a notably horrible massacre, but, on the other hand, they appeared youthful and innocent. In the media discourse, any sense that the shooters could be understood (even if their actions were undoubtedly to be condemned) was suppressed, as efforts to understand and justify are too easily conflated, especially in the emotionally charged atmosphere following school rampages.

Ultimately, the Columbine shooters remain widely infamous yet poorly understood, despite efforts to examine their life histories and motivations (see Brown and Merritt 2002; Cullen 2009; Larkin 2007). Aside from the meaning that such discourse has for our understanding of the Columbine event (as discussed elsewhere Muschert and Spencer 2009a and 2009b), the emergence of the rampage school shooter as a cultural trope (Tonso 2009) allowed for the transference of the anxiety about youth superpredators away from urban minority youths and criminal gangs onto white suburban youths, particularly in the school setting. This development was new, because it focused the more generalized sense of anxiety about youth violence specifically in schools. Parents, teachers, and administrators now worried that suburban superpredators, largely under the radar of agents of social control, populated the classrooms of high schools across America. In effect, the Columbine shooters became the poster boys for a new brand of violent youth offender (Muschert 2007a), one that necessitated widespread changes in security practices in secondary schools.[1]

It is within this cultural backdrop that the current regime of discipline in American schools continued its development, one increasingly characterized in particular by low risk tolerance. In the post-Columbine period, security measures in schools are increasingly punitive, especially when compared with security measures in place just two or three decades ago. We now observe comparatively harsher penalties for misbehavior (including zero-tolerance policies), mandatory school exclusions such as suspension or expulsion for a variety of offenses, greater presence of security personnel (including police), and greater use of surveillance technologies. These practices mirror similar developments observed in the criminal justice system, and the alarming implication is that students are increasingly exposed to prison-like regimes of control (Hirschfield 2008; Kupchik 2010; Monahan and Torres 2010). All of this has occurred during a period of declining rates of juvenile delinquency, including delinquent acts in schools (Kupchik 2010). The image of the rampage school shooter, though a wildly inaccurate exemplar of a typical youth offender, nonetheless serves as a potent image that underlies our worst fears about what could happen in schools. To the extent that this image of youth offenders is inaccurate, our efforts to maintain security in schools may be equally off base.

Low Tolerance of Risk and
Increased Desire for Risk Assessment

The facts are that schools are the safest location that exists for American children, school shootings are rare events, and rampage attacks in the infamous model of Columbine High School where multiple victims are killed are even less likely (Donohue, Schiraldi, and Ziedenberg 1998). However, such incidents warrant serious concern, for when they do occur, they not only produce casualties but also leave many survivors and bystanders with post-traumatic stress (James 2009; Schwarz and Kowalski 1991) and create extensive fear among the larger public (Altheide 2002; Burns and Crawford 1999; Harding, Fox, and Mehta 2002). It is just this combination of low probability and high potential cost (which Muschert and Peguero 2010 call "compositional risk" and "degree of risk," respectively) that has altered the landscape of discussions about school safety and security. Contemporary schools in the United States often deliberately assess risk and craft school disciplinary and security policy with the mindset that school rampage shootings are possible and even likely (Madfis 2012). This may reflect what Tversky and Kahneman (1986, p. 49) refer to as the "anchoring" heuristic whereby people identify harm and estimate likelihoods by basing their knowledge on a particular starting point that may not reflect reality. As the media disproportionately focuses on particularly sensational and violent events such as school shootings, these types of occurrences are misperceived to be more commonplace. Certainly rare but devastating events must be taken seriously (as Posner 2004 points out), but it is not necessarily a given that high potential costs (even the lives of innocent youths) automatically supersede low probabilities.[2] Given the current news/entertainment environment, in which media conglomerates capitalize on the most rare and sensational events in order to instill fear and maintain viewership (Kappeler and Potter 2005), however, the perception that a series of school rampage shootings at the turn of the twenty-first century constituted a full-fledged crime wave became rather commonplace. The fact that the vast majority of school rampage attacks occurred in middle- and upper-class suburban and rural areas made the threat all the more tangible and frightening to schools previously unconcerned with school violence (Kimmel and Mahler 2003; Lawrence 2007; Simon 2007).

Therefore, when the genuinely high potential cost of school rampage fused with the perception of high probability, school rampages came to be viewed as a risk that could not be tolerated and must be avoided at nearly any cost. Students' civil liberties and schools' limited financial resources were both worth sacrificing in the name of school safety. As a result, all schools, even those in comparatively more affluent suburban and rural regions of the nation with few persistent problems with crime or violence, have experienced sweeping changes in largely two forms: (1) the implementation of risk and threat assessment procedures designed to predict the occurrence of similar events in the future and (2) the increase in various forms of punitive disciplinary policy and school security. Both of these developments make perfect sense within a larger cultural context wherein society is increasingly concerned with the prediction and alleviation of risk (Beck 1992; Giddens 1999; Luhman 1991). In these formulations, the modern "risk society" entails a mind-set where there is a preoccupation with the future and the systematic manipulation of risk is achievable, global, and primary.

The administration of justice, in particular, has moved toward an "actuarial justice" mind-set that reorients penology toward "techniques for identifying, classifying, and managing groups assorted by levels of dangerousness" (Feeley and Simon 1994, p. 173). Rather than opting for intervention as a means of retribution or rehabilitation, this so-called "new penology" sees crime as inevitable and seeks instead to manage risk and regulate danger (Rigakos and Hadden 2001). Likewise, Steiker (1998, p. 774) argues that our justice system increasingly attempts

> to identify and neutralize dangerous individuals before they commit crimes by restricting their liberty in a variety of ways. In pursuing this goal, the state often will expand the functions of the institutions primarily involved in the criminal justice system—namely, the police and the prison. But other analogous institutions, such as the juvenile justice system and the civil commitment process, are also sometimes tools of, to coin another phrase, the "preventive state."

This preventive imperative and the actuarial mind-set that criminal conduct is an unavoidable but manageable risk have certainly "expanded" into school disciplinary and security practices. With this frame of mind, it may be inevitable for certain students to possess the desire to fatally harm their peers, but the risk of rampage killing may be mitigated through the systematic prediction of prospective school shooters and by monitoring and securing the physical space of school buildings. It is to the first of these new developments, the diverse field of violence risk assessment, to which we now turn.

On Violence Risk Assessment

According to scholars documenting its origins, the field of violence risk assessment has advanced from early empirical studies in the 1970s that attempted to predict violence to a more complex, multi-disciplinary research literature that deals not only with the estimation and assessment of future violence potential, but also with how best to manage and intervene with high-violence risk individuals (Andrade 2009). Knowledge gleaned from this field is frequently used by numerous practitioners, both for "adult and juvenile courts, parole and probation departments, and correctional facilities, as well as for child protective services agencies, school departments, community mental health centers, and more" (Andrade, O'Neill, and Diener 2009, p. 3). While all methods of risk assessment engage in the "scientific effort to identify ways to improve estimates of future violence," the approaches vary substantially (Grisso 2009, p. xvi). Reddy and colleagues (2001) codified and categorized these varied approaches as profiling, guided professional judgment, automated decisionmaking, and threat assessment.[3]

Profiling

Profiling, often qualified as criminal profiling (Douglas et al. 1986; Kocsis 2007; Turvey 2008), behavioral profiling (Petherick 2006), or offender profiling (Canter and Youngs 2009; Keppel 2006; Palermo and Kocsis 2005), is practiced in a number of diverse forms but broadly refers to investigative techniques or assessment strategies used to identify current and potential offenders. In its original form, as developed by the FBI's Behavioral Science Unit, hypotheses regarding offenders' behavioral, demographic, and personality characteristics were generated from data left at crime scenes (Douglas et al. 1986). The realm of profiling has expanded, however, to include the "prospective identification of would-be criminals" wherein "the typical perpetrator of a particular type of crime—such as serial murder or school shootings—is compiled from characteristics shared by known previous perpetrators" (Reddy et al. 2001, p. 161). This prototypical profile is then used to identify the types of individuals likely to become perpetrators and to assess an individual's likelihood of future offending. To this end, the FBI created a prospective profile of the "school shooter" (Band and Harpold 1999), while McGee and DeBernardo (1999) generated their own profile of the "classroom avenger." While various profiling techniques have gained some measure of empirical support (Homant and Kennedy 1998; Kocsis et al. 2000; Pinizzotto and Finkel 1990), the profiling of young students has proved particularly problematic. Many students who fit general profiles never commit school violence of any kind, while numerous students who have planned and even completed attacks at their schools did not closely match prior profiles (Sewell and Mendelsohn 2000). Such student profiles have recently fallen out of favor, and a systematic investigation of targeted school shooting incidents revealed that there "is no accurate or useful 'profile' of students who engaged in targeted school violence" (Vossekuil et al. 2002, p. 11).

Guided Professional Judgment and Warning Signs

Another technique used to appraise students' violence risk is guided professional judgment, which has also been referred to as structured clinical assessment (Reddy et al. 2001). This approach entails evaluation through the use of checklists of risk factors or warning signs for violence (Borum 2000; Otto 2000). Such assessment is sometimes conducted by licensed mental health professionals (Reddy et al. 2001), though school and law enforcement officials have also utilized the various checklists that have been publicized over the years by the Justice and Education Departments (Dwyer, Osher, and Warger 1998), the International Association of Chiefs of Police (1999), and the collaboration between MTV and the American Psychological Association (American Psychological Association 1999). As some of these checklists featured warning signs such as a "minimal interest in academics," this approach has been criticized for utilizing criteria that are vague and broad enough to apply to the majority of any student body (Fox and Burstein 2010, p. 69; Fox, Levin, and Quinet 2008). While standardized psychological tests and instruments used by mental health professionals have been found to be somewhat accurate in certain contexts with violence in general (Reddy et al. 2001), there is no empirical evidence that suggests that they are successful in predicting targeted school violence with preselected victims (Borum 2000).

Automated Decisionmaking

Risk assessment approaches classified as automated decisionmaking have been broken into two camps, actuarial formulas and artificial intelligence, both of which "produce a decision . . . rather than leaving the decision to the person conducting the assessment" (Reddy et al. 2001, p. 166). The actuarial form of automated decisionmaking is based on purportedly objective algorithms utilizing empirically based criteria, which produce outcome scores to determine judgments about the future likelihood of violence (Vincent, Terry, and Maney 2009). Though the use of actuarial measurements has shown some success (Borum 2000), their accuracy is somewhat questionable (Mossman 1994). The use of artificial intelligence programs represents the other automated approach to risk assessment. Computer programs render decisions in a manner thought to reduce human error and bias. One such technology developed by a California company for the Bureau of Alcohol, Tobacco, and Firearms, the MOSAIC Threat Assessment System, is frequently used on the campus of Yale University even though it remains extremely controversial (Fox and Burstein 2010; Sachsman 1997). Both types of automated decisionmaking have been criticized for not being sufficiently malleable or flexible (Reddy et al. 2001; Sewell and Mendelsohn 2000; Vincent, Terry, and Maney 2009) and for an inordinate focus on statistical associations or objective conclusions over complex understandings of causality (Grubin and Wingate 1996).

The Threat Assessment Approach

Finally, the threat assessment perspective is a prolific approach that has been developed in recent years to advance understanding about the causes and manifestations of targeted school violence. Initially developed as a "set of investigative and operational techniques that can be used by law enforcement professionals to identify, assess, and manage the risks of targeted violence and its potential perpetrators" (Fein, Vossekuil, and Holden 1995, p. 1), the last decade has seen a multitude of school violence research conducted under the rubric of threat assessment (Cornell 2003; Cornell and Sheras 2006; Cornell et al. 2004; Deisinger et al. 2008; Fein et al. 2002; Jimerson, Brock, and Cowan 2005; O'Toole 2000; Randazzo et al. 2006; Rappaport and Barrett 2009; Reddy et al. 2001; Strong and Cornell 2008; Twemlow et al. 2002; Vossekuil et al. 2002). Threat assessment differs from previous attempts to discern dangerousness due to its focus on the substantive analysis of existing threats rather than predicting future behavior based on typical personality profiles, warning signs, or other aggregate data pertaining to individual characteristics. This approach argues that people who perpetrate acts of targeted violence lack a single homogeneous profile, but the evaluation of the backgrounds, personalities, lifestyles, and resources of those who threaten may aid in determining the gravity of threats (O'Toole 2000). Perhaps most significantly, this perspective asserts that not all threats are equivalent—that is, "there is a distinction between making a threat . . . and posing a threat. . . . Many people who make threats do not pose a serious risk of harm to a target. Conversely, many who pose a serious risk of harm will not issue direct threats prior to the attack" (Reddy et al. 2001, p. 168). Critical details, such as how direct, detailed, developed, and actionable the threat is, help to further assess seriousness. Though the utility of threat assessment is limited in its application only to those incidents in which individuals communicate threats in advance (Borum et al. 2010), the approach must be credited with providing a more nuanced and restrained approach to student threat.

While the assessment of violence risk is a diverse and developing field, there are numerous issues and unanswered questions regarding their application in practice at schools around the country. Verlinden, Hersen, and Thomas (2000, p. 27) noted that there is a total lack of "data at this point to assist a clinician in selecting the 'best' strategy for risk assessment for violent school assaults." Similarly, Reddy et al. (2001, p. 160) pointed out that "it is not currently known how many schools use which type of assessment" and that little data exists that clearly evaluates "their effectiveness—perceived or actual." These unanswered questions aside, even the more sophisticated threat assessment approach may be critiqued as a form of "administrative criminology" exclusively and perhaps inordinately concerned with the management and control of risky populations over and above the comprehension and alleviation of underlying forces that lead people to engage in violent and threatening behavior in the first place (Young 1994).

Demand for Discipline and Security in Schools

Muschert and Peguero (2010, p. 122) argued that one of the principal consequences of the Columbine Effect is to permit "mechanisms of social control to expand." This expansion of social control has manifested itself in schools across the country through punitive zero-tolerance disciplinary policies, the proliferation of police officers and surveillance cameras, and various forms of school security designed to prevent crime through environmental design. These developments, which Hirschfield and Celinska (2011, p. 1) have collectively referred to as "school criminalization," all represent a swift and widespread "penetration of law enforcement personnel and technology into urban, suburban, and rural schools" (Hirschfield 2010, p. 39).

Zero-Tolerance Disciplinary Policies

One of the most frequently cited reactions to the various school shooting massacres of the late 1990s was the implementation of various zero-tolerance disciplinary policies that mandate strict penalties for student misbehavior, regardless of individual or situational circumstances. Though the original formulation took the form of the 1994 Gun Free Schools Act, which required schools to expel for a minimum of one year any student caught carrying a firearm in school, various states and individual school districts broadened the scope to include zero-tolerance policies for aggressive behavior, possession of other objects deemed weapons, and various controlled substances (Ayers, Ayers, and Dohrn 2001). As a result, schools have expelled, suspended, or sent to alternative schools large numbers of students for sharing over-the-counter medications with their peers; for bringing utensils and toy weapons, some made of paper or plastic, to school grounds; or for making relatively questionable gestures or comments that were deemed violent or threatening. More than a decade ago, Skiba and Peterson (1999) documented several of the more egregious examples that showcased the "dark side of zero-tolerance" spawned by fear of Columbine and other similar shootings. One particularly egregious incident involved the suspension of an eight-year-old child for pointing a chicken finger at a teacher and saying, "Pow, pow, pow" (Times Wire Reports 2001). Though zero-tolerance policies have been widely condemned in recent years by various academics (Ayers, Ayers, and Dohrn 2001; Casella 2003b; Skiba 2000), the American Bar Association (American Bar Association 2001), and the American Psychological Association (American Psychological Association Zero-tolerance Task Force 2008), such punitive absolutism persists. In 2009, a six-year-old boy from Newark, Delaware, was suspended for bringing his Cub Scouts camping utensil to lunch (Urbina 2009), and, in 2010, a thirteen-year-old female honor roll student in Houston, Texas, was expelled and labeled a "terrorist" for pointing a "finger gun" in the general direction of one of her teachers ("Student Suspended" 2010).

Surveillance Through the Proliferation of Police Officers and Security Cameras

The last few decades have seen a massive increase in the surveillance of school students, whether that means through additional resource officers officially stationed as police liaisons or security cameras that record student movements through school hallways and egresses. Whereas there were fewer than 100 police officers in American public schools at the end of the 1970s (Brady, Balmer, and Phenix 2007), more than 14,000 full-time resource officers were working in public schools by 2003 (Hickman and Reaves 2006). Thus, 60 percent of teachers in suburban middle and high schools (and 67 percent of teachers in majority-black or Hispanic schools) reported armed police officers working at their schools (Public Agenda 2004). While some officers certainly view mentorship and advising as part of their school role, they often "bring to these non-traditional policing tasks a cognitive and professional orientation that leads them to define, symbolically if not legally, student problems as crime problems" (Hirschfield and Celinska 2011, p. 3).

Not unlike police officers in schools, security cameras were a rare sight thirty years ago anywhere but in prisons and retail establishments. They did not arrive in schools until the 1990s, and while urban school districts were the first to implement cameras, wealthy suburban schools are now usually the proud owners of the most sophisticated and expensive surveillance technology (Casella 2006). During the 1999–2000 school year, only 19 percent of all public high schools used security cameras to monitor their students (Dinkes, Kemp, and Baum 2009, p. vii). By the 2007–2008 school year, 55 percent of all public schools (and 76.6 percent of all public high schools) possessed security cameras (Ruddy et al. 2010). While cameras may have numerous security and monitoring benefits, as well as the potential for various invasions of personal privacy, the security industry markets technological surveillance as an inevitable "way of the future" (Casella 2003a, p. 88), and many school administrators share this perception (Madfis 2012).

School Security Designed to Prevent Crime Through Environmental Design

Part of a larger field referred to as Crime Prevention through Environmental Design (CPTED), attaining school safety via the use of architectural designs such as large windows, skylights, and straight hallways to increase visibility has become extremely lucrative. The advent of gates, specialized door locks, and the limiting of entry and exit to one location during school hours have similarly been adopted to secure areas in numerous school buildings (Casella 2006). Typically affluent communities prefer these environmental designs (as well as surveillance through police and cameras) to the daily use of metal detectors and random weapon searches. These latter invasive security measures are more commonly found in urban schools with predominantly minority students (Hirschfield 2010). Despite variations by ethnicity or socioeconomic status, all of these forms of security through environmental design adopt the same mind-set. They make crime more difficult to commit by restraining the physical environment with increased visibility and decreased access, but operate under the assumption that people's desire to commit such crimes cannot be diminished. Much like the various violence risk assessments, dangerous people are to be managed and risks controlled rather than prevented or alleviated.

Concluding Discussion

The repercussions of the Columbine Effect in the realm of school security persist despite the fact that more than ten years after Columbine, rates of youth violence and school violence in particular continue to stay far lower than that of the early 1990s (Fox and Burstein 2010). Our chapter has focused somewhat critically on the punitive side of the Columbine Effect including the discursive field from which such policy responses have emerged. Though such a critical stance is surely in line with the spirit of this volume, we would also like to conclude with an exploration of what we see as some feasible alternatives to the contemporary regime of risk control in post-Columbine schools.

The various punitive disciplinary policies and increased security and surveillance technologies discussed in this chapter were often conspicuously implemented in direct response to the fear of extreme violent events like Columbine. However, they are routinely applied in schools to stigmatize and penalize students for relatively petty crimes like drug use, disorderly conduct, and vandalism, not violence (Madfis 2012). In practice, this serves to expand the "school-to-prison pipeline" where the punishment of school misbehavior is transferred from the educational system to the juvenile and criminal justice systems (Advancement Project 2005; Wald and Losen 2003). As a result, the most vulnerable young people, such as minority or poor students, are disproportionately penalized (Kupchik 2010; Michigan ACLU 2009), and this widens the effects of exclusion by setting at-risk students further behind. Such developments take place, of course, within the contemporary regime of social control and interface with twenty-first-century conceptions of risk and control. Thus, the culture of control in schools disproportionately addresses the low risk of misbehavior by an imagined crop of superpredators inhabiting the hallways of our middle and high schools. These potential offenders are apparently indistinguishable from the millions of other students, just as the Columbine High School shooters Harris and Klebold were indistinguishable from their classmates. Within the context of low risk tolerance in society in general, schools are a location where risk tolerance is almost nil. This has served as a catalyst for neoliberal attempts to manage undesirables in schools, especially in middle-class or affluent communities. The unintended consequence of many recent efforts to securitize schools is that the culture of punitive discipline in schools is incongruent with the general culture of transgression, which involves a large number of minor events, most of which are far from life threatening. Thus, in preparation for the momentously horrific repercussions that could potentially occur if a school shooting event were to take place, schools increasingly treat students as if they could potentially develop into versions of Harris and Klebold. Rationally, we know that this is very unlikely to occur. It amounts to a present-day version of throwing out the baby with the bathwater, by creating an airport-like (if not prison-like) school environment that may ultimately undermine the primary pedagogical goals of educational institutions.

In contrast, are there any reasonable alternatives? This question can be answered in two ways: first by addressing the effect Columbine has on the discursive field of school violence, and second by pointing to some policies that run counter to the punitive tendencies we have outlined. Reimagining the discourse of school discipline can be particularly difficult, especially to those deeply involved in school administration or with disciplinary roles. However, such a reimagining is possible. First, we argue for an increased reliance on rational evidence in school disciplinary and security decisions. Of course, this suggests the use of social science data in instituting and evaluating procedures and their effectiveness, but also that evidence should become increasingly useful in the administration of discipline in schools. An increased reliance on empirical evidence would help to clarify the reasonable risks associated with school attendance, and thus could help those involved in various levels of disciplinary administration in schools to articulate the relative rationality of various efforts to maintain security. In addition, an increased reliance on empirical research in open dialogue among stakeholders can help to clarify the manner in which some policies lead to unintended consequences and, in the worst cases, hurt more than they help.

Second, we believe that journalists need to engage in more responsible and representative coverage of school discipline and its transgression, though we are not particularly optimistic about the likelihood of any such positive transformation. Most media attention to school misconduct is driven by extreme and unrepresentative events that then create and enhance misconceptions about what is common and pervasive. One alternative would be media coverage of school discipline that highlights its normal and mundane functioning, rather than just those horrible and rare cases in which order breaks down. Such routinized attention to conventional school discipline would help to publicize the successes and failures of the contemporary regime of control as well as individual policies. In practical terms, this means that journalists could provide an educational service by informing the public about the everyday functioning of school disciplinary mechanisms and by reporting on common infractions (such as bullying, sexual harassment, intimate partner abuse, truancy, and substance abuse violations). This could even entail focusing on changing patterns of behavior, rather than on individual cases of transgression. Such reporting would enable readers to develop a sense of how the system generally responds to common infractions, thereby providing a more balanced view of security needs and functioning within schools.

Another, somewhat less lofty, goal would be for socially responsible reporters to, at the very least, situate the rare and shocking events they cover in the appropriate context, and thus acknowledge larger routine patterns of discipline and transgression. Unfortunately, any such informative coverage exploring the mundane but representative school experience runs counter to all contemporary media practices and policies that strive to shock consumers and increase profit—the very notion of reporting typical patterns of school order and misbehavior is completely anathema to current crime reporting. Though such fair-minded reporting could lessen moral panics that frame the rare as common and the overwhelmingly safe as teeming with dangerous potential, such coverage would likewise detract from the scandal and intrigue of salacious story lines, and so we have little faith that any substantial progress will soon be made. Nonetheless, the role of the media is a significant one, and so it must remain a focus of empirical scholarship and, perhaps eventually, dramatic reform and transformation.

There are indeed policies that run counter to the dominant punitive regime of school discipline. While these programs should be subjected to the same empirical assessments as punitive policies, they offer reasons for hope. Though a detailed examination of these policies is beyond the scope of this chapter, we mention a few in order to provide a balanced picture of both the field of school disciplinary measures and the long-term effect that rampage school shootings have had on American schooling.

First, one must acknowledge the problem of false positives inherent in much of the reaction to school rampages. Warning signs, profiles, and other risk assessments inherently overestimate student riskiness and cast suspicion on many innocent students who happen to have broad characteristics in common with some school shooters (Fox, Levin, and Quinet 2008). Likewise, many school safety measures (such as the implementation of police, metal detectors, and surveillance cameras) alter the school environment for every student, not merely those thought to be at risk for serious violence. As such, it is worth looking toward other long-term preventative solutions that may result in false positives in program assessment, yet would only benefit, rather than harm, most students even when a wide net is cast. These include bullying prevention (which was greatly augmented following Columbine), conflict resolution and peer mediation education, decreasing student-to-teacher or student-to-guidance-counselor ratios, and increasing extracurricular activities and rates of involvement (Fox, Levin, and Quinet 2008; Levin and Madfis 2009).

Second, such less punitive and long-term strategies take an entirely different tack as they focus on preventing students from having the desire to harm their peers in the first place, rather than merely managing the behavior of risky individuals through assessment and security. As Levin and Madfis (2009, p. 1241) point out:

> Increasing the number and effectiveness of capable guardians and engaging in target-hardening tactics to diminish their suitability and easy access does nothing to diminish the third and most vital [factor], the motivation of offenders. To this end, the focus must also be on long-term prevention techniques to ensure that students do not develop the desire to engage in a school massacre in the first place.

Such programs promote tolerance and empathy in school through the lesson of the Columbine tragedy. Assemblies such as Rachel's Challenge and the Names Can Really Hurt Us Program of the Anti-Defamation League (ADL) and performances of dramatic plays such as *A Line in the Sand* and *The Columbine Project* hope to alert students to the severity of teenage social hierarchy and increase awareness of how it feels to be bullied and marginalized at school. As a nuanced part of the Columbine Effect, these projects stand out as restorative efforts to influence some of the underlying tensions in schools that may foment conflict.

In this same vein, another promising change to emerge from the wake of Columbine is the newfound focus on bystander awareness (not only among agents of control such as police and disciplinarians, but also among students, parents, faculty, and other staff), which has the potential to not only prevent future rampage attacks, but also to reduce bullying and school violence more generally. One of the most touted findings to come out of research on school rampage was that many killers informed others about their violent plots in advance. Vossekuil et al. (2002) found that at least one person had some prior knowledge about the plans of perpetrators in 81 percent of targeted school-shooting incidents, while multiple people have some awareness in 59 percent of their sample. This discovery led to discussions about a student "code of silence," which prohibits students from coming forward with pivotal information about their peers' dangerous intentions (Halbig 2000; Merida 1999; Syvertsen, Flanagan, and Stout 2009) and the creation of anonymous hot lines and e-mail systems to break through this code (Teicher 2006). Today, various bystander prevention programs exist in schools across the country that work to break the student code of silence and encourage young people to be more active about speaking up and stopping the problematic behaviors of their peers (Lodge and Frydenberg 2005; Twemlow, Fonagy, and Sacco 2004).

Clearly, the motivation of this volume is to explore the role of Columbine and other extreme cases of violence in American schools as catalysts for the development of school disciplinary practices, most of them punitive. While the overall picture of discipline in schools may be negative, one that drives our youths toward increased compliance and complaisance in the presence of formal agents of control in their daily lives, there are perhaps reasons for hope as well. Among these are the following: moves on the part of school administrators to incorporate evidence-based practices in their disciplinary regimes (Kupchik 2010, pp. 193–222), the increased attention among scholars from a wide array of academic perspectives and backgrounds on the issue of school violence and its control, and the presence of the comparatively more pro-social educational or mediation measures mentioned above. Taken together, these signal that there is a sufficient and fertile group of scholars and practitioners willing and able to engage in meaningful discussion about how discipline and security can be maintained in schools in ways that avoid undermining primary pedagogical goals and unintended negative consequences for students and schools.

Notes

1. An underemphasized aspect of discourse studies concerning the evolution of the school shooter is the melding of the victim and perpetrator roles in the "ideal type" of school shooter, a dynamic that Cerulo (1998) calls "doublecasting." In effect, the school shooter simultaneously represents the worst kind of offender (the superpredator) and a victim who is worthy of compassion (one who has suffered at the hands of bullies). Thus, the issues of attribution of blame or waiving of responsibility are never easy ones in cases of school shootings. Though this ambiguity is, in part, explored elsewhere (see, e.g., Muschert 2012; Spencer 2005; Spencer and Muschert 2009), this area remains rich for future exploration.

2. For example, one might argue that while bullying may not typically be fatal, it affects the lives of a far larger segment of American schoolchildren than school rampage. Therefore, if one were to employ Bentham's ([1789] 1970) utilitarian principle concerning the greatest good for the greatest number of people, school programming and policy should be directed away from concerns about school rampage and toward bullying prevention.

3. Violence risk assessment has elsewhere been delineated into clinical, actuarial, and structured professional judgment (Vincent, Terry, and Maney 2009).

3

Negotiation of Care and Control in School Safety

Curtis A. Brewer and Jane Clark Lindle

This volume testifies to the complex nature of school violence. As Henry (2009) explained, "school violence can be acts, relationships" or "processes that occur in a school or a school-related setting" (p. 1253). The results of such engagements create reductions of a person or a group "from what they are" or limit them "from becoming what they might become for any period of time" (p. 1253). In addition, organizational structures and social groups perpetrate violence, causing physical harm as well as emotional and psychological harm. Schools are community-based institutions widely experienced by society's members and intentionally created to address the formation of social and academic skills among individuals and groups (Bronfenbrenner 1979; Dewey 1964, 1989). However, opportunities for developing pupils' pro-social skills also breed potential for emotional or physical violence to individuals and groups (McLaren 2007). Columbine's school shootings heightened our awareness of this complicated and layered process.

The aftermath of Columbine exposed school violence as a multilevel phenomenon requiring a heuristic to permit a multilevel analysis. Henry (2009) explained how it is "important to identify a wide range of violence at different levels of society that affect the school and to see how these are reciprocally interrelated in the school setting as a process over time" (p. 1248). Many authors (e.g., Henry 2009; Lindle 2008; Muschert and Peguero 2010; Noguera 1995) have argued that schools' reactions to threats of violence lead to processes and policies that, in themselves, may be a form of violence. Therefore, as Henry (2009) proposed, we should comprehend how violent acts, "including extreme expressions, such as rampage school shootings, are outcomes of multiple sub-violent, violent, and symbolically violent processes" (p. 1261) perpetrated by society and the school, as well as groups and individuals.

In this chapter, we take a closer look at the range of school administrators' reactions to the threats and consequences of school violence and how they are coupled to demands for ensuring safe climates for learning (Kinney 2009; O'Donovan 2006; Reeves, Kanan, and Plog 2010). Such school officials require reasonable options for responses to a variety of dilemmas embedded in the daily conflicts that manifest in the school microcosm. As Muschert and Peguero (2010) pointed out, the "line between caring and undue control is unclear" (p. 123). This investigation hopes to illustrate the social and professional demands for finding equilibrium along this *line* in educators' practices.

That is, achieving equilibrium along this line must be understood as a negotiation between practices of risk management and the educative requirement of schooling. On the one hand, that educational requirement rests on an ethic of care that leads to cultivating relationships between and among teachers and learners (Akiba 2010; MacNeil and Prater 2010; Shapiro and Stefkovich 2011). Arguably, such educative relationships require both trust and caring (e.g., Beatty 2007; Noddings 2006; Sebring et al. 2006). On the other hand, safety and legal demands on schooling may be reduced to institutional and bureaucratic routines impacting administrative performance and circumventing social contracts between communities and schools (Ball 2001, 2003; Beatty 2007). In other words, educators must *walk a line* between caring and control, while attending to the effects of a wide range of violence and potential violence from different levels across society. If we are to understand school violence, then we need to understand the relationships, choices, and practices of school personnel entrenched within the wider social contexts of schooling.

We illustrate the experience of school administrators as they negotiate the dilemmas associated with the line between caring and controlling by presenting four scenarios that are regularly found in schools. In order to help make meaning of these scenarios we will first briefly describe a framework that builds from previous work (Lindle 2008; Young and Brewer 2008). Through the scenarios and the application of the framework, we highlight the ways in which school administrators seek balance between the educative ethic of caring and the social and legal duties for controlling risk in a social institution characterized by environments of uncertainty and punctuated with moral panic, set within a wider cultural framework of both violence and nonviolence.

Theoretical Framework

As will be made evident by others in this volume, violence and our reactions to it are interactive and reciprocal. This pattern is especially manifest in high-modern societies where there is a pervasive sense of uncertainty and risk (Beck 1992; Giddens 1991; Young 2007b). Work in this vein has argued that daily life in many Western democracies qualitatively differs from past societies due to few shared ontologies or other norms. The fluidity of social norms, the foregrounding of market processes (Ball 2001, 2003; Lumby 2009; Lyotard 1984), and the growing understanding of uncertainty as central to study of the universe, or multiverse (Carr 2007), have left people with ambiguity and fear at personal, social, and existential levels (Giddens 1991).

As Young (2007b) describes in his aptly titled book *The Vertigo of Late Modernity,* uncertainty is experienced across manifolds of societal interactions. Social conditions that foment uncertainty can also generate "symmetrical" energy and fear among various groups, such as those who will revel in the transgression of unstable norms, those who desire the reestablishment of rigorous norms, as well as those who find legitimacy in a policing role (Young 2007a, p. 56). Such emotive energy and its various media representations can generate moral panic (Cohen 1972). Subsequently, emotive activities emerge in moral panic phenomena and become more plausible for various cultures and subcultures across time (Tudor 2003). Moral panic punctuates macro-cultures such as that of a nation like the United States, but also policy subcultures like that which frames public debate about purposes of schooling (Young and Brewer 2008) or the local cultures that exist within schools and districts (Lindle 2008).

Thus, the phenomenon of moral panic often permeates this environment of uncertainty and fearfulness (Cohen 1972). Widespread fear can be cultivated when deeply held popular expectations about the tranquility of schools are juxtaposed against the realities of easily accessible democratic institutions (Aviel 2006; Lindle 2008). This juxtaposition is often highlighted by the practices of media and politicians who capitalize on, and sensationalize, social ills (Brooks, Schiraldi, and Ziedenberg 2000; Cohen 1972; Donohue, Schiraldi, and Ziedenberg 1998; Macallair 2002; Welch, Price, and Yankey 2002). When a society's social norms are fluid, and when faced with distance between assumptions about safety and sensationalized media depictions of complexity in securing schools, people often call for policies out of proportion with the reality of past events (Brooks, Schiraldi, and Ziedenberg 2000; Cohen 1972; Donohue, Schiraldi, and Ziedenberg 1998). Concurrently, some students revel in the spotlight and purposefully flout safety policies to show their sense of injustices. As Young (2007a) succinctly stated, "You cannot have a moral panic unless there is something morally to panic about" (p. 60).

As the study of the Columbine Effect (Muschert and Peguero 2010) has indicated, the pervading popular wish for students to be safer at school than elsewhere is a false assumption. Most students' socialization occurs at their schools, which are microcosms of their communities (Honora and Rolle 2002; Salzinger et al. 2006). Violence is a social phenomenon, and schools are social institutions embedded in society, local culture, and mores. Schools house multiple actors (students, teachers, administrators, parents, general public), all of whom can enact roles of both victims and bullies (Schreck, Miller, and Gibson 2003; Thompkins 2000; Watts and Erevelles 2004). All of these actors share in generating moral panic around school safety, and given complex actors and their interactions, school leaders face multiple dilemmas.

In our attempt to represent the dilemmas that school personnel face, two assumptions guide our perspectives. We assume first that, in modern society, the attempt to implement safety is shaped by two important contentious desires: (1) a desire to formally control risks (Foucault 1979; Robers, Zhang, and Truman 2010) and (2) a professional ethic of caring necessary to create relationships conducive to learning (Goodman 2008; Noddings 2006; Shapiro and Stefkovich 2011). Our second assumption is that tensions between these two desires shape reactions to school violence at multiple levels. For school personnel, these tensions percolate through three levels: (1) macro (state or national level), (2) meso (community or school district level), and (3) micro (school and interactions that take place within the school). We also assert that in schools all three of these levels affect people's attempts to negotiate their dilemmas. Obviously, we owe a debt to Henry's (2009) framework, although we diverge from Henry's approach. To explain the situation of school personnel, we collapsed multiple levels—1 (individual), 2 (group), and 3 (organizational)—into a single level (the school) because school personnel interact among these simultaneously. We do this to highlight ways in which school leaders' experience of the line between care and control includes all of the levels at once. School conflicts represent interactions among individuals who frequently connect to groups and communities. In short, school personnel live at the nexus of controlling risk as well as creating the kinds of caring relationships necessary for learning and must walk a line constituted by forces at all levels (Beatty 2007; Muschert and Peguero 2010; Zorn and Boler 2007).

Figure 3.1 depicts a linear divide representing the nexus of control or caring across levels of social interactions. In Figure 3.1, this line is a vertical dotted line, on the left side of which risk control results in prescriptively routine interactions. The right side shows caring relationships as ongoing negotiations among individuals or groups. Our argument is that a lack of balance in remaining near this line can contribute to and encourage elements of school violence and routines of subviolence.[1]

For example, cultural mores favoring absolutes and overly legal responses lead to overreliance on formal risk management at the societal (macro) level, yielding three-strike laws with dire punishments that prohibit second chances or rehabilitation. Such absolute

Figure 3.1. Dynamics of School Safety

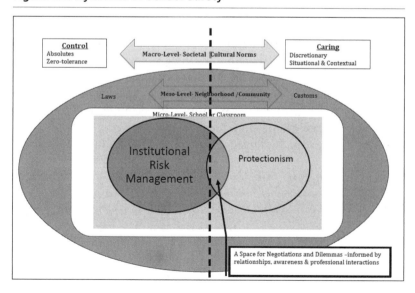

sentences enact violence in terms of "alienation, collective abandonment, and vengeance ideology" (Henry 2009, p. 1255). At the community or neighborhood (meso) level, overreliance on risk control can lead to prescriptive laws or district policies. Prescriptive policies allow no professional discretion yielding forms of violence including "polarization, social disorganization, labeling and subordinating and the impoverishment of the creativity of the learning environment" (p. 1255). Within schools and classrooms (micro) level, an overreliance on organizational rules and policies, such as tracking or zero-tolerance, sacrifices professional accommodation of student needs and thus ultimately does violence to students' chances for academic success. Without any mediating, professional judgment, rules, and routines can lead to forms of violence such as "corporal punishment, overreliance on expulsion, systematic protection of poor teaching; the limiting of educational potential and alienation of students, teachers, or parents" (p. 1255).

However, the right side of the vertical line is not a complete antidote to the potential for conflict and violence in schools. Many forms of caring can be disabling instead of enabling (Dewey 1964, 1989; Goodman 2008; Noddings 2006). An imbalance in favor of discretion and an overappreciation of situational aspects can also result in violent and subviolent processes. At the macro-level, overidentification with situational aspects of social phenomena can lead to paralyzing uncertainty and moments of extreme moral panic. The resulting violence is "the fragmentation of society and a sense of a broken world" (Henry 2009, p. 1255). In communities and neighborhoods, at the meso-level, assumptions about the uniqueness of every social situation can lead to reliance on market forces or community traditions to make decisions. At risk here is both protection of equal rights and the possibility for creativity; that is, many local customs could create a caste system that undermines minority rights, diminishing individual choice in favor of a status quo for elites. In contrast, equal rights and choice often may be protected better through institutional structures. Finally, at the micro-level, an overreliance on discretion by those in power can lead to the development of cliques and gangs intended to make power moves countering the established powers (Thompkins 2000; Watts and Erevelles, 2004). Such engendering of power plays and protectionism can lead to emotional and physical violence as well as "predation" (Henry 2009, p. 1255). In this way, schools can be complicit in violent and subviolent processes because safety is guaranteed only for select groups or individuals. In the worst cases of completely discretionary practices, common safety is unpredictable and moral panic arises.

We argue that administrators who are most successful at mitigating school violence are those who succeed in finding a balance near Figure 3.1's vertical dividing line. The figure's center depicts a negotiated space between control and caring. In this space, school personnel can utilize elements of formal control, their own emotional awareness, and relationships along with their ethical professional judgments to prevent multiple levels of violence (Beatty 2007; Zorn and Boler 2007). They must make and enact decisions that negotiate the span between control and caring case by case.

Demands on school personnel for ensuring safe learning spaces reach beyond risk management to social and emotional health among teachers and students, ultimately requiring that school leaders care (Beatty 2007; Goodman 2008; Zorn and Boler 2007). Very early research in the field of educational leadership explicitly checked the connection between controlling students and the socioemotional conditions for schooling (Willower, Eidell, and Hoy 1967, 1973). These studies indicated that a focus on rigid control damages relationships (Packard 1988). Some evidence suggested that both administrators and teachers resent rigid policies that prevent use of their professional judgments (Daly 2009; Fries and DeMitchell 2007). Some school policies can increase school personnel's fears (Ricketts 2007; Smith and Smith 2006; Williams and Corvo 2005). School personnel whom students perceived as bullies increased student absenteeism and thus damaged the necessary relationships for learning (Akiba 2010; Astor et al. 2002; Gregory, Skiba, and Noguera 2010). School personnel fear for their own safety, and a failure to acknowledge those feelings exacerbates damage to school's relationships as well (Beatty 2007; Roberts et al. 2007; Smith and Smith 2006; Williams and Corvo 2005). School personnel's professional roles require a balanced awareness of how they develop and nurture social capital while meeting requirements for formal risk management. Thus, their work represents a precarious and constant duty to balance control and caring.

Given this perspective, we agree with Twemlow and Cohen's (2003) editorial assertion that "at the end of the day all violence prevention programs come down to relationships: our ability to listen to ourselves, to recognize other's experience and use this information to solve problems, to learn and be creative together" (p. 121). We also assert that school personnel have a greater responsibility to undertake such a task given that they have access to more information and to more problem-solving tools than other actors do at any of the social levels in the model. However, as shown in the following scenarios, most school administrators do not work in a simple open space where choices neatly fall into instances of caring or control. Instead, school personnel face multiple dilemmas in which all options produce some degree of consequential violence. Despite constraints, their professional judgments must achieve a nuanced balance in their caring control of risks.

Negotiating the Daily Dilemmas of School Safety

How can school administrators walk the model's line in schools' daily common conflicts and dilemmas? As a societal creature, schools' social architecture envelops relationships among all who access campuses. Thus, while each encounter carries distinguishing features, daily school conflicts share common dilemmas. The subset of daily challenges on which we focus include the following four dilemmas: (1) controlling self versus caring for others, (2) official safety enforcement positions versus classroom-based environments for learning, (3) control of policy demands versus caring relationships, and (4) securing spaces versus overlapping networks.

Controlling Self vs. Caring for Others

A basic awareness of their legal responsibilities underlies many school leaders' understanding of their work (Kinney 2009; O'Donovan 2006). In fact, international attention to the outcomes of schooling has unleashed what some have called a *policy epidemic* (Levin 1998). Among the consequences of burgeoning educational policies is an array of "policy technologies" designed to create power networks (Ball 2003, p. 216). Amid these technologies, one, known as performativity, degrades social relationships into prescriptive judgmental functions, a dehumanizing efficiency of hierarchies (Ball, 2003; Beatty, 2007). Within the proliferation of educational policies, many have argued that school policies that combine safety with student achievement goals have subjected professional educators to enact their roles as performances, leading to robotic performativity (Ball 2001, 2003; Beatty 2007; Lumby 2009; Lyotard 1984; Perryman 2006). Performativity rests on the control side of our model. Arguably, inexperienced school personnel may focus inordinately on their own job security and turn to performativity over caring judgments.

Imagine the common case of a ninth grade student sent to the assistant principal (AP) for discipline who is accused by a teacher of threatening her in class. In too many of these cases, the accused student is an African American male and the teacher is white (Gregory, Skiba, and Noguera 2010; Osher et al. 2010). Typically, APs for discipline are white males, but those demographics are changing faster than demographics of accused students and offended teachers. Typical interviews between the student and AP last five to fifteen minutes, generally involving student denial of any incident or threat, shifting to a claim that the teacher does not understand him, and perhaps some discussion of how the teacher had started the incident. This latter move permits the AP to assert that the student has admitted at least that there is conflict, and the AP may seize the opportunity to affirm a confession. If the AP takes a coercive stance, the student may confirm a confession, which then becomes grounds for suspension or arrest. Punishment severity may be a result of the strength or weakness in the AP-student relationship.

Further sources influence this scenario. School policy may require that APs contact both teachers and parents or guardians before issuing punishment. The AP may take the student's statement at face value and then seek the teacher's version independently. At some point, APs must decide which version, student's or teacher's, applies in any resolution strategy. Under these conditions, the AP-teacher relationship may outweigh the AP-student relationship, or vice versa. In other schools, policy requires teacher and student explain their versions in front of the AP and each other. This practice requires each party to make his or her case. In such situations, again, students may not fare well due to the resources of the teachers, who are more experienced. For example, some male students may either choose not to, or lack the verbal skills to, engage in the style of argument typical among middle-class school personnel. Further, males' verbal communication skills are qualitatively different from those of females (Tannen 2001). In this exchange, the strength of relationships among the AP, teacher, and student play a role in the degree to which the student's argument is deemed credible in comparison to that of the teacher.

The longevity of the relationships plays another role based on the AP's experience and social capital in the school. Students are not a permanent population within any school; they are transient, and if all goes well, leave their schools in three to five years. On the other hand, teachers hold territorial and social capital when the students arrive and after they leave. Rampant turnover of school administrators also means that many teachers hold both territorial and social capital over principals and assistant principals. Relationships with teachers are imbued with power considerations and expected performances for both students and administrators. APs may feel the need to protect their jobs and careers by building and nurturing relationships with teachers instead of students.

In contrast to the appeal of considering social capital with teachers, leaders must recognize that any interaction between teacher and a particular student affects relationships with other students. What is the collateral violence that other students experienced in the exchange between teacher and student? To what degree did the conflict interrupt other students' rights to a safe learning environment? If the AP recognizes other students' rights, then the investigation may extend beyond teacher and student to the student body.

Another concern for this common scenario is discernment of the nature of the infraction; the accusation in this scenario is that the student threatened the teacher. In the daily occurrences of disagreements between students and teachers there exists a broad interpretive range for understanding language or gestures. Adolescents use extreme language; adolescent males often compete in escalating the extremity of their expressions. At what point does youthful hyperbole shift into a threat? When do threatening words become bullying? To what extent do the threat of words and style of communication reflect wider cultural and structural power differences across race, class, and gender dimensions as embodied in the youth's performativity? Between adult and youth, who holds the balance of power to bully? Such questions should form the nexus of the AP's decisionmaking in this scenario. Depending on the degree to which the AP shares background and experiences with other adults in this scenario, to what degree can any student expect a caring outcome or an automatic, controlling one? To what degree can the other students expect protection in their learning?

Further consideration in the choices of control or compassion must include the emotions of the AP. Too often a self-protective choice of performativity leads to loss of emotional awareness (Beatty 2007; Zorn and Boler 2007). The model's control side points to potential for a lack of caring about self or others (Beatty 2007; Zorn and Boler 2007). Oddly enough, when self-protection creates a motive for adopting routines, performativity provides a slippery slope to losing one's self (Ball 2003; Beatty 2007); hierarchical and functional responses yield dehumanizing costs. On both sides of the line, extreme responses of control or caring offer no certainty or stability.

Official Safety Positions vs. Classroom-Based Environments for Learning

Positions assigned for school safety and discipline accumulate in schooling's hierarchy. Hierarchy can interfere with caring relationships essential to learning. Disciplinary hierarchies may disrupt the caring spaces among teachers and students.

The disruption occurs in two ways through two enforcement roles: (1) assistant principals (APs) and (2) school resource officers (SROs). Generally, each school system can vary greatly in its job descriptions for APs and SROs. In both roles, violence prevention can be accomplished through visibility by roaming hallways and other school facilities; this may also create a sense of insecurity caused by surveillance. Additionally, both roles share enforcement duties. These roles diverge as APs handle chronic disrupters referred from classrooms, while SROs may hold both instructive and enforcement roles by their presence in schools (Center for the Prevention of School Violence 2009; National Association of School Resource Officers 2010).

The way these positions work together and, to a degree, differently may be illustrated in returning to our scenario. In most schools, the AP will handle the referred student and conduct the investigation. If the investigation revealed the student to have made a threat to kill the teacher, which the teacher and other witnesses took seriously, then the AP and SRO might work together in determining whether the threat was credible beyond those perceptions. The questions they might have to answer include: to what degree is the relationship between teacher and student damaged? Is that damage great enough that the student would return to class and disrupt further? Or even more seriously, is the teacher-student relationship wrecked to the extent that the student would physically attack the teacher if seen in any venue on or off school grounds?

Another part of the investigation would determine whether the student has a plan and the means to carry out the threat. For this part of the investigation, the student's locker and backpack might be searched. With evidence from that search, the SRO might turn over the case to civic law enforcement or work with them to search the student's home or other community-based locales.

These roles may be necessary in the extreme situation of a highly credible threat where the student-teacher relationship is completely broken. Yet both APs and SROs are supposed to prevent such extreme cases. How can they do so? What kind of expertise can either of these roles contribute to the teacher and student bond? To what degree do third parties enable and nurture good relationships between the other two parties?

The answers in education's institutional bureaucracy typically are not APs or SROs, and unfortunately, probably not school counselors, social workers, or psychologists. Too often, schools do not have a social worker, and even more unfortunately, many students are not eligible for such support. Most social workers work outside the school and are not directly involved between teachers and students. Many school-based counselors and psychologists have had their work diverted by testing requirements and policies. Despite their preferences, many school counselors find their work more focused on educational policy demands for test and record keeping rather than direct work with students or teachers (American School Counselor Association 2005). The issue of developing and nurturing student-teacher relationships remains relatively unsupported and falls exclusively on teachers and students. Unhappily, bureaucracy inhabiting the macro-, meso-, and micro-levels enforces control, not caring relationships. Policy also falls on the control, rather than caring, side of the model. This failure in balance permits a hollow promise of security and simultaneously a greater sense of uncertainty.

Policy Demands Control vs. Caring Relationships

Another consequence of schools' institutional and hierarchical nature is embedded in measures of successful schooling. Repeated studies of schools with higher-than-expected levels of achievement note correlated characteristics including the following: (a) rigorous curriculum, (b) safe and orderly environment, (c) instruction leadership and academic focus, (d) collaboration, and (e) community support, including parent involvement (Lezotte and Passalacqua 1978; Marzano 2003; Purkey and Smith 1983; Sebring et al. 2006). Despite the axiom that *correlation is not causation,* a common strategy for trying to turnaround poor academic performance is to work serially on these features, rather than simultaneously (Marzano

2003). In addition, the literature on how low-performing schools changed "leaves open the question of whether persistently low-performing schools can be significantly improved" (Orr et al. 2008, p. 673) or even where to start. The policy pressures for high achievement shown as supported by safe schools can serve to push out and marginalize students who may be struggling learners, in the most need of strong relationships with teachers (Beachum et al. 2008; Thompkins 2000; Watts and Erevelles 2004). Others have explained that the pressures of policy demands also draw those involved toward a more controlled, rather than caring, approach to their work (Ball 2003; Lumby 2009; Perryman 2006). The risk to individuals is loss of personal and professional identity (Beatty 2007; Lumby 2009; Perryman 2006).

In the scenario of the student who allegedly threatened the teacher, the potential influence of policy demands may constrain the teacher's ability to build a relationship with the student. In the drive for higher achievement, a student who requires extra attention and effort may appear to be a threat to the teacher's career. Such a threat may result in a teacher's belief that he or she needs to control which students remain in the class due to a perception that he or she can be more successful with some students than with others. Such teachers may forge a campaign to remove a specific list of students from occupying extra time or other resources (Valenzuela 2005).

These removal efforts need not spiral into verbal or physical confrontations. Instead, less observable violence to students may occur. Push-out strategies may include recommendations that a student be placed in a different classroom ranging from comparable classrooms to testing the pupil for placement in specialized programs or tracking. Each of these results can lead to a different and less rigorous learning environment. Moreover, push-out options may escalate to students dropping out of school (Beachum et al. 2008; Gregory, Skiba, and Noguera 2010; Ou 2010). This routine of moving students out of classrooms is not one that rises to bureaucratic levels associated with school safety, such as SROs or APs. Nevertheless, removing students to alternative tracks or specialized classes may be a form of violence to their rights to education.

The push-out phenomena could be among the options for the AP during the investigation of our scenario. The pressures of a policy focus on safety might influence a time-saving judgment not to investigate the perceptions of threat from more than one participant or witness or even to generate further evidence. Instead, the controlling reaction may be to accept teacher's word over that of the student and institute a suspension as an efficiency end. Thus, time control, encouraged by a need to perform on state accountability tests, becomes a mechanism for pushing out accused students. The challenge in these situations is to maintain the ethic of caring despite the pressure to fulfill policy prescriptions for performance or surveillance networks (Beatty 2007; Perryman 2006).

Securing Spaces vs. Overlapping Networks

Performance networks represent policy tools for achieving controlled outcomes (Ball 2003; Beatty 2007). While most educational policy includes requirements for a safe learning environment, the acts of inspection and visible measures of security in school facilities heighten teachers' and students' fears (Astor et al. 2002; Perryman 2006; Reddy et al. 2001; Ricketts 2007; Roberts et al. 2007; Smith and Smith 2006).

Additionally, most schools face issues of security that are not limited to physical spaces. Past concerns about property invasion by threatening actors, whether students, teachers, parents, or strangers, are one form of violence, but now the invasion of school relationships may come from social networks beyond school walls, in cyberspaces (Caplan 2003; Shapiro and Stefkovich 2011). As with many waves of moral panic concerning damaged relationships among students and school personnel, at this writing, media attention has focused on cyber-bullying and bullying in general (Duncan 2011; Hinduja and Patchin 2011). The boundaries surrounding cyber-bullying, Internet and social networking, and the responsibilities of school personnel have not been enunciated clearly yet (Caplan 2003; Hinduja and Patchin 2011; Shapiro and Stefkovich 2011).

Our model argues that the lack of clarity is the middle space for negotiating between controlled or caring responses. Our single scenario is slightly more informed about the damaged relationship between student and teacher, once the influence of overlapping networks is introduced. Does the posting of either person's discontent with the other in some social media, an instant message (IM), or other transient chat increase the interpretation of the words the student or the teacher used in the school-based incident to the level of threats and bullying? And how would either an AP or SRO be able to access or investigate cyber-words that may have preceded the school incident?

Implications for Practice and Research

Our descriptions of school personnel's dilemmas illustrate the fine line that administrators must walk in ensuring an environment safe for the necessary relationships of teaching and learning. In particular, administrators and other school leaders must balance the desire for risk control with the professional ethic of care across many social levels. In addition, they must be aware of and prepare for the ways in which outside forces can permeate school's physical or cyber-spaces to do violence to relationships among learners and school personnel. Also, we have argued that these constant forces cannot be viewed as mere trespassers because communities and individuals have a right to be in schools. We have offered a model and made a case for a continual steadying of the margins between control and care required in daily schooling practices. At this point, we suggest approaches for practical application and, further, offer recommendations for research, which may provide grounding for our model.

Recommendations for Research

Demographic patterns have emerged, as schools' disciplinary practices and their impact have been reviewed (Beachum et al. 2008; Gregory, Skiba, and Noguera 2010; Osher et al. 2010). These patterns may signal systematic social damage to relationships among the individuals involved in school-wide safety concerns and between teaching and learning relationships. Other recent studies (Freiberg and Lapointe 2006; Horner, Sugai, and Anderson 2010; Upreti, Liaupsin, and Koonce 2010) focus on effectiveness of program components and measures, which admittedly are systems-based, hierarchical packages for school implementation. These analyses diagnose several persisting challenges with ensuring school-wide safety and suggest some systematic remedies. Many of these studies point to the need for investigations of the deeper issues of social capacity for repairing relationships.

Early research in educational administration provided a brief window into teacher and student relationships surrounding student behavior. These studies, known as the Pupil Control Ideology studies (Willower 1978), date back to the late 1960s. Although this line of research's methods and concepts have been critiqued (Packard 1988), this prior agenda conceptualized a theory of dichotomous reactions to perceived threats from student behavior ranging from a custodial orientation to a more humanistic one. The underlying assumptions about the source of threat, student deportment, provided a limited view of the dispersion of risks to school safety. One of the foundational flaws in the theory building of this line of work was a deliberate elimination of pedagogical perspectives (Packard 1988). On the other hand, these studies made some practical contributions. For example, at least one of the so-called remedies of the day was corporal punishment, which seemed the ultimate control mechanism for student unruliness (Packard 1988). These studies contributed a stable finding that the extreme violence of spanking or paddling only damaged the school climate (Hoy 1971; Packard 1988). Even though these studies tried to place the issues of student misbehavior within the complexity of schools as organizations, unlike our proposed model, these studies stopped at the schoolhouse doors. We argue for a research agenda that includes families, neighborhoods and other agencies and organizations connected to schools. This research agenda would focus on walking the line in the emotive environments central to understanding school personnel's role in preventing or perpetrating school violence.

Grounded research elicits the connections and patterns among people and events (Clarke and Friese 2007; Corbin and Strauss 2008). This research approach permits more than surveying statistics of infractions, referrals, and dispensation of student discipline and could yield a deeper investigation of the antecedents and consequences of incidents from their moment in physical school locations to the connected social and cyber-networks among schools, neighborhoods, and communities. Such an approach can draw on multiple perspectives from the primary actors in an incident to those in close proximity, but not necessarily close relational associates, and still also including close friends and families. From these perspectives, school personnel can learn more about their roles in negotiating relationships to protect the learning environment and in enhancing teacher-student relationships.

Recommendations for Practice

The location of the school personnel in the processes of school violence has led us to offer a few recommendations for school leader preparation and practice. Most school personnel are bound by state-issued certification or license, which requires them to uphold state and federal statutes. Moreover, all school personnel hold contracts with local school boards or district trustees that also impose an allegiance to local ordinances and policies. While these are the parameters of work for school personnel, most are prepared for these educative roles with a basic ethic of care, which is maintained by ongoing professional development and participation in professional organizations. However, as other agencies' personnel, such as SROs or caseworkers, become involved in schools, their professional training may hinder the educative ethos. Their work in schools might be shaped by deeper awareness of how their presence forms a risk, no matter how small, to the strength of relationships necessary for learning.

The model offered here may serve as a resource in continuous education requirements so school personnel negotiate the constrictions of their licenses and contracts with creative thinking and reflective care necessary for professional judgments required on the job. The model's service increases as a heuristic for instructional cases, possibly generated through the research agenda grounding it in lived situations in schools.

Among the immediately practical suggestions, which our model projects, is a focus on the importance of encouraging well-trained professionals to exercise their informed judgments in the best interest of *each* student as well as *all* students. Zero-tolerance policies provide narrow prescriptions for complex situations and enfeeble those who have the duty and background to make decisions. While human error is a risk in any profession or institution, zero-tolerance policies raise the risk for error and, in the case of school safety, likely ensure escalation of the disruption to learning.

Conclusions

As pointed out by Muschert and Perguero (2010), the discourse known as the Columbine Effect has "resulted in an increasing number of school administrators implementing school antiviolence policies" (p. 142). However, the implementation of such policies is in itself a complicated process constituted by social forces originating from many levels. The moral panic of the Columbine Effect revealed that school leaders gain emotive energy and fear from the act of policing (Young 2007a). Our scenarios point to a difficult and requisite professional obligation to create balance in a world of uncertainty. This balance cannot be achieved by either an ethic of care or allegiance to a risk-management system. Instead, it is the practice of teetering on the line between control and caring despite the onset of vertigo due to moral panic (Young 2007b).

Notes

This chapter included many contributors from our nontraditional graduate students, who also serve their communities as school leaders, including Betty Bagley, Kristen Hill, Sheila Hilton, and Matthew Moore, among others, for whose support, comments, and insight we are very grateful.

1. Our recognition of balance resonates with Tittle's (1995) control balance theory. However, our perspective diverges in two distinct ways: (a) our concern is not with the generation of deviance nor does it use a behavioral lens and instead engages macro-sociological literature to describe the ways that perceptions of safety can degrade into fear; and (b) our major thesis is located at the fulcrum of Tittle's model in dimensions that Tittle does not address where balance teeters based on micro, meso, and macro negotiations among individuals and groups.

4

The Dynamics of School Discipline in a Neoliberal Era

Aaron Kupchik and Thomas J. Catlaw

As several other chapters in this volume illustrate, over the past two decades schools across the United States have incorporated a host of new security and punishment practices, such as police officers, surveillance cameras, zero-tolerance policies, use of drug-sniffing dogs, metal detectors, and others. Muschert and Peguero (2010) discuss how these practices have been spurred by the Columbine Effect, whereby heightened and widespread fear following the attack at Columbine High School increased the attention paid to school violence (see also Addington 2009). While we agree that "events such as Columbine do exert a high leverage in the discourse about school violence" (Muschert and Peguero 2010, p. 124), in this chapter we frame contemporary school security and punishment as part of a broader historical trend in local and national governance.

Certainly Columbine and other school shootings during the 1990s stoked fear, especially among middle-class, suburban, white parents, who previously viewed school violence as a problem only for urban schools serving poor and racial or ethnic minority youth. In the aftermath of Columbine, policy makers had virtually no choice but to respond to this fear by enacting policies with a promise to prevent future violence in schools. Furthermore, events like Columbine provide powerful rhetorical leverage for justifying and framing how school violence is conceived by policymakers and the general public—much as events like September 11 informed the reception and shaping of antiterrorist policy. But given a wide range of available responses to Columbine—including options for increased counseling, greater funding for schools, academic initiatives, and strategies that increase students' democratic participation in school governance—it is notable that schools' efforts to prevent violence have focused only on a fairly limited cluster of practices that promote exclusion and punishment.

These now commonplace antiviolence practices are fundamentally antidemocratic in how they are applied. Research finds that their primary action is to express and augment the authority of teachers and administrators over students, and in the process deny students the opportunity to discuss their behavior or participate in school governance (see Kupchik 2010; Lyons and Drew 2006; Noguera 2003). Policies such as police presence, mandatory arrests, and zero tolerance seek to detect misbehavior and exclude students from school when caught violating laws or school rules. Their intended effect is therefore to remove problems rather than solve them. Students' concerns, and even their reasons for misbehaving, are often ignored as school staff implement rules without consideration of context. In sum, rules and punishment have become so central to school governance that they are goals unto themselves, often displacing even pedagogic goals (Kupchik 2010).

It is somewhat ironic that schools across the United States have responded to fears of crime by implementing authoritarian policies, since the literature on school misbehavior clearly establishes that schools with a communal social climate experience less crime and disorder than other schools (e.g., Gottfredson 2001; Welsh 2000). A communal social climate is one in which students feel a part of their school community—where they believe they are respected and listened to, and where they feel a bond between adults and children. Because they undermine students' relationships with school staff and potentially alienate them from school, contemporary school security practices contradict a growing body of research on how to keep schools safe (Cornell 2006; Kupchik 2010; Muschert and Peguero 2010; Skiba et al. 2006). Moreover, there is little evidence showing any effectiveness of rigid security or harsh punishments in deterring future misbehavior (Muschert and Peguero 2010).

In the following pages we discuss why schools have acted so similarly in their efforts to promote safety, despite evidence that their efforts may have little effect or even backfire. Reducing students' democratic participation in schools through authoritarian discipline was not the only solution available to the moral panic over school violence, but it is by far the most common one. Though a Columbine Effect certainly has been important, the tragedy at Columbine did not ensure policy action in the particular form that we have seen. As we argue, contemporary school security and punishment practices are informed by and implemented against the backdrop of longer-term trends in US governance and policymaking generally. These broader governance trends, termed "neoliberalism," constitute the interpretive context within which schools and policymakers make sense of events such as Columbine and assess the menu of practically available and politically appropriate responses.

It is, of course, the case that *all* schools in the United States have been governed against this backdrop, but that not all have responded in identical ways or in ways that mirror the neoliberal strategies described next. Moreover, as we note in this chapter, the governance trends themselves display tremendous diversity as they are enacted in unique national and local settings. Thus, our intent here is not to explain post-Columbine, antidemocratic school policies via a grand neoliberal causal narrative. Rather, we wish simply to situate policy and institutional responses to school violence among the more general, and more mundane, practices of governance that have emerged within the same historical period; to illustrate the complementary, reinforcing logics among these governing strategies that are designed to cultivate and manage disorder; and to explore the implications of these strategies for democratic participation.

Our perspective parallels Henry's (2009) call for a multilevel view of school violence, in which violence is the "outcome of several causal processes" (p. 1248) and occurs at several levels. Though we consider school policies rather than school violence, we apply Henry's perspective by considering how school policies reflect broad trends in governance observed across social institutional spheres, rather than trying to locate the sources of these policies only in schools, students, or fearful parents. We also borrow heavily from the insights of Garland (2001) and Simon (2007), both of whom explain the emergence of punitive criminal justice policies (including school policies, for Simon) as a consequence of a shifting structural and cultural terrain that transformed governance over the past several decades. We apply their ideas as well as literature from the field of public administration to help understand the emergence of punitive school security and punishment policies.

Transformations in American Governance

In this section we explore the broader, historical context within which the governance of schools has developed. We argue that it is only in the context of the growing use of markets for moral education, expert incentive design, and the recentralization of authority in administrators and executives that the complex background of contemporary school security and punishment practices is fully intelligible.

The last four decades have been characterized by a radical transformation in the ideology, policies, and techniques of American governance. Succinctly put, the progressive style of government that came to prominence in the late nineteenth century emphasized the regulation and disciplining of individuals and society by expertise exercised through bureaucratically organized governmental institutions (Dean 2010). But today both the idea of the governability of society and the reformability of individuals by government largely have been abandoned. In their place, a paradoxical, punitive regime of governance has emerged. This regime is marked both by fragmentation and centralization and emphasizes several sometimes conflicting practices and ideals, including individual choice and strong authority; the use of contracts and privatization for the provision of public goods; and, perhaps more importantly, an abiding concern for the production of security while advancing a broad strategy of what Catlaw (2007) calls "governing through disorder" and Simon (2007) calls "governing through crime."[1]

This new regime of governance is often dubbed "neoliberalism" or "advanced liberalism" (e.g., Dean 2010; Rose 1997).[2] When implemented in specific countries, states, and even agencies, neoliberalism looks very different, depending on the historical and political setting. Still, it is possible to identify in neoliberalism a distinct set of policies and managerial and administrative practices and strategies that emphasize the role of markets for the provision of public goods and a "smaller" government. On the policy front, neoliberalism calls for a reduction of both the size of government and spending by the state in the area of social welfare services and economic regulation—cornerstones of progressive governance. The prescribed role of government is limited to the provision of those military, police, and legal institutions that protect private property, encourage entrepreneurial initiative, and create conditions for the development and efficient functioning of markets. Neoliberal policy is informed not merely by the elevation of markets but also by a critique of government. As Brown and Jacobs (2008, pp. 22–24) summarize the neoliberal brief: "government mainly fails"; "government is incompetent" and in any case, the social world is so opaque that we cannot possibly have enough knowledge to make policies with which we can govern society;

government cannot advance the fiction of the public interest since it is inevitably captured by special interests and bureaucrats are utility-maximizing rent-seekers themselves; government unjustly and unjustifiably curtails individual freedom; and government only gets worse, beginning a "spiral" that "aggravates capture and kindred public sector pathologies."

On the managerial and administrative front, neoliberalism is known as the new public management and includes a now-familiar toolbox of reforms and strategies that seek to inject a market-logic into the administration of government. We briefly consider some of the common reform measures here (see Kjaer 2004, pp. 25–37). First, an active, expert manager or executive is placed at the controls of governmental management in lieu of, or at the expense of, forms of popular, democratic control. Second, publicly owned enterprises are sold or transferred to private hands. In the United States, where state-managed industries were rarer than in other countries, privatization is undertaken primarily through contracting out government functions or service provision to private and nonprofit entities. Third, government bureaus are often broken up into smaller units based on task or function, for example, revenue collection. Fourth, the policy- and decisionmaking authority is decentralized to subnational governments or communities. Fifth, competition is seen as a way to enhance efficient use of public funds and accountability, and to obtain better outcomes. Thus, for example, public sector agencies are encouraged to compete with one another and the private sector for the public's "business." Within government, internal or quasi-markets may be created. School choice or voucher programs are a visible example.

Our task here is neither to explore the possible causes for the eclipse of progressive or democratic governance nor to criticize the disconcerting assumptions of neoliberalism. Rather, our concern is, what does the celebration of markets have to do with school security practices? More precisely, how does the backdrop of neoliberal government help us to contextualize the preference for, and application of, one set of school security and punishment practices over another? To begin with, neoliberalism elevates "security" as a primary value (Catlaw 2007; Dean 2010) and, in this sense, is consistent with the classical liberal justification for the government itself: security for the individual and his or her body and property from the dangers of the state of nature. But, at the same time, there are other ways to conceptualize and enable security, such as the strategies of social insurance and welfare that protect individuals from illness or economic downturn. Neoliberalism for its part eschews such welfarist strategies in favor of security through exclusion, often through incarceration (Wacquant 2009), just as schools in particular attempt to maintain security through suspension, exclusion, and arrest rather than by responding to students' underlying problems with counselors or remedial education (Kupchik 2010).

The preference for exclusionary and punitive school discipline policies can be understood by looking at some of the conflicting elements of neoliberal *theory* as it is commonly *practiced* and how it creates a coherent, if vindictive, regime of governance (see Wacquant 2009). Neoliberalism is enabled by the presence of both a strong naturalism and strong constructivism. In other words, on the one hand, it is characterized by a nostalgic, seemingly neutral rhetoric about scaling back government in order to "return" to a less regulated, simpler, more "natural" society before the advent of the welfare state (Catlaw 2007). On the other hand, neoliberal governance is highly active in the *construction* of markets and institutional spaces based on market logics where there were none previously (Foucault [2004] 2008; Harvey 2005, p. 79), such as government, civil society, and even the family. With its active, constructionist orientation, neoliberalism breaks definitively with nineteenth-century laissez-faire in which government was theorized to merely oversee the workings of the self-regulating, prepolitical market. Under neoliberalism, government is active and aggressive, not merely in restoring those domains "violated" by social government to their pre-welfarist condition, but also to construct new markets spaces and market-based relationships.

Consider two examples. First, the Pentagon's Defense Advanced Research Projects Agency (DARPA) developed the "Policy Analysis Market," based on an idea developed by the private San Diego firm, Net Exchange. This project sought to create an online foreign policy futures market with the hope of predicting violence and political developments in the Middle East. In simple terms, the idea was to mobilize the so-called wisdom of crowds (Surowiecki 2004) expressed by the prices of futures contracts. The contracts would effectively be bets on the likelihood of some event happening, like the overthrow of a regime or, controversially, political assassinations. High prices would indicate high probabilities of events actually happening since the price would reflect the underlying "rationality" and collective information pooling of the marketplace. While the notion of betting on violence and killing proved to be unpalatable to Congress and the public, thereby forcing the Defense Department to internally shut down its Middle East market, the Pentagon continues to explore this project. Though the work has shifted, Net Exchange continues to develop related foreign-policy instruments. Another example is the Central Intelligence Agency's (CIA's) venture capital (VC) firm, In-Q-Tel. Believing that government could not adapt quickly enough to technological innovations used by perceived threats, the CIA established this nonprofit VC that provides seed money to start-up high-technology firms with promising, innovative intelligence-related product designs. These illustrate not only the invention of new "markets" but also the use of markets and market rationalities as governing strategies.

This realignment of governance corresponds closely to aspects of school security. A primary justification for school security is to deal with today's presumed "out-of-control" youngsters, who are compared nostalgically to the youth of previous generations (Kupchik 2010). Surveillance and security are promised as means to restore order and return to a school in which teachers were able to focus entirely on academic content. Yet these nostalgic ideas of teachers' duties and students' behaviors are not accurate, as even early schoolteachers focused a considerable amount of attention on the physical discipline of students (Tyack 1974), and most forms of student misbehaviors and crimes have been decreasing for nearly twenty years (Robers, Zhang, and Truman 2010). Moreover, school security policies can at times lead to the construction of new functional departments, such as in schools with multiple "deans of discipline," who perform functions previously reserved for teachers, principals, and assistant principals.

It is important to appreciate that neoliberal markets are not merely places for the exchange of goods and services, but rather places and practices for the moral education of citizens, an education thought to be corrupted by the interventions of welfarism (see Lakoff 2002). Central to this moral education is the self-discipline instilled by competition. We can see this at work in how government is instructed to use markets to reform itself through the new public management. Welfarist government (like the citizen under welfarism) is depicted as flabby, wasteful, and irresponsible. The introduction of market competition is intended to address this and to *teach* a steely ethic of responsibility, autonomy, prudence, and principled free choice. Again the connection to schools is obvious, since school security is promised to have educational value, in that it teaches proper conduct to youth. The facts that police teach programs such as Drug Abuse Resistance

Education (DARE), which has repeatedly failed to show any positive effects (Rosenbaum et al. 1994), to young children, and that police in many schools are required to teach a certain number of hours each school year (Kupchik and Bracy 2010), make this clear.

Finally, markets are used as a sorting mechanism that removes those organizations—and people—who cannot acquit themselves of the demands of market competition and the privileges of freedom. Schools have perhaps learned this lesson better than any other organization, as evidenced by rates of suspension and expulsion in recent years, particularly for racial and ethnic minority youth (see Kim, Losen, and Hewitt 2010).

An important issue, though, is how this overreliance on the use of markets, and the individualism it encourages, creates disorder and disruption in society (Polanyi 1944). As Harvey (2005) rightly notes, the instability produced by deregulation and marketization necessitates the use of nationalist and xenophobic political rhetoric in order to fabricate some minimal level of social cohesion.[3] More generally, neoliberalism exhibits centralizing tendencies and a bias toward formal authority figures—in spite of its emphasis on decentralization, individualism, and choice—in order to manage its disruptive effects. Though it rejects the progressive notion of a governable society and its "elite" expertise, neoliberalism nevertheless also avers that social contexts are essentially rationally programmable as market spaces (Rose 1997, p. 53). This is familiar in the ubiquitous contemporary demand to "get the incentives right." In contrast to democratic collaboration, social spaces are reimagined as "design spaces" in which expertly devised incentives induce certain "freely chosen" behaviors of rationally self-interested actors. Thus in decentralizing or hollowing out government through privatization or contracts (Rhodes 1994), neoliberalism *re*centralizes power in the hands of managers, administrators, and executives, and also inscribes into everyday life a subtle contempt for average citizens and workers, who are the objects of these incentive schemes. Catlaw (2007) has called the combination and consequences of these tactics that seek to produce and manage social disruption "governing through disorder" (see also note 1).

In sum, notwithstanding the variation in its implementation, the broad strategies of everyday neoliberal governance are clear. First, neoliberal governance exhibits a tendency toward centralization of authority in administration, management, and executives. Second, neoliberalism seeks to incite a kind of individual agency and ethic of self-regulation through markets but at the same time to control and manipulate that agency to the predefined ends of those in authority. Third, the practices of authority are basically concerned with managing the obvious tension between administrative control and inciting individual agency. This is the core problem of *security*—security, that is, of the borders of local sites (like workplaces, schools, government agencies) and the policing and monitoring within them, since these spaces are, after all, populated with agents who may, at any time, get out of control. The abiding concern for security is no doubt a major reason why crime has become such a central and, for authority, valuable resource for contemporary governance, as Jonathan Simon argues in his recent book, *Governing Through Crime* (2007; see also Wacquant 2009). Fourth, a growing sense of insecurity and distrust (see Nye, Zelikow, and King 1997) means that the problem of security and the perpetual threat of disorder offer authority new grounds to legitimatize itself (Garland 2001; Simon 2007). Finally, in this world, authority does not reform or rehabilitate; it punishes and removes those who make "poor choices" or fail to be disciplined by the market. In doing so it changes the relationship between citizens and government in an important way. To paraphrase school administrator William Finnegan (in Simon 2007, pp. 222–223), authority now tells us what it expects from us and removes us if we give it trouble.

These neoliberal practices and values can be seen clearly in the particular strategies schools now use to promote safety—including surveillance, policing, zero tolerance, suspension, expulsion, drug-sniffing dogs, and others. Of course it makes sense that during a time of insecurity and reorganization, schools would adopt the principles of governance that reign outside schools. The same politicians who advocate neoliberal policies in other domains also set school policies, and school administrators take their ideas and plans from the toolkit of strategies that are popular and available at the time (Simon 2007).

But the close alignment between school security and neoliberal governance means that what is currently happening in schools has its roots in governance practices that are shared by other institutional spheres and that are several decades old (see Hirschfield 2008; Simon 2007). Thus it would be a mistake to assume that the events themselves at Columbine inspired the punitive, undemocratic regime of school security and punishment that we see today. Certainly Columbine directed additional attention to the problem of school violence, and it served as a justification for the expansion of school security and punishment. But these were trends that were already well established.

Perhaps more importantly, though, Columbine was a call to action without any intrinsic direction. It was neoliberal governance that provided this direction, which is aimed at punishment and exclusion rather than counseling or other welfare-oriented responses to students' needs.

Developing Neoliberal Citizens

Considering school security and punishment as a part of broader trends in governance also allows us to consider more clearly their potential political and social consequences. Police in schools and zero-tolerance policies may or may not prevent one kind of violence that Henry (2009) refers to as level-one violence among students; further empirical research is needed to answer this question. But it adds violence at other levels and from other sources, such as from teacher to student, from administrator to teacher and to student, and from school board to schools (see Henry 2009; Muschert and Peguero 2010). Moreover, because they are embedded in a series of governance strategies born out of a particular view of the role of citizens, they are likely to shape young citizens in certain ways.

Of course scholars have long recognized that schools' choices about their curricula, organization, and other practices matter in many ways that surpass their impacts on course instruction (Dewey [1909] 1959; Durkheim [1903] 1961; Gutmann [1987] 1999). As many have pointed out, schools impart lessons to students by socializing them into future social, political, and economic roles (often called the "hidden curriculum"; Giroux and Purpel 1983). According to David Tyack (1974), for example, early nineteenth-century public schools taught youth skills, such as physical discipline, punctuality, and respect for authority, that they were to need in their likely roles as factory workers. Paul Willis's (1977) study of working-class boys in England likewise illustrates how youth are taught in school how to relate to authorities in a way that reproduces their parents' class status (see also Apple 2004; Bowles and Gintis 1977).

In addition to labor market roles, schools also teach youth a great deal about their likely future opportunities for social and political action (Brady, Verba, and Schlozman 1995). Schools teach middle-class norms and expectations, and reward these behaviors as if they are the result of effort and intelligence alone, rather than shaped by students' class status (Bourdieu and Passeron 1990). As a result, students who learn skills at home such as the ability to debate and ask acceptable questions of authorities—skills that are much more likely to be taught in middle-class homes than working-class homes (Lareau 2003)—are perceived to be more astute than others. Through this process of recognizing markers of social-class status, schools sort students into those perceived to have high potential for future success and those perceived to have low potential, and teach them skills relevant for their projected paths. When we apply this understanding to school security and punishment, it is clear that school policies do more than prevent violence (or fail to do so); they also teach youth about how to relate to authority as they socialize students into future political roles.

What lessons are youth likely to learn from the hidden curriculum embodied in contemporary school security and punishment? As we have suggested already, under neoliberal governance, democracy is not on the agenda. Even the rhetorically prized individual liberty is circumscribed by the narrowing of individual agency in the market ethic and the centralization of authority. Contemporary school policies are quite clear and consistent with this in their message about how youth should relate to authorities: they communicate a complete lack of social and political power. As Casella (2001), Kupchik (2010), and Lyons and Drew (2006) describe, school policies undermine students' ability to shape the school environment, and thus negatively impact school social climate. They pit students against the school by enacting a vision of students as potential criminals who can neither be trusted nor allowed to shape school policy or participate in its practice. Disciplinarians do not listen to students when they punish them and students' concerns are not addressed by security and crime prevention efforts.

Beyond socializing students into certain relationships to authority, the neoliberal school is likely to have other "political spillover" effects.[4] We hypothesize that neoliberal school security and punishment practices have a dampening effect on students' future civic participation. There is little empirical research on this subject, though the scant evidence that is available supports our hypothesis.[5] One study, by David Campbell (2006), finds that students who attend schools with more inclusive and democratic social climates are more likely than others to vote years later. His research suggests that schools that empower students to be active citizens of a school also teach them to be active citizens of a nation in the longer term. McFarland and Thomas (2006) find somewhat similar results—that active engagement in certain kinds of extracurricular activities among students is associated with active political participation years later. Both studies support the idea that school inclusiveness is associated with future political and civic participation, and suggest that certain school policies that alienate students may squelch their future democratic participation.

Calvin Morrill and colleagues (2010) likewise support our expectations with their recent research on legal mobilization in schools. Morrill and colleagues used surveys and in-depth interviews of high school students in three states to better understand students' responses to both hypothetical and actual rights violations in schools, such as suspension without due process or racial discrimination by a teacher, and how these responses vary across race. They found that African American students are more likely than white students to claim that they would pursue legal remedies (e.g., a lawsuit) in response to a hypothetical rights violation. But this effect disappears once the researchers account for actual past experience with perceived rights violations. They interpret this result as evidence that African American students learn from their experiences in school to be resigned to injustice. Their qualitative analysis of in-depth interviews sheds greater light on this finding: "Interviews with African American youth revealed the unfairness and resignation with which African American youth regarded how their schools handle rights violations and discipline" (Morrill et al. 2010, p. 683). We therefore would speculate that as school security and punishment become increasingly severe and restrictive, the number of students who experience such feelings and the intensity with which they feel them will increase.

Democratic Alternatives

Such a negative outcome is not inevitable or the only possibility for the governance of schools and the cultivation of citizenship today. Though neoliberal forms of governance dominate contemporary American society, there are grounds to be optimistic that a more democratic alternative could find support and take root if it is chosen and encouraged. While neoliberalism seeks to maintain centralized authority and perversely create a sense of danger and disorder to justify itself (see Garland 2001; Simon 2007), it also encourages individual agency that could be oriented to different collective ends and

purposes. Furthermore, while neoliberal forms of governance dominate American society, they are not the only visible and important
forms. Since the advent of neoliberalism in the early 1970s, American governance has been marked by a powerful counterdemand for
public participation and public engagement (Held 1996; Nalbandian
2005). And notwithstanding pessimism about the levels of civic
engagement in the United States (e.g., Putnam 2000), there is evidence that citizens are engaging in higher levels of elite-challenging
behavior than ever before, and institutions characterized by hierarchical authority have seen their popular support decline dramatically
over the last three decades (Nye, Zelikow, and King 1997). Hundreds
of federal, state, and local governments are now required to include
citizens in rulemaking and administrative processes (e.g., Kathi and
Cooper 2005). Furthermore, though not widespread, some schools
also have sought to engage students as fuller participants in the governance of their education (e.g., Apple and Beane 1999).[6] Though all
that glitters is not gold in these initiatives, they do represent an
important political space for encouraging a more active, engaged
practice of citizenship than the one offered by neoliberalism.

However, to think about democratic citizenship in this manner
requires us to consider the idea beyond the conventional, albeit
important, forms of democratic participation like voting and volunteering and to focus on the effects of the hidden curriculum in contemporary schools on citizenship. This, in turn, requires a more
robust definition of "democracy." To this point, in their comprehensive analysis of the theoretical and empirical scholarship on "everyday democracy," Rawlings and Catlaw (2011, p. 51) summarize:

> Democracy . . . refers to a particular qualitative process or way of talk-
> ing and interacting with others. This process emphasizes openness to
> the other; flexible habits of mind; a concern for individual creativity,
> autonomy, and personal efficacy; involvement in the tasks close at hand
> in our lives, which, in turn, seems to facilitate the development of a
> sense of self in relation to others; and close attention to the concrete
> empirical situation. It is concerned . . . with the particular *texture* of
> contextual interaction or contact and a kind of mutual learning through
> activity and interaction that such contact provides.

This understanding is consistent with Apple and Beane (1999), who
identify seven capacities that democratic schools should cultivate,
including an appreciation for an open flow of ideas, "faith in the
individual and collective capacity of people" to solve problems, critical reflection, "concern for the welfare of others and the 'common

good,'" and a "concern for the dignity and rights of individuals and minorities" (p. 7). The cornerstone of cultivating these capacities is *participation*—that is, engagement of students in school-related planning, decisionmaking, problem solving, and other activities that affect them at both the classroom and school levels. Exemplary democratic schools tend to view students as active, rights-bearing individuals rather than "objects to be acted upon" (Dobozy 2007).

These practices, which would give students more direct and immediate influence in formulating the policies and practices that affect them, clearly are not emphasized in neoliberal forms of governance that dominate schools today. Such everyday democratic practices require that those in authority cease to view security as their underlying goal and youth as potential threats to maintaining order. While schools may never be able to completely prevent events like Columbine, they can change the way in which we respond to them. We can create a more communal social climate in which students feel a part of their school community—where they believe they are respected and listened to and where they "jointly construct [with adults] the moral and social fabric of the common culture" (Schwartz 1987, p. 5).

Conclusion

Our goal in this chapter has been to clarify the context underlying the emergence of the particular school security policies that have become prominent in American public schools in recent decades. As we discuss, contemporary school security and punishment practices can be seen as part of the trends in neoliberal governance, broadly.[7] Though the ways in which neoliberalism and school governance intersect in concrete situations is, of course, complex, it is sufficient for us to recognize that school policies are embedded in, and draw heavily from, a larger political context for their direction. As schools have implemented new practices and policies, they have done so in a way that mirrors changes in workplaces, government, and other public spaces and quite visibly draws from a common array of tactics and policies.

We also discuss potential long-term consequences of school security. Our concern is that because they are authoritarian and undemocratic, contemporary school practices may dampen students' future civic participation, including discreet practices such as voting or volunteering as well as subtler behaviors such as the practices of "everyday democracy." Whether our concerns are valid is an empirical question that, to the best of our knowledge, no current research considers.

Despite the urgent need for empirical research on this question, we urge caution in how this research is done. At first glance, it is not self-evident that our hypothesis is correct, since there has been little decline in young adult voting or youth volunteering since the spread of punitive school security and punishment (see civicyouth.org). But such a view is insufficient. As we noted earlier, while dominated by neoliberal forms of governance, there are counter, democratizing trends in contemporary American society. Moreover, instead of considering overall trends, it is necessary to use longitudinal data to better understand the trajectories of individual youths who encounter varying school policies, and to compare the youth of different levels of social and cultural capital and how they respond to authoritarian school practices.

Our hope is that through continued scholarship and advocacy via projects like the current edited volume, we will see significant shifts in school security and punishment policies. Regardless of how they shape long-term democratic participation, these policies have been shown to be unfair and counterproductive. They exacerbate racial and class inequality, thus exacerbating violence done by schools to students (Henry 2009), while showing little to no evidence of improving school safety (see Kim, Losen, and Hewitt 2010; Muschert and Peguero 2010; Skiba, Michael, and Nardo 2000), issues that themselves should be worrisome for a democratic polity. Granted, it seems unlikely that schools will back down from the implementation of neoliberal governance any time soon for several reasons. Policies that arise from neoliberal governance have become institutionalized and expected in schools, and may protect them from the threat of litigation. But more importantly, they adhere to the strategies and policies that dominate the world of governance today. At the same time, we might draw optimism, generally, from the countering trend of democratization and, in particular, from American schools, which in the past have been at the forefront of many major changes in society, such as racial integration.

Notes

1. Catlaw sees "governing through disorder" as a broader description of the ways in which authorities have sought to maintain social control; the manufacture and use of crime would be an important subset of this trend, as would the

related use of fear (Robin 2004). An example of governing through disorder that does not involve crime per se would be everyday management strategies that seek to inculcate competition among employees through "pay for performance," with the effect of eroding workplace relationships and destabilizing job stability.

2. See also David Garland's (2001) discussion of social order in "late modernity."

3. Consider as well Henry's (2009) discussion of how school policies can contribute to violence against students.

4. See Rawlings and Catlaw (2011) for an overview of this and related literatures.

5. For the most part, empirical studies of the effects of democratic capacity building and political socialization have been case studies of individual schools or classrooms (e.g., Angell 1998; Apple and Beane 1999) or investigations of the effects of various democratic practices on students while students were in school (e.g., Feldman et al. 2007). While these studies are invaluable for demonstrating the range of approaches and techniques available for democratic schooling and their immediate effects, they do not shed light on the long-term effects of democratic schooling on political and civic participation after graduation from high school. Empirical examination along these lines has been exceedingly rare (see Pasek et al. 2008; Zaff et al. 2003). This was the conclusion reached by Ehman (1980) in his review of the literature on schooling and political socialization some thirty years ago, and it remains the case today.

6. Though it is unlikely to be comprehensive, a global listing of "democratic schools" has been compiled by the Alternative Education Resource Organization (http://www.educationrevolution.org/demschool.html).

7. See Wacquant (2009) for a detailed discussion of how punishment practices broadly, especially mass incarceration, need to be considered in the context of neoliberalism as well. For a consideration of how mass incarceration is used as a tool of governance and maintaining social integration, see Catlaw (2007, ch. 6).

Part 2
Contemporary Policies

5

Surveillance and Security Approaches Across Public School Levels

Lynn A. Addington

While researchers have devoted great attention to working to understand the causes of school violence, less is known about the decisions to adopt particular policies to address the problem. One important factor contributing to changes in policy and security practices is likely a response to actual or feared escalation in school violence. The fatal shootings at Columbine High School provide a clear illustration of this reaction. The aftermath of Columbine prompted a variety of policy proposals and changes across the United States to address the perceived epidemic of school violence. One set of responses centered on increasing school security with an emphasis on the use of visible security measures. These "visible security measures" include the presence of surveillance devices (such as metal detectors and security cameras), the use of identification of students and staff (such as IDs or uniforms), and the employment of trained personnel (such as law enforcement officers and private security guards). Although these measures have an unknown effectiveness and a high financial cost, they appeared to be popular methods for school administrators seeking to tangibly demonstrate the safety of their school to worried parents (Addington 2009; Muschert and Peguero 2010). Federal government funding and targeted marketing from private security companies also promoted the use of security officers and cameras (Addington 2009; Casella 2006). Little is known about the long-term changes in school security in the dozen years since Columbine, especially in terms of the use of security across school levels and the characteristics associated with schools opting to employ particular security devices. Addressing this omission can help inform the policy debate over school security. Critics argue that the overzealous use of security measures in relatively safe schools negatively affects students and their educational environment. In contrast, advocates point to the necessity of these same measures in troubled schools struggling to combat serious violence. This chapter seeks to contribute to this discussion by assessing various factors associated with changes in policy and security practices.

Background

The use of security practices and equipment in US schools is not new, but it has evolved over time. Decades before Columbine, schools utilized a variety of security measures; however, their original purpose largely focused on deterring property crimes (such as the theft of school equipment) and problems arising from graffiti and vandalism of the school building (Lawrence 2007; National Institute of Education 1978). Starting in the 1980s, schools redirected these efforts to preventing school violence and crime against individual victims. Practices such as the use of metal detectors and security guards initially were limited to "problematic" urban schools, such as those in New York, Chicago, and Los Angeles (Crews and Counts 1997; Hirschfield 2010; Vera Institute of Justice 1999). In more recent years, what "school violence" entails and the characteristics of schools opting to employ these security practices have broadened. The definition of school violence has expanded from physical assaults and robberies (US National Institute of Education 1978) to include a range of behaviors ranging from lethal assaults to bullying and verbal threats.[1] During this same time, utilization of school security grew from urban schools to those located in suburban and rural areas. Although schools in these areas started adopting measures such as police and surveillance cameras, they did so in a different manner than their urban counterparts. Here schools, especially in the affluent suburban areas, took steps to minimize creating an institutional atmosphere, as frequently occurs in inner-city schools (Hirschfield 2010).

While US schools increased security over time, little attention has been devoted to systematically studying these trends since Columbine or their effects (see Muschert and Peguero 2010, for a discussion). Studies that have examined security changes since Columbine present a similar picture: the greatest increases have occurred in the monitoring of students by security guards or police and through surveillance by cameras (Addington 2009; Snell et al. 2002). Other popular measures, such as requiring visitors to sign in and using staff supervision in the building, showed little increase as they were commonly used before Columbine. More extreme measures, such as metal detectors, were not frequently used before or after Columbine (Addington 2009).

Concerns about the expanding use of surveillance measures in schools have prompted inquiry into their possible negative repercussions on the schools and their students. A common observation is that security measures, such as police, cameras, and metal detectors, create a prison-like, institutional atmosphere, especially for schools located in low-income or inner-city areas (Hirschfield 2010; Noguera 1995). Although suburban schools might try to create a more positive school security experience (Hirschfield 2010), the employment of police and security cameras cannot help but convey to students an underlying message of accusation or vulnerability since "all students [are being] treated as if they were either sources or targets of potential danger" (Erikson 2001, p. 119). This environment can generate student fear, resentment, and other negative reactions that can interfere with promoting an effective learning environment. Commentators have suggested that the overzealous use of security measures in relatively safe schools is associated with negative repercussions such as increased student fear and a greater threat to student civil liberties (Addington 2009; Bracy 2010; Schreck and Miller 2003).

Given these negative consequences, more work is needed to better understand the use of security in US public schools, particularly with regard to comparisons across school levels and an understanding of the characteristics of schools that opt to utilize particular types of security measures. Studies of school security overall, and since Columbine, focus on middle and high schools. This emphasis is understandable since crime and violence problems occur most frequently among older students. As a result, little is known about the utilization of security in elementary schools (see Fox and Burstein 2010). Obtaining a better understanding of the use of security measures across various grade levels will provide a context for assessing students' experiences with security and surveillance over the course of their educational careers.

Little attention also has been given to exploring the characteristics of schools that adopt particular security policies (Nickerson and Spears 2007). Descriptive studies suggest that security measures such as metal detectors and guards are employed most frequently by schools struggling with issues of crime and delinquency, especially those located in inner-city, high-crime areas (Devine 1996; Noguera 1995; Vera Institute of Justice 1999). Few studies, though, have systematically explored factors related to a school's decision to adopt a particular form of security or policy (Pagliocca and Nickerson 2001). Understanding the characteristics associated with the presence of specific types of security measures can help to contextualize post-Columbine changes in security. Of particular interest is whether security measures such as police, surveillance cameras, and metal detectors continue to be present primarily in schools addressing demonstrated problems with violence, or whether these tactics are commonplace in schools located in relatively safe areas.

To address these gaps in the current literature, this chapter explores two primary research questions. The initial question is: what are the trends since Columbine in the use of security in US schools overall and across particular school levels? The second question is: what school characteristics, if any, are associated with the use of particular security measures?

Methodology

Data

To answer these research questions, this study uses data from the School Survey of Crime and Safety (SSOCS) Restricted-Use Data File.[2] The following description largely relies on information provided by Neiman and DeVoe (2009) and Ruddy and her colleagues (2010). The first SSOCS data collection was conducted in the 1999–2000 school year.[3] These data have been collected on a biannual basis since 2003. The SSOCS data are compiled from a nationally representative stratified sample of public schools in the United States. The survey is sent to school principals. The principal (or other knowledgeable school official) answers questions concerning the frequency of crime at the school, nature of the school environment, characteristics of school safety programs, and the school's disciplinary responses. The data collection mode is a mail-based survey with a telephone follow-up to bolster response rates.[4] The sample is based on the National Center of Education Statistics (NCES) Schools and Staffing Survey sampling frame and purposefully oversamples middle and high schools due to the survey's focus on crime-related issues.

The present study uses all years of currently available data: 1999–2000, 2003–2004, 2005–2006, and 2007–2008. Four levels of schools are included in the SSOCS data: elementary, middle, high, and combination schools. Since the present study is interested in comparing schools with traditional grade levels, all combination schools are removed from the sample. The Appendix provides the respective sample sizes for each year of data.

Variables Used

The variables of interest for this study include: school level, types of security, and characteristics of the school. School level and types of security are examined for all four years of SSOCS data. More in-depth analyses are conducted using school characteristics for the most recent year of data (2007–2008). The SSOCS Restricted-Use File includes variables derived from the SSOCS survey instrument as well as variables obtained from the Common Core Data (CCD), which constitutes the NCES's annual census of data from all public schools in the United States. The Appendix provides frequencies for all study variables.

School level is characterized as elementary, middle, or high school. As noted, schools designated as combination schools are removed from the sample. The school level variable is based on information collected by the CCD.

Six types of visible security measures are included in this study. Four of these measures come directly from SSOCS items that ask about characteristics of school policies used during the current school year. These four measures are: (1) requiring visitors to sign or check in (*visitor sign-in*), (2) controlling access to school buildings during school hours (*locked doors*), (3) requiring students to wear badges or picture IDs (*student IDs*), and (4) using one or more security cameras to monitor the school (*security cameras*). The fifth measure combines two of these items (whether the school requires students to pass through metal detectors each day and whether it performs one or more random metal-detector checks on students) into a single "any use of metal detectors" item (*metal detectors*).[5] The final measure concerns the use of security officers, which include law enforcement or school resource officers as well as other paid security officials.[6] Several questions are asked about the use of security officers. For purposes of this study, a school is counted as using security officers if these officials are used at any time during school hours (*security officers*).

The four school characteristic variables (school size, urbanicity, neighborhood crime levels, and the school's violent crime rate) all concern school crime. School size, urbanicity, and neighborhood crime levels are attributes identified by previous research as associated with high levels of disorganization or crime and delinquency in schools. Larger schools experience greater disorder and disciplinary problems than smaller schools (Lawrence 2007). *School size* is based on CCD information and is coded into four categories: under 300 students, 300 to 499 students, 500 to 999 students, and over 1,000 students. Urban schools, particularly those in inner-city districts, experience higher levels of crime and delinquency as compared to those in nonurban locations (Gottfredson 2001). *Urbanicity* also is based on CCD data concerning the location of the school. The four categories are city (inside urban area and principal city), suburb (inside urban area but not in principal city), town (inside urban area but outside city), and rural. Schools located in higher-crime neighborhoods tend to experience more crime and violence than those in lower-crime areas (Gottfredson and Gottfredson 1985). *Neighborhood crime* concerns the school principal's perception about the level of crime in the neighborhood where the school is located. Possible response categories to this SSOCS item are low, moderate, and high crime levels. The level of school crime also is measured directly. *Violent crime rate* is a variable created using the number of violent incidents at the school for the current school year as reported by school officials to SSOCS questions. Violent incidents include rape, attempted rape, sexual battery, robbery (with and without a weapon), attacks (with and without a weapon), and threats of attacks (with and without a weapon). This number is divided by the total number of students at the school provided by the CCD. In following the practice in NCES publications, this rate is multiplied by 1,000 and reported as a school violence rate per 1,000 students for the year.

Analyses Conducted

Initial exploratory analyses are conducted using descriptive analyses and contingency tables. To compare predictors of use of school security measures, binary logistic regression models are estimated. Analyzing SSOCS data requires giving special attention to the appropriate weights, imputed data, and complex sample structure. All analyses presented use weighted data. Weighted data allow inferences to be made about the population. In addition, the SSOCS weights minimize nonresponse bias, reduce sampling error, and adjust for oversampling of middle and high schools (Neiman and DeVoe 2009). Although the vast majority of the individual SSOCS items of interest for this study have high response rates (over 95 percent), NCES provides imputed data in both its public-use and restricted-use files for all years but the initial year of data collection (1999–2000). Details of the imputation process are provided by Ruddy and her colleagues (2010). For the analyses using the 1999–2000 SSOCS data, complete case analysis is used since the variables of interest have less than 1 percent missing data (Allison 2002). Finally, SSOCS data are collected using a stratified random sample. To obtain the correct standard errors and interpretations of the significance tests, this complex sampling design needs to be considered. All analyses presented utilize the jackknife replication method to adjust for the complex sample following the practice by NCES (Ruddy et al. 2010). Readers interested in a detailed discussion about this method are directed to Heeringa, West, and Berglund (2010).

Findings

Figure 5.1 depicts the overall trends in school security since the 1999–2000 school year. For all schools, the use of security cameras increased the most and the most steadily of all six measures. Reports in the use of security cameras rose from 19.1 to 54.7 percent, which represents an almost 300 percent increase from 1999–2000 to 2007–2008. The use of security guards also showed a marked increase, rising from 31.8 to 42.8 percent (or an increase of over a third). Both visitor sign-in and locked doors remained consistently popular measures and used by a large percentage of schools. This pattern is not surprising given that both measures are fairly inexpensive and easy to implement. Reports about the use of metal detectors and student IDs also had a consistent pattern following Columbine, but here only a small percentage of schools utilized these measures. The finding of a small, and unchanged, percentage of schools using student IDs is interesting since anecdotal reports indicated these measures were more widely used after Columbine (Addington 2009).

To explore these trends in more depth, three measures were selected for further study: security cameras, security guards, and metal detectors. These three are selected because all three require

Figure 5.1 Trends in the Use of Particular Security Measures over Time, SSOCS (various years)

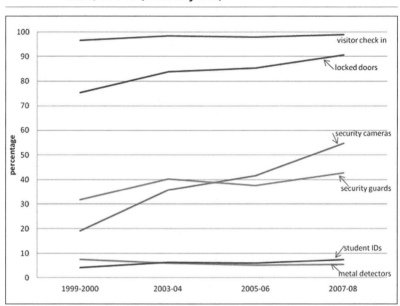

some monetary expenditure by the school.[7] In addition, security cameras and guards are of interest since both increased dramatically since Columbine. Metal detectors, on the other hand, provide a useful comparison as their limited use remained consistent and this measure is typically viewed as one of the more extreme forms of school security.

Table 5.1 disaggregates the use of each measure by school level for all four years of data. Trends are observed similar to the overall trends depicted in Figure 5.1. A few points are noteworthy. For metal detectors, no significant difference is observed across any level over the four years. More metal detectors are used in middle and high schools as opposed to elementary schools for all four years. With regard to security cameras, an increase is observed across all school levels, but this increase is the greatest for elementary and middle schools (both of which saw a threefold increase) as compared to high schools (where the use doubled). The greatest use, however, occurs at the high school level. For school security guards, a similar pattern to the growth in use of cameras is observed. Elementary and middle schools saw the largest increase in use over the time period (about a

Table 5.1 Percentage of Schools Using Particular Security Measures by School Level Across Years, SSOCS (various years)

Type of Security/ School Level	Year			
	1999–2000 (95% CI)	2003–2004 (95% CI)	2005–2006 (95% CI)	2007–2008 (95% CI)
Metal Detectors				
Elementary	3.5 (2.1–4.9)	2.6 (1.4–3.9)	2.3 (1.1–3.4)	2.4 (1.3–3.5)
Middle	13.8 (11.3–16.3)	10.7 (8.7–12.8)	9.2 (7.4–11.1)	10.1 (8.3–11.9)
High	15.1 (12.5–17.8)	13.9 (11.9–15.8)	11.4 (9.3–13.5)	11.7 (9.8–13.7)
Security Cameras				
Elementary	14.1 (11.2–17.0)	28.5 (24.8–32.1)	31.4 (27.6–35.2)	45.9 (41.4–50.3)
Middle	20.5 (17.5–23.5)	41.8 (38.5–45.2)	52.5 (49.4–55.6)	66.0 (62.8–69.1)
High	38.6 (34.9–42.4)	60.3 (56.4–64.3)	69.7 (66.3–73.0)	76.6 (73.1–80.0)
Security Officers				
Elementary	20.8 (17.5–24.2)	27.5 (24.3–30.6)	21.5 (17.9–25.1)	28.4 (24.5–32.2)
Middle	46.7 (42.9–50.5)	61.2 (57.9–64.5)	61.3 (58.6–63.9)	62.4 (59.0–65.8)
High	60.2 (56.1–64.2)	69.3 (65.8–72.8)	73.0 (69.6–76.4)	76.9 (74.3–79.5)

33 percent increase in both cases). The use of security guards in high schools increased by about 25 percent, and these schools had the highest percentage of use.

The remainder of the analyses focuses on the most recently available year of data (2007–2008). Given the exploratory nature of this study, an examination of two sets of contingency tables is useful to better understand the relationship between school level, type of security, and school characteristics. Table 5.2 presents the association between school level, type of security measure and level of crime in the neighborhood where the school is located. For metal detectors, across all school levels, a greater percentage of schools in high-crime neighborhoods use metal detectors as compared to those in low-crime neighborhoods. For security cameras, no statistically significant differences are observed across any of neighborhood crime levels. Fewer schools located in low-crime

Table 5.2 Percentage of Schools Using Particular Security Measures by Level of Crime in School Neighborhood, SSOCS 2007–2008

Type of Security/ School Level	Level of Crime in School Neighborhood		
	High (95% CI)	Moderate (95% CI)	Low (95% CI)
Metal Detectors			
Elementary	12.8 (2.3–23.3)	3.0 (0–6.0)	1.2 (0–2.3)
Middle	29.2 (16.7–41.7)	17.3 (11.3–23.4)	6.8 (4.9–8.6)
High	37.8 (17.3–58.4)	25.7 (19.7–31.8)	6.7 (4.9–6.0)
Security Cameras			
Elementary	57.1 (40.4–73.7)	50.6 (40.7–60.5)	43.6 (38.6–48.6)
Middle	58.5 (43.3–73.7)	73.6 (67.0–80.3)	64.6 (60.7–68.5)
High	72.9 (54.6–91.1)	74.6 (65.9–83.3)	77.3 (73.8–80.8)
Security Officers			
Elementary	50.7 (32.7–68.7)	37.0 (27.9–46.2)	24.0 (20.0–28.1)
Middle	83.6 (70.6–96.5)	71.8 (64.6–79.0)	58.4 (54.4–62.3)
High	89.4 (76.7–100)	86.7 (79.6–93.9)	73.8 (70.4–77.2)

neighborhoods use security officers as compared to ones located in moderate- or high-crime areas, especially for middle and high schools.

Table 5.3 presents the association between school level, type of security measures, and urbanicity of school location. For metal detectors, no differences are observed across elementary schools in the four locations except that schools in cities use metal detectors more than schools in towns. In middle schools, cities and suburbs use metal detectors more than schools in towns or rural areas. In high schools, schools located in cities use metal detectors more than in the other three locations. For security cameras, no statistically significant differences are observed across any of the school levels for any of the four locations. For security officers, more elementary schools located in cities use this measure compared with those located in suburban or rural areas. No statistically significant

Table 5.3 Percentage of Schools Using Particular Security Measures by Urbanicity of School Location, SSOCS 2007–2008

Type of Security/ School Level	Urbanicity of School Location			
	City (95% CI)	Suburb (95% CI)	Town (95% CI)	Rural (95% CI)
Metal Detectors				
Elementary	5.6	1.1	0	1.6
	(2.4–8.8)	(0–2.7)	(0)	(0–3.8)
Middle	22.9	4.9	7.9	6.6
	(17.0–28.7)	(2.5–7.3)	(3.1–12.6)	(3.0–10.0)
High	30.3	7.1	5.0	5.5
	(23.6–37.1)	(4.1–10.1)	(1.4–8.5)	(2.9–8.6)
Security Cameras				
Elementary	45.4	49.6	48.8	40.7
	(36.8–54.0)	(43.5–55.8)	(35.5–62.0)	(33.4–48.0)
Middle	63.6	67.1	71.2	62.9
	(55.9–71.4)	(61.7–72.4)	(62.5–80.0)	(56.3–69.6)
High	74.4	78.2	79.0	75.4
	(67.4–81.4)	(72.5–84.0)	(71.4–86.6)	(69.8–81.1)
Security Officers				
Elementary	40.0	22.8	35.7	19.3
	(31.8–48.3)	(17.1–28.6)	(24.8–46.5)	(12.8–25.8)
Middle	82.2	63.7	50.1	51.6
	(76.8–87.5)	(58.0–69.4)	(40.8–59.5)	(43.6–59.6)
High	91.4	85.0	68.7	64.0
	(86.2–96.6)	(79.8–90.3)	(60.1–77.3)	(58.4–70.0)

difference is observed between cities and towns for elementary schools using security officers. For middle schools, more schools located in cities use security officers than those located in the other three areas. For high schools, more schools located in cities and suburban areas use security officers than schools in towns or rural areas.

Table 5.4 presents the binary logistic regression models predicting use of particular security measures. Each measure is modeled separately. For all three types of security, middle and high schools are more likely to use the measure than elementary schools. For all three measures, school level is also the strongest predictor. With regard to the use of metal detectors, schools located in cities are more likely to use these devices than schools in rural areas. Schools located in areas of high or moderate crime are more likely to use metal detectors than schools located in low-crime areas. With regard

Table 5.4 Binary Logistic Regression Models Predicting Use of Particular Security Measures, SSOCS 2007–2008

Predictors	Metal Detectors		Security Cameras		Security Guards	
	Odds ratio	Standard error (p value)	Odds ratio	Standard error (p value)	Odds ratio	Standard error (p value)
School Level						
Middle school[a]	6.2	2.0 (<0.001)*	2.2	0.25 (<0.001)*	3.7	0.52 (<0.001)*
High school[a]	6.8	2.4 (<0.001)*	3.5	0.53 (<0.001)*	5.7	0.85 (<0.001)*
School Size						
300 to 499 students[b]	2.3	1.4 (0.17)	1.4	0.27 (0.10)	1.5	0.39 (0.10)
500 to 999 students[b]	1.3	0.66 (0.65)	1.5	0.25 (0.02)*	2.4	0.50 (<0.001)*
Over 1000 students[b]	2.0	0.92 (0.14)	1.7	0.32 (0.006)*	10.3	2.8 (<0.001)*
Urbanicity						
City[c]	2.8	1.0 (0.006)*	0.87	0.14 (0.40)	1.9	0.40 (0.002)*
Suburb[c]	0.71	0.31 (0.44)	1.1	0.14 (0.30)	0.96	0.17 (0.82)
Town[c]	0.69	0.28 (0.36)	1.3	0.25 (0.24)	1.4	0.30 (0.08)
Neighborhood Crime						
High crime[d]	4.6	1.6 (<0.001)*	1.6	0.43 (0.07)	2.2	0.81 (0.04)*
Moderate crime[d]	2.2	0.51 (0.001)*	1.3	0.24 (0.13)	1.4	0.26 (0.05)*
School Violence Rate						
Number of incidents/1,000	1.0	0.0004 (0.62)	1.0	0.0003 (0.21)	1.0	0.0003 (0.49)

Notes: * p < 0.05
N = 76,388 (weighted cases), 2,451 (unweighted cases)
a. elementary school comparison group
b. under 300 students comparison group
c. rural comparison group
d. low-crime comparison group

to the use of security cameras, however, a different pattern is observed. Here, other than school level, none of the school characteristics that predict the use of metal detectors are significant. Instead, school size is a significant predictor. Schools with larger populations (500–999 students and over 1,000 students) are more likely to use cameras than schools with fewer than 300 students. The use of security guards shares predictors that are statistically significant for the other two security types. As with security cameras, schools serving larger student populations are more likely to use guards than schools serving student populations under 300. As with metal detectors, schools located in cities are more likely to use these services than those in rural areas. Schools located in areas of high or moderate crime are more likely to use guards than schools located in low-crime areas.

Discussion

The trends in the use of particular visible security measures echo previous studies. For all school levels, the largest increases are observed in the use of security cameras and security guards. Visitor sign-in and locked doors are the most frequently used since Columbine, but these measures also were popular before Columbine, most likely due to their ease of use and minimal cost. Despite media reports to the contrary, schools did not widely adopt additional metal detectors or student IDs.

Beyond merely confirming the trend toward greater deployment of security guards and cameras, this study highlights the dramatic increase in their use. This rapid change, combined with the unknown effectiveness of these measures, reiterates concerns over the negative repercussions raised by previous commentators. To the extent security measures are ineffective, they create a false sense of security (Lawrence 2007, pp. 161–62) and a dangerous environment, directly as well as indirectly, by diverting money and resources from preventative measures that do work. The expanded reliance on surveillance by police and cameras also reiterates the need to better understand the effect these measures have on students' civil liberties (both in the short and long term) as well as assessing the implications for the overall learning environment.

With regard to examining security across school levels, this study confirms that high schools use security more frequently than any other school level. While it is not surprising that elementary schools employ security measures the least, elementary schools do use visible security measures. Almost half (45.9 percent) of all elementary schools use security cameras and over a quarter (28.4 percent) use security guards. Among elementary schools in high-crime neighborhoods, for the 2007–2008 school year, these numbers rise to

57 percent using cameras, 50.7 percent using guards, and almost 13 percent using metal detectors. While the greatest use is seen in high-crime areas and could be interpreted as a reasonable response to a demonstrated danger, the ubiquitous spread of these measures, especially in elementary schools, could be conditioning a generation of students to accept enhanced surveillance as "normal." Given the use of these measures in elementary schools, future studies of school security and its repercussions should consider the possible effect on students who encounter measures like police, cameras, and metal detectors at school throughout their entire educational careers.

The characteristics of schools associated with the use of various types of security provide a new context for assessing post-Columbine trends. Across all three measures examined, high schools are more likely to use security than middle or elementary schools. With regard to particular measures, the use of security cameras is only associated with school level and school size. While larger schools tend to have more problems with crime, the models controlled for school violence rate. This finding suggests that security cameras might be used for other reasons, such as managing crowds or other types of disorder that occur in larger schools (especially those over 500 students). Expanding the use of cameras for purposes beyond prevention of school violence suggests possible "security creep" (Marx and Steeves 2010). Security creep raises privacy concerns in cases where a measure is being used just because it is more convenient but no more effective than a less invasive practice, such as changing hallway traffic patterns or renovating school buildings (Addington 2009; Casella 2006).

Metal detectors, on the other hand, are not associated with school size but rather have characteristics that may be related to an identified problem with crime. The relationship between metal detectors and level of crime in the school's neighborhood as well as urban location suggests that schools might be trying to prevent dangers from coming into the school. Gottfredson and Gottfredson (1985) identified this phenomenon as the "importation hypothesis," which states that crime and violence are imported into schools by surrounding high-crime neighborhoods.

The use of security guards is predicted by a mix of these factors. This finding suggests that schools may use security guards for a variety of reasons, including addressing concerns about dangers being imported from a dangerous neighborhood, assisting with other types of disorder found in schools with large student populations, and possibly allaying parental concerns. Unlike technical devices such as metal detectors or cameras, police officers can address a range of internal and external safety concerns and be adapted to meet particular problems facing the school (McDevitt and Panniello 2005). In addition, the hundreds of millions of dollars in federal grant money made hiring police an attractive security option for some schools that might otherwise have preferred an alternate option for addressing a particular problem (Addington 2009).

In interpreting the urban location and its positive relationship with the use of metal detectors and security guards, it may be useful to view urban public schools as "a special case," as noted by Gottfredson (2001). Urban schools struggle with delinquency and student behavior problems and simultaneously are plagued with a lack of resources. These schools tend to be unsuccessful in addressing these problems and in implementing effective prevention programs due to overburdened administrators, understaffing, and the school climate (Gottfredson 2001; Gottfredson et al. 1997). As a result, urban schools may be more likely to rely on security measures as a way of handling these problems. This reliance becomes a vicious cycle that reinforces the ineffectiveness of alternative strategies (that require mutual trust and respect between staff and students) and continues to promote a negative learning environment.

One characteristic that was not associated with the use of any security measure is the actual school violence rate. This result is somewhat surprising and cannot be readily explained. It may be that once other variables related to school crime are controlled for, the violence rate is not associated with use of security. Another reason might be the reliance on the cross-sectional nature of the data. The school violence rate might show a significant relationship before the security measure is adopted. Identifying a change over time would require longitudinal observations for particular schools, and the SSOCS sampling strategy does not purposefully follow schools over time. In addition, how the violence rate is measured might affect the findings. The measure used may undercount school violence for two reasons. First, it relies on reports by school officials of incidents that have come to their attention. Second, the SSOCS data are collected between February and June. School officials report on the incidents that occurred during the current school year. As a result, those who report in February will have a lower amount of crime than those reporting in June.

Conclusion

The trends identified by this study suggest that schools of all levels increased their use of security after the Columbine shootings. Of particular concern is the dramatic increase in the use of security cameras and the fact that these cameras appear to be used by schools not plagued by demonstrated crime problems or located in dangerous areas. This trend is problematic for two reasons.

One reason concerns the long-term negative consequences on student civil liberties, which starts for some students when they enter elementary school. School security measures that focus on the surveillance of students are leading to an erosion of student civil liberties, particularly their privacy rights at school (Addington 2009). Although students cannot expect absolute privacy at school, increasing infringement is occurring with regard to what privacy they do have. Of particular concern is the situation of students attending relatively safe schools. Here surveillance measures can morph from being used for preventing violent school crime to purposes such as preventing graffiti in bathrooms or taking attendance, which are more effectively (and less intrusively) served by other policies (Addington 2009; Marx and Steeves 2010). In addition because students typically have no voice in these policies or how they are implemented, they may be given an underlying message that it is acceptable for those in positions of power to encroach on and fail to protect the privacy interests and civil liberties of the disenfranchised.

A second concern is the danger created if reliance on technology leads schools to ignore more effective ways of addressing violence. As discussed by Henry (2009), school violence has a variety of causes, which cannot be addressed by one easy solution. In fact, the most effective programs are those that recognize that school violence issues arise from a complex set of problems and organizational relationships and are not amenable to simple solutions (Peterson, Larson, and Skiba 2001). These programs incorporate proactive ways to deter conflicts from escalating into violence through anti-bullying programs and conflict resolution classes, create more positive and inclusive communities, and promote a school atmosphere where all have a stake in safety and a responsibility to maintain a secure school (Gagnon and Leone 2001; Greene 2005; Juvonen 2001; Peterson, Larson, and Skiba 2001). These programs, however, are not as immediately visible as a security guard or camera. More work is needed to compare trends in the adoption of visible security measures with these more effective, but more understated, antiviolence programs.

Appendix

Table 5.A Percentages (or Means) of Study Variables, SSOCS Weighted Data

	Year			
	1999–2000	2003–2004	2005–2006	2007–2008
School Level				
Elementary school	64.7	65.8	64.0	64.4
Middle school	20.0	19.6	20.5	20.0
High school	15.4	14.6	15.4	15.6
Security Type				
Visitor sign–in	96.6	98.4	97.9	99.0
Locked doors	75.4	83.8	85.4	90.7
Metal detectors	7.4	5.9	5.1	5.4
Student ID	4.1	6.3	6.0	7.5
Security cameras	19.1	35.7	41.6	54.7
Security officers	31.8	40.2	37.6	42.8
School Characteristics				
Crime in School Neighborhood				
High				6.4
Moderate				19.0
Low				74.6
Urbanicity				
City				26.8
Suburb				30.7
Town				14.4
Rural				28.1
School Size				
Under 300 students				21.4
300 to 499 students				29.7
500 to 999 students				37.4
Over 1,000				11.5
School Violence Rate				34.1*
Weighted n	77,145	74,087	75,800	76,389
(Unweighted n)	2,089	2,670	2,587	2,451

Note: Percentages may not equal 100 due to rounding.
*mean of continuous variable

Notes

1. In addition, the definition of bullying itself has expanded over time from only physical incidents to also including psychological forms and social isolation.

2. SSOCS is sponsored by the US Department of Education's National Center for Education Statistics (NCES). To protect the confidentiality of participating schools, the public-use SSOCS data remove identifiable information such as

school size and other characteristics relevant to this study. These characteristics are included in the restircted-use data files. Public-use SSOCS files are freely available on the NCES's website. Accessing the restricted-use SSOCS files requires obtaining a data license from NCES.

3. One motivation prompting the development and collection of SSOCS data were the series of school shootings that occurred in 1997–1998, the school year that preceded the Columbine shootings. These events highlighted the need for the US Department of Education to have a systematic way of collecting school crime data (US Department of Education, 2003).

4. The unweighted unit response rates were: 68.5 percent (1999–2000), 74.7 percent (2003–2004), 77.5 percent (2005–2006), and 74.6 percent (2007–2008).

5. Metal detectors used by schools can include various formats such as walk-through machines and handheld wands. Handheld wands are the version most commonly used by schools (Garcia 2003).

6. A growing number of law enforcement officers are being assigned as "school resource officers" and receiving special training for deployment in a school setting (McDevitt and Panniello 2005).

7. The SSOCS data do not indicate whether funding comes out of the school's existing operating budget or additional funds from a federal, state, or local grant. If additional funding is from a grant, it is possible the decision to employ a particular security measure is based on an attempt to obtain extra funds, which might not reflect a policy priority. Future research should address this issue.

6

Zero-Tolerance Policies

Aviva M. Rich-Shea and James Alan Fox

Donald Black, in his seminal work *The Behavior of Law,* suggests that not only is law a quantifiable variable within a society that ebbs and wanes, but it is very possible to quantify the amount of "law," or formal social control, that a given society accepts or utilizes. According to Black, "law" is about government social control that can be measured by the number and scope of prohibitions, obligations, and standards, in addition to the quantity and rate of legislation, litigation, and adjudication. Black also contends that this quantifiable variable of "law," or formal processing, varies across time and space and throughout societies, regions, and communities. Most importantly, Black asserts that "law varies inversely with other social control" (1976, p. 6).

Black's perspective on law is echoed by Bazemore, Leip, and Stinchcomb (2004) in their argument regarding the nexus between formal and informal social control in the context of the school. They asserted that when informal social controls break down, formal controls and processes will move in and take over. These observations arose from studying a large law-enforcement-led truancy intervention program (Bazemore, Leip, and Stinchcomb 2004) in an unidentified urban county in the southeastern United States as an example of the erosion of the boundary between formal and informal social control.

The authors employ the term "reaching down" to describe the expansion of a disciplinary approach based in the criminal justice system, which they see as increasingly criminalizing normative childhood misbehaviors. They view this trend as a result of the failure of institutions of informal control that were once rooted in families, neighborhoods, and schools to contain youth behavior. Additionally,

Bazemore and colleagues see three trends propelling the juvenile justice system to widen its jurisdiction over low-level misconduct it previously ignored: (1) zero-tolerance (ZT) policies increasingly enforced by school-based police officers; (2) the injection of law enforcement into social service and public health functions through new system collaborations; and (3) the rise of new specialty courts for matters such as smoking, truancy, or curfews. The result is that, through the use of on-site arrests and summonses, problematic conduct such as defiant behavior and interpersonal conflict is being elevated to a criminal offense, thereby pushing students into the criminal justice system (see also Stinchcomb, Bazemore, and Riestenberg 2006).

In this chapter, we focus on the first trend cited by Bazemore—the confluence of zero-tolerance disciplinary policies and school resource officers (SROs). We examine the genesis of these two programs, how they continue to be fueled by the fear of "another Columbine," and their impact on students. In addition, we review some of the widespread challenges to maintaining an orderly educational environment that have been obscured by an obsession with defending against active shooters.

Zero Tolerance as a Philosophy of Student Discipline

In 1994, Congress passed the Gun-Free Schools Act, a response to inner-city gang-related shootings fueled by the crack cocaine epidemic and its concomitant "turf wars" (Feld 1998; Fox and Burstein 2010). This act made states' receipt of federal funding for K–12 education contingent on their passage of legislation requiring that any student found in possession of a firearm on school property be expelled for a minimum of one year. By the end of 1995, all fifty states had enacted laws compliant with this directive (Brady 2002). As the 1990s progressed, rates of juvenile offending dropped dramatically. Regardless, the get-tough policy push was just gathering steam, and it began to accelerate rapidly with the passage of zero-tolerance approaches to student discipline (Ayers, Ayers, and Dohrn 2001; Blumenson and Nilsen 2002; Casella 2003b; Insley 2001).

States quickly expanded the list of behaviors subject to expulsion and suspension. Although the Gun-Free Schools Act only mandated punishment for possession of firearms, many school systems extended that to any type of weapon (Pinard 2003), such as knives (including penknives and plastic knives and then scissors and nail files). In over 80 percent of public high schools, policies were expanded further to include possession and use of drugs, alcohol, and tobacco, and ultimately to many other behaviors, such as fighting, and defiance or disobedience of school rules (Hirschfield 2008). The school-based mass shootings that occurred in suburban communities between 1996 and 2001 increased the pressure for all school administrators (ADMs) to institute a tough disciplinary policy. The risk of "another Columbine" could not be tolerated.

Skiba et al. (2006) conducted a meta-analysis of research on the effectiveness of zero-tolerance policies titled, *Are Zero Tolerance Policies Effective in the Schools? An Evidentiary Review and Recommendations, A Report by the American Psychological Association Zero Tolerance Task Force*. The task force examined the impact of ZT policies on school safety, consistency in discipline, improvement in school climate, and student behavior. Its evidentiary review showed no evidence that ZT increases school safety or reduces inconsistency in school discipline. The task force also found that school climates deteriorate and academic achievement declines in the face of increased school exclusions. Among their most salient findings, the team reported that not only do ZT policies not deter misbehavior, but students to whom they are applied subsequently have higher rates of misbehavior, exclusions, and school dropout.

Other social scientists have critiqued ZT from a number of different points of view. Lorenz (2010) argued that since it lacks any consideration for due process or for the intent of the accused, ZT, therefore, lacks any legitimacy as law. Gorman and Pauken (2003) focused on the potential for zero tolerance to alienate students from the adults at their schools because it is antithetical to "the development of caring trusting relationships between children and adults" (p. 32). Another concern voiced by experts in both adolescent development and education is that zero-tolerance policies do not take the developmental stage of the adolescent into account. Therefore, they argue, these one-size-fits-all formal methods undermine the developmental process of adolescence and exert a negative influence on the child's need to develop autonomy and competence in an environment that provides both the structure and support for student engagement and academic success (Gregory and Cornell 2009).

Emergence of the School Resource Officer

The concept of community policing was developed in Flint, Michigan, during the 1950s (Girouard 2001). The goal was to bring more police officers out of their patrol cars and onto neighborhood streets to encourage police-community interaction. Community policing offered a new paradigm that focused on community-police collaborations with a problem-solving orientation. This was a departure from the traditional focus on preventative patrol and incident-based crime control. Community policing emphasized the importance of maintaining social order and reducing the criminogenic effects of disorganized or disorderly communities (Gowri 2003). By addressing incipient signs of disorder such as vandalism or graffiti, community-policing advocates aimed to prevent disorder from escalating into more serious forms of criminality. This approach is exemplified by George Kelling and Catherine Coles in their book, *Fixing Broken Windows* (1996). The goal is to develop trust between police and neighborhood residents. The police officer often becomes a service delivery provider in the first line of defense against crime by encouraging orderly communities. As an extension of this new community-policing model, police officers were sent into public schools.

The Omnibus Crime Control and Safe Streets Act of 1968 was the first official law to identify the role of the school resource officer, "a career law enforcement officer, with sworn authority, deployed in community-oriented policing, and assigned by the employing police department or agency to work in collaboration with school and community-based organizations" (Girouard 2001). This concept of the SRO was well received in a few states during the 1960s and 1970s, but interest leveled off during the next two decades until the late 1990s, when the Department of Justice aggressively accelerated the funding of the placement of SROs.

Driven by President Clinton in response to the massacre at Westside Middle School in his home state of Arkansas, the federal Office of Community Oriented Policing Services (COPS) initiated the "COPS in Schools" program to fund the hiring of SROs "to engage in community policing in and around primary and secondary schools" (Office of Community Oriented Policing Services 2008). The COPS in Schools program had two primary objectives: (1) to improve student and school safety, and (2) to help police agencies build collaborative partnerships with local schools.

Between 1999 and 2005, the COPS office awarded more than $750 million to over 3,000 agencies to hire SROs, along with an additional $23 million to train SROs and administrators in participating schools. The COPS office also awarded an additional $11.5 million through the Safe Schools/Healthy Students Initiative and the

Office of Justice Programs' Gang Reduction Project (Office of Community Oriented Policing Services 2005, 2008). Today it is estimated that there are approximately 17,000 SROs in schools nationwide (Thurau and Wald 2010).

Research on the Impact of the SRO

School resource officers are police officers assigned full- or part-time to public schools. They are armed and in uniform, and remain primarily under the jurisdiction of their local police departments. There are three primary roles assigned to the SRO. The first is *law enforcement*, which involves maintaining order within the school and taking action as needed. The second role is that of *mentor or counselor*, which is designed to help the SRO connect with the students in order to facilitate trust and help the students to view the SRO in a problem-solving capacity. *Teaching and/or coaching* is the third role of the SRO. This is usually accomplished through coaching sports teams and teaching drug or gang control classes or perhaps health classes, and is intended to serve an educational function.

The Office of Juvenile Justice and Delinquency Prevention issued guidelines for SRO programs that delineate these three roles and areas of responsibility (Girouard 2001). The actual percentage of time an officer spends on each of these three areas varies drastically from school to school, district to district, and state to state. McDevitt and Finn (2005) conducted a four-part study of SROs involving survey data, and determined that SROs spent 60–65 percent of their time on law enforcement activities, 25–30 percent on mentoring or counseling, and 10–15 percent on teaching or coaching students.

The placement of police officers in schools marks the confluence of intertwining influences of law, policy, and sociological trends. Although the driving force is federal policy, any SRO implementation is based on disciplinary policy in the local school. The school administration is faced with the decision of how to incorporate an officer of the law into its strategies for ensuring an orderly educational environment. Questions must be answered concerning the boundaries between rule breaking and law breaking and to what extent the criminal justice system becomes a venue for student discipline. Organizational dynamics between the local police department and the school principal's office bear heavily on the degree to which authority over juveniles in the town is reconciled with authority over juveniles in the school. The amount of social capital commanded by parents' organizations and other local community groups can influence the balance between informal and formal social control of misbehaving students.

Apprehension about the consequences of having a permanently assigned armed law enforcement presence in schools has been expressed by many diverse groups. These concerns range from the possibility of exacerbating disproportionate minority involvement and contact with police and courts to referring students to the courts for behaviors that have traditionally been handled well by school administrators and parents, to the criminalization of normative childhood behaviors (e.g., classroom "clowning," schoolyard fighting), and to the impact of SRO intervention on increased suspensions, expulsions, and ultimately school exclusions (Advancement Project and the Civil Rights Project 2000; Ayers, Ayers, and Dohrn 2001; Bazemore, Leip, and Stinchcomb 2004; Insley 2001; Morrison 2003; Reyes 2003). Various researchers have investigated the consequences of having police in schools and uncovered evidence that these fears are not unfounded.

Brady, Balmer, and Phenix (2007) looked at school-police partnerships in a study of the impact and effectiveness of a NYC program developed to combat crime in some of the city's most crime-ridden schools. This program, NYC Impact Schools Initiative, was based on the "broken windows" (Kelling and Coles 1996) approach to crime control and a "zero-tolerance" policing strategy that emphasized the containment of low-level disruptive and problematic behaviors, with the goal of deterring their escalation. Following the model of targeting hotspots of violence and criminal activity within the city's communities, schools that were determined to be hotspots of delinquency and violence were chosen to participate in this pilot program, which saturated the identified schools with police officers.

Brady and colleagues used school-level data in the form of suspensions, attendance, and criminal incidents reported by the Department of Education to the New York City Police Department and employed a comparison group of schools without a police presence that enrolled similar numbers of students with a similar racial mix. Data were collected for the year (academic year 2002–2003) prior to the implementation of the initiative and then again a year and a half later (academic year 2004–2005). Between these two points in time, the suspension rate per 1,000 students at the Impact schools rose from 78.5 to 114.1, a 45 percent increase, while the control group experienced a more modest change of 21 percent from 73.8 to 89.5.

Differences over the same time period for rates of noncriminal police incidents per 1,000 students showed a similar pattern—a sharp rise of 54 percent in the Impact schools as opposed to virtually no change in the control group. Clearly, the added police were doing the job set out for them, and the rate per 1,000 students for major crimes fell 15 percent. The control group, however, showed a larger decrease of 28 percent. One cost of the initiative was that the attendance rate at the Impact schools fell by 9 percent against a drop of only 4 percent in the control group.

Hallett (2004) took a critical look at one aspect of the SRO program in Jacksonville, Florida, namely the Monitoring at Risk Students (MARS) program run by the Jacksonville Sheriff's Office. Based on a weekly download of student conduct violations from the Duval County Public Schools, MARS identified students with five or more incidents for police department monitoring and used a weighting system to target "top offenders" for direct contact by the local SRO. Hallett pointed out that over 95 percent of the reported incidents did not constitute criminal activity, but rather tardiness or common oppositional behavior such as failure to follow directions or classroom disruption, even for those students labeled top offenders. He noted that MARS appeared to be initiated and operated with little or no oversight from the school system or the community, whereas North Carolina, with one of the oldest and most comprehensive SRO programs in the country, strictly prohibited the use of student education records by SROs, owing to the strong involvement of the state School Board. Hallett concluded that Jacksonville would be better served by following US Department of Justice indicators (e.g., abuse, neglect, exposure to domestic violence, poverty, developmental disability) to identify "at-risk" students instead of singling out children who misbehave in class.

As part of an initiative by the US Department of Education and the National Academy of Sciences, Katherine Newman led a team of researchers in an in-depth study of two communities that had suffered mass school shootings: Heath, Kentucky, and Westside, Arkansas. They conducted 163 interviews of a wide range of people touched by these tragedies, including students, school personnel, families of the victims, families of the perpetrators, officials of the justice system, psychologists, and members of the media. In response to these incidents, both communities placed full-time police (school resource officers) in their high schools. In a positive review of this policy of more formal social control, Newman (2004, p. 282) noted its acceptance despite consequences similar to those that concerned Bazemore:

> There are unintended consequences to having law enforcement personnel on campus. The presence of an SRO clearly leads to more student interaction with the criminal justice system. Where school authorities might have invoked their own "law" in the past, these days all violations that can be construed as "criminal," including fighting in the hallway, have become the province of the Sheriff's Office. The Westside SRO told us, "Fighting is illegal. Fighting is battery." Local juvenile court officials process more students from schools with an SRO than without one. Kids who might have had a discipline record at school now have an arrest record in the courts. This can create problems for them later, because employers are often troubled by delinquency. However, as with all interventions, *the consequences of the change are mixed, and on balance we think the pros outweigh the cons.* (emphasis added)

In an ethnographic study of two high schools ("City High" and "Central High"), Bracy (2010) examined strategies that administrators and SROs used to conduct searches, interrogations, and background checks on students without technically violating their Fourth Amendment, Fifth Amendment, and privacy rights. Bracy related a situation of an administrator enforcing a closed campus school policy mandating that students who leave must be searched upon returning to the building. Armed with reasonable suspicion owing to this violation of school rules, the administrator called in the SRO to stand by and watch while the administrator conducted the search. This allowed the police officer to observe while obviating his more stringent requirement of probable cause to carry out the search himself.

The administration and SRO took a similar approach to student interrogations by operating in tandem, which, at least in their minds, eliminated the need to Mirandize the student. Moving on to student privacy rights, an SRO explained how he can check the arrest record of a transfer student that the registrar "had a bad feeling about" (Bracy 2010, p. 307). If he found anything of interest, he did not formally disclose it, but did advise "that they might want to look into this student more, and they can have the district request . . . a background check" (Bracy 2010, pp. 307–308).

Bracy presented some telling insights into the disciplinary mindset of the administrators at the two study schools. In addition to the closed campus policy enforced by mandatory searches, City High relied heavily on out-of-school suspensions. Central High, where suspicion and distrust can prompt an investigation into a new student's background in the criminal justice system, subsequently subjected this same student to regular searches because "word on the street is that this student is 'sometimes strapped' [carrying a weapon]" (Bracy 2010, p. 308). Central also endorsed a zero-tolerance approach with mandatory arrests of all students involved in fistfights, without regard for the circumstances.

Theriot (2009) investigated the impact of SROs on school-based arrests by comparing the number of arrests over a three-year period at thirteen middle and high schools with SROs and fifteen middle and high schools without SROs in the same district. He observed, first, that having an SRO more than doubled the rate of arrest for disorderly conduct, even when controlling for school-to-school differences in economic disadvantage. Theriot saw this as evidence of the criminalization of student behavior, previously discussed by Bazemore and alluded to by Newman. He did point out, however, that since an officer can exercise a great deal of discretion in making the charge of disorderly conduct, school administrators and SROs could work out policies and procedures to minimize the chance that an oppositional student would end up arrested. In addition, when compared to schools without SROs, schools with SROs had significantly lower arrest rates for the serious crimes of assault (by 52 percent) and weapons charges (by 73 percent). Echoing Johnson's (1999) observations ten years earlier, Theriot surmised that these reductions could be due to the deterrence effect of having a law enforcement officer on patrol within the school environment. He also suggested that having an SRO could make students feel safer and less inclined to carry a weapon for protection, and that this perception of safety would reduce aggression and fights between students.

Other researchers have noted the positive effects of having a police officer involved in school discipline. Johnson (1999), for example, conducted a case study of the effectiveness of an SRO program introduced into one middle school and four high schools in Birmingham, Alabama, in order to provide a safe school environment by reducing the prevalence of weapons, drugs, and gang-related activities. She administered surveys to seventeen SROs and seventeen school personnel (five principals, five assistant principals, seven teachers), as well as conducting informal interviews with another thirty teachers and forty-six students, in order to gain everyone's perceptions of the SRO program that had been introduced the previous year. In addition, Johnson compiled data on responses and arrests from school incident reports compiled by SROs from January to May 1996, and collected data on suspensions published by the study schools for academic years 1994–1995 (pre-SRO), 1995–1996 (post-SRO), and the first half of 1996–1997.

The SROs maintained an active and visible presence in the schools throughout the day, checking students' IDs and backpacks, securing exterior doors, monitoring student movement between classes and in the lunchroom, interacting with and counseling students, and intervening immediately in dangerous situations such as fights, drug-related activity, and gang identification. In their incident reports for January to May 1996, the SROs reported 97 responses involving drugs, 49 responses for weapons, and 157 responses concerning gang-related activities, resulting in 145 total arrests. There was no comparable data for any other time period.

The SROs strongly believed that their presence and activities had a positive effect on school safety, citing perceived reductions in weapons, gang-related activities, drugs, misdemeanors, and felonies. While not quite as unanimous as the SROs, the majority of school officials endorsed the program, observing reductions in the use of weapons, fighting, drugs, gambling, illicit sexual behavior, and dress code violations. Overall, the students expressed the belief that the presence of a uniformed police officer in their school gave them a sense of security, that it encouraged students to curtail misbehavior, and that the sight of a student being immediately arrested and handcuffed was clearly a deterrent. Johnson reported a decline in total suspensions for all Birmingham middle and high schools from 7,316 in 1994–1995 (pre-SRO) to 6,470 in 1995–1996 (post-SRO) as an indication of the SRO program's effectiveness. She did not address, however, the 4,067 total suspensions logged for August–November 1996, which projected to over 8,000 for the 1996–1997 school year, a significant increase over the pre-SRO year.

In their study of SROs in sixteen Massachusetts school districts, Thurau and Wald (2010) noted a similar widespread perception on the part of SROs that their permanent presence in a school over a period of several years resulted in a reduction in arrests, although the researchers were unable to compile corroborating data. The officers attributed the decrease to the relationships that they had formed with students.

Barnes (2008) conducted an evaluative study of the SRO program in North Carolina, the largest statewide SRO program in the country. Mail surveys were sent to all known SROs (n = 137) and ADMs (n = 133) in all 117 school districts and responses were received from 75 and 77 percent of recipients, respectively. Surveys were designed to assess perceptions of the SRO program and its implementation. Barnes also conducted an analysis of crime data comparing the incidence of violence before and after the introduction of SROs. The study concluded that both the SROs and the ADMs liked the partnership they developed, and felt it changed some student behaviors by inhibiting students from bringing contraband to school. However, the Barnes study found that neither the SROs nor the ADMs perceived a safer school environment as a result of the program. Further, the analysis of crime data revealed no reduction in crime in the schools studied.

Jackson (2002) evaluated the impact of interaction with SROs on young people's attitudes toward police, attitudes toward offending, and perceptions that they would be caught were they to engage in delinquent behavior. He surveyed a sample of 271 students from one school that had recently adopted an SRO program and two nearby non-SRO schools that served as control groups. Surveys were administered to the same students both at the beginning of the school year and again nine months later. Jackson compared the responses of students from SRO and non-SRO schools, and also examined change over time in the aggregate responses of students from the SRO school. The results showed no significant differences in student attitudes toward police or offending, but did show that students in the SRO school perceived the likelihood of being caught for wrongdoing as lower than students in the non-SRO schools. Jackson went on to suggest that "this finding may be due to the school administrators and staff relinquishing their rule enforcement responsibilities upon the arrival of the SRO, whereas, the control school, due to the lack of an SRO, still utilizes a combined effort of education, detection, and punishment from all school faculty and staff" (p. 646).

Martin Scheffer (1987) published a case study on the Boise, Idaho, SRO program, which at that time was twelve years old and implemented in all of the city's elementary, middle, and high schools. Scheffer described the duties of the SRO as mainly prevention, education, and counseling. This program deemphasized the formal social control function of law enforcement for the SRO, and presented an approach similar to what Theriot suggested as a way to handle misbehavior without arrest. In fact, he suggested that SROs can be "instrumental in reducing the number of minor and first offense cases from reaching the courts" (p. 53). This was accomplished through the use of Behavioral Agreements between the student and the SRO: "The Behavioral Agreement is an informal effort to avoid the risk of

further stimulating a youth's delinquency either in response to the official labeling processes or because court sanctions are often interpreted as meaningless to minor and first-time offenders" (p. 54).

A report issued by the Center for Problem-Oriented Policing (2002) reviewed the effectiveness of an SRO program developed for two small Illinois communities (Salem and Vandalia) through a collaboration of the Illinois State Police (ISP) and high school administrators, court probation units, local police, and mental health groups. The program hired and trained ten off-duty ISP officers as part-time SROs "to interact with students, design and implement a graduated enforcement protocol, provide classroom teaching, and participate in counseling sessions for students and parents" (p. 3).

The genesis of this effort was a mental health survey repeated over several years of eighth and twelfth grade students in all seventeen school systems in the county, which depicted high rates of depression and illegal substance abuse, accompanied by vandalism and thefts. A joint task force of the ISP, school administrators, and mental health providers identified four factors for local youth involvement in criminal behavior: (1) perceived lack of formal sanctions for law-breaking, (2) easy access to illegal substances, (3) lack of informal social control due to limited community and parental involvement, and (4) low self-esteem and depression. In response, the ISP proposed the SRO-based community collaboration described here, which was accepted enthusiastically by school and mental health professionals in Salem and Vandalia. In this model, "SROs served four basic functions: enforcement, counseling, teaching and technical assistance" (p. 9).

At the end of the first year, the program reported a significant reduction in violence, drug use, and truancy at both schools. At Salem Community High School, serious misconduct cases dropped by 86 percent and overall truancy fell by 85 percent. While teachers at Vandalia were sending more students to the administration for discipline, expulsions for alcohol use dropped by 100 percent, for truancy by 68 percent, and for drug use by 50 percent. Perhaps the most telling finding was the following: "More than 90% of the juvenile problems which surfaced in the first year were addressed outside of the court system. Problems were immediately identified, and appropriate sanctions or treatments were imposed with the help of the school, parents, and counselors" (p. 16).

Although researchers do their best to put a positive disciplinary spin on the presence of police officers in schools, a closer look reveals otherwise. Johnson (1999) reported a decline in total suspensions in the first year of an SRO program, but she did not address the even greater increase in the second year. She also noted that the SROs in her study made 145 arrests in the five months during which she collected data. As noted by others (Barnes 2008; Thurau and Wald 2010), the SROs and administrators had positive views of the program, but they could offer no concrete data on its effects other than their own opinions. The students at Johnson's schools felt a sense of security with the presence of uniformed police officers, reinforced by the threat of immediate arrest for stepping out of line. This attitude harkens back to Newman's justification that the "pros" of school safety "outweigh the cons" of "more student interaction with the criminal justice system." The CPOP (2002) review reflects the same line of thinking: that resolving roughly 10 percent of the juvenile problems in the courts is a small price to pay for effective in-school discipline based on a graduated enforcement protocol designed and implemented by off-duty state police officers.

One of the more telling findings was Jackson's observation that students in a school with an SRO felt that they were less likely to be caught for breaking the rules than students in schools without police. His explanation connects directly to Black's theory of law and Bazemore's thesis that when formal social controls are imposed, informal social control breaks down. With an officer on duty, school administrators and staff no longer operate their network of informal discipline.

While Scheffer (1987) presents an SRO program based on informal control via behavioral agreements, this study takes place over a decade prior to Columbine. Police chief Gary Rudnick (2011) observes that since the vigorous response to school shootings of the federal COPS program, the underlying focus of SRO training is on the rare occurrence of an active shooter, not on creative approaches to keep students on the straight and narrow and out of the criminal justice system. Rudnick goes on to note that this emphasis obscures the more widespread challenges to maintaining an orderly educational environment, such as the incidence of serious crime (physical assault, possession of weapons and drugs, theft), the mainstreaming of students with disabilities of all types, students living in dysfunctional environments, bullying, irate parents, faculty frustrated with maintaining classroom decorum, and the pressures of No Child Left Behind. Perhaps it is the intolerable complexity of these issues that influences so many school administrators to simplify discipline by hiring a school resource officer to help enforce a code of zero tolerance.

This nexus of ZT and SROs led one of us to conduct research (Rich-Shea, 2010), interviewing twenty-five school administrators and fifteen SROs, representing fourteen schools with SROs and eleven control group schools without SRO programs in Massachusetts.

To start, the presence of an SRO was consistent with formal social control based on punishment for rule violations, a punitive turn in school policy. As reflected in Massachusetts Department of Education data for 2008, SRO schools applied formal social control in the form of suspensions at a rate twice that of schools without SROs. From 2003 to 2006, the difference was in the range of 20 percent to 25 percent, but from 2006 to 2008, schools in the non-SRO control group significantly cut their usage of formal discipline, while the SRO schools stayed the course. In addition, all the administrators at the SRO schools had a stated zero-tolerance policy as the foundation of their disciplinary approach, while less than half the non-SRO ADMs reported a comprehensive policy based on zero tolerance.

As part of the interview-based survey, all administrators were asked how they would handle four different hypothetical scenarios of student misbehavior: a classroom disruption, a lunchroom disruption, a knife fight, and a student with a weapon for defensive purposes. In response to the two scenarios of oppositional student behavior, 90 percent of ADMs with SROs would ultimately arrest, twice the rate of non-SRO ADMs. This is certainly consistent with Theriot's (2009) research on school discipline based on the utilization of SROs, which showed "reaching down" to criminalize student defiance and disruption with formal punishment for disorderly conduct or disturbing school assembly.

The presence of an SRO, furthermore, was not consistent with informal social control based on relationships. In response to all of the hypothetical scenarios except for the knife fight, from 40 percent to 73 percent of the non-SRO ADMs resolved the situation by involving the student's parents, while less than one-fifth as many SRO ADMs would do the same. The divide between SRO schools and non-SRO schools regarding involvement of the parents in the disciplinary process surfaced in the surveys and interviews as well. Working with and involving parents was also a common theme in the profiles of the large non-SRO schools. This difference in approach is echoed by Black (1976): "When there is little or no parental involvement, or if the involvement is seen as negative by the police, more law is applied by the police officers, which in effect implies that the quantity of law applied varies based on the quality and type of parent involvement" (pp. 122–123).

There were other indications that the presence of SROs reinforced a punitive disciplinary approach. In many schools, the SRO was used as the ultimate threat to a misbehaving student, as school staff would warn, "You are this close to being arrested." Often this warning would be operationalized with the SRO called into a chaotic scene where the teacher or administrator was unable to maintain control. It was the SRO then who led the student away, sometimes in handcuffs, for formal processing. This way, the SRO became a disciplinary layer between the administration and students, rendering that relationship just a bit more distant and impersonal. At a school without an SRO, it was not so easy for the administration to wash its hands of uncooperative students and have them disappear. The responses to the hypothetical scenario of a knife fight illustrated this divide, with more than half the non-SRO ADMs personally intervening, while only one of the SRO ADMs would do the same. Another way that SROs reinforced an authoritarian environment was in carrying out routine duties such as checking tardiness, enforcing dress codes, or monitoring the lunchroom. The presence of an armed officer in uniform conveys an image of potential consequences far more severe than anything just another assistant principal could muster.

Other findings showed that SROs were employed to further a punitive disciplinary approach. In schools where there was any communication between the ADM and the SRO, the SRO was expected to provide information on out-of-school student contact with the police and criminal justice system to help identify the troublemakers. More directly, for the 2008–2009 school year, the study SROs reported making 114 arrests and issuing 107 summonses, a large percentage of which were for disturbing school assembly or disorderly conduct.

To summarize the research, compared to non-SRO schools, SRO schools tend to criminalize normative childhood behavior, such as defiance—redefining it as disorderly conduct or disturbing school assembly. However, it is not clear that this is a result of the presence of the SRO. The more fully the ADM embraces a ZT approach, the more likely the school is both to have an SRO and to use the SRO to institute more formal methods of social control. The SRO appears to be a tool in the formal social control toolkit utilized disproportionately by authoritarian school administrators.

Various researchers have noted that the confluence of ZT and SROs produces a punitive school climate and forms the bedrock of the school-to-prison pipeline. Black's theory of law—"Law varies inversely with other social control"—provides the theoretical framework to describe the effects of this imposition of formal disciplinary methods to the detriment of community-based informal social control.

Citing their own groundbreaking research, the authors show that the more fully the administration embraces a zero-tolerance approach, the more likely the school is both to have an SRO and to use the SRO to institute more formal methods of social control. The SRO operates as a tool in the formal social control toolkit utilized disproportionately by authoritarian school administrators.

7

Safe Schools Initiatives and the Shifting Climate of Trust

Valerie Steeves and Gary T. Marx

The Columbine shooting left a large footprint in the Canadian consciousness, especially when, eight days after Columbine, a fourteen-year-old student walked into an Alberta high school and shot a fellow student to death (Canadian Broadcasting Corporation [CBC] 2000b). Although media painted the shooting as a US problem that was moving north of the border (e.g., CBC 2000a), the first reported school shooting in North America occurred in Canada in 1975 (Cobb and Avery 1977); and, in the three and a half decades that followed there have been twenty-six reported school shootings in the country (Howell 2009; *Toronto Star* 2007).

However, Columbine, and the Montreal Massacre that preceded it, significantly changed the public debate (Rathjen and Montpetit 1999). As Muschert notes, Columbine has become a metaphorical "keyword for a complex set of emotions surrounding youth, fear, risk, and delinquency in 21st century America" (Muschert 2007a, p. 365). In this context, the term "Columbine Effect" refers to the ways in which school shootings impact practices and beliefs about school violence and security (Muschert and Peguero 2010, p. 119). Certainly by the time of Columbine, there was a high level of agreement among Canadian teachers, students, school officials, and police that zero-tolerance policies would enable schools to prevent another tragedy (Gabor 1995). Across the country zero-tolerance policies were adopted almost universally, setting out specific offenses that would lead to automatic suspension or expulsion (Day et al. 1995).

In this chapter, we examine the impact of these formal policies and related behaviors in two Canadian schools. We ask, "What security policies were put in place in the two schools in the years following Columbine?" We then turn to some ethnographic observations to describe changes in teacher and student behavior in response. In doing so, we build on Henry's insight that school violence is the result of a complex set of influences that operate at the institutional and individual levels (Henry 2009). We argue that the policies enacted in response to Columbine to reduce individual acts of violence have reshaped the social relationships between administrators, teachers, and students, and inadvertently created a school climate that undermines students' trust in the ability of school administrators to respond to violent incidents.

The Schools

The two schools examined, Briargreen Public School (Briargreen) and Sir Robert Borden High School (SRB), are located in Nepean, a suburb of the city of Ottawa. Briargreen is an elementary school with a population of approximately 450 students. It is also a feeder school for SRB, a suburban high school with a population of approximately 1,500 students. Both schools are located in a quiet, well-off, and ethnically and racially diverse suburban community (Statistics Canada 2010a, 2010b), are surrounded by large playing fields, and have well-funded and well-maintained libraries, and arts and sports facilities.

The community around the schools is relatively crime-free. In 2006, the city of Ottawa had the lowest violent crime rate of the thirteen largest urban areas in the country (Statistics Canada 2008). The crime rate in the suburb Nepean is even lower, with few or no murders and little gun violence reported in an average year (Ottawa Police Service 2010a, 2010b). In keeping with national norms, the schools are also at low risk for violence. National data from 2006 indicates that 13 percent of youth crime in Canada is committed on school property and only 7 percent of that crime involves weapons. An even smaller proportion—less than 1 percent of that 13 percent—involves guns (Taylor-Butts and Bressan 2009).

The Board Policies

Despite the low risk of violence, zero tolerance was introduced to the two schools on May 15, 1998, when the board passed a safe school procedure (PR521.SCO; supplemented in 2001 with a safe school policy, P.032.SCO; for details of all school policies, see the Appendix), a weapons policy (P.036.SC; PR.525.SCO), and "Guidelines for Dealing with Reports of Strangers Approaching Students" (P.042.SCO; PR.532.SCO). In keeping with similar policies adopted in both Canada and the United States (Cameron 2006; Gabor 1995), these documents assert that "assault, threat and intimidation are of serious concern to staff, trustees, students and parents" (P.036.SCO, s. 2.1). Relevant actors, including the school board, school staff, teachers, students, parents, community partners, and community agencies, must work together to ensure the success of "prevention and intervention programs" (P.032.SCO, s. 4.0).

Moreover, failure is not an option: "facilities must be safe places in which to learn and work" (P.036.SC, s. 2.1). Accordingly, weapons are "strictly prohibited" (s. 2.1) and possession, threatening with, and use of weapons lead to automatic suspension (PR.525.SCO, s. 4). Codes of conduct are required to advise students of specific behaviors that will not be tolerated and the consequences that will ensue should the codes be breached (PR.521.SCO, s. 4.2).

The Safe School Initiative underlines the belief that schools are no longer safe places. The fact that there is little violence in the schools does not permit complacency; as Matthew notes, the logic of zero-tolerance policies implies that "even schools that have not experienced violence, thefts, and other problems should consider increased [security] measures" (Matthew 2010, p. 123). Strangers pose a particular risk of danger, in spite of the fact that school shooters are typically students who are part of the school community (Langman 2009). Accordingly, "the presence of intruders on any of its property or at school-sponsored events" will not be tolerated (s. 4.4); and students must be constantly supervised both at school and at school-sponsored events (P.042.SCO, s. 2.1(a)) in order to "ensure the Board provides a safe environment" (s. 1).

The policies draw heavily on criminal justice language and metaphors. For example, the definition of weapons is explicitly drawn from the Criminal Code (PR.525.SCO, s. 2.1), and incidents involving weapons must be noted in the student's permanent record (ss. 4.1(f), 4.2(f), 4.3(f)), parts of which are required to be retained for fifty-five years after the student leaves the school. Staff members and students are also required to report to the principal the names of students or visitors who they believe threaten the security of the school (s. 4.8(a), (b)).

However, there is an absence of due process to interpret the meaning of these provisions. Principals may deem a variety of items, including scissors, knives, sling shots, hockey sticks, and baseball bats, to be weapons (s. 2.2(b)), and prohibitions apply beyond the physical borders of the school. Safety requires that all members of the school community—including parents and students—comply with the rules whether they are on school property or at school-authorized events off school property (P.036.SCO, s. 2.1; P.032.SCO, s. 3.2). Criminal justice–style responses are accordingly amplified and extended into the community, without the constraints of judicial oversight.

Given this ethos it is not surprising that police officers are given a privileged role because of their expertise with respect to security. In addition to automatically involving police in certain circumstances, such as the (threat of) use of weapons at school (PR.525.SCO, ss. 4.2, 4.3), the board and the schools are required to "maintain a close working relationship" with the police (P.042.SCO, s. 2.1(c)) and to create "procedures consistent with the recommendations of the Ottawa Police Services" (PR.532.SCO, s. 1.0). Responsibility for implementing the guidelines is shared by the school principal and the police (s. 3.0), and principals are required to notify police of "violent acts committed or likely to be committed, whether on or off Board property" (PR.521.SCO), s. 4.7(c)). Police may be called in to assist regardless of the student's age because, although a child under twelve cannot be charged with an offense, "the school or Board is not similarly constrained in imposing discipline" (P.043.SCO, s. 4(i)).

These provisions extend police surveillance in two ways. First, schools must report actions that have not yet taken place, broadening the traditional scope of intervention beyond post de facto response to preemption based on suspicion. Second, schools are co-opted to watch students both on and *off* school property, extending police surveillance beyond the confines of the school. The goal of this surveillance is to identify potentially violent children so that authorities can intervene to prevent violence from occurring.

The policies are intended to work together to "effectively interlink public education and criminal justices systems" (Monahan and Torres 2010, p. 1). The Ontario Ministry of Education states: "The police play an essential role in making our school and communities safer" (2012). Perhaps the most visible symbol of this interlinking is the lockdown drill, which schools are advised to conduct at least twice each semester (PR.521.SCO, s. 4.9 (b) (xi)). In addition, the police are embedded into the school community through the presence of police officers who work as school resource officers (SROs). However, as the previous analysis indicates, the police presence extends well beyond the lockdown and the SRO; police involvement in school administration and policy setting reflect a commitment to increasing security by adopting criminal justice protocols that, in effect, reshape school discipline by "[borrowing] from policing mentalities and practices" (Kupchik and Bracy 2010, p. 24).

Individual schools, such as Briargreen and SRB, communicate the policy requirements to their students through school codes of conduct. Both Briargreen's Our Student's Pledge and SRB's Code of Behavior extend the Safe School principles to include routine behaviors. For example, Briargreen's Our Student's Pledge indicates that "profane language, aggressive behavior, contact sports, body contact, and throwing snowballs" are "inappropriate" and "not acceptable." Similarly, "Game Boys, skateboards, roller blades, hockey sticks, solid rubber balls, small hardballs, lacrosse sticks, and aluminum and wooden bats" are not allowed at school "for obvious safety and security reasons" (section g). SRB's Code of Behavior indicates that students may be suspended for swearing at a teacher, being under the influence of alcohol, smoking, or being in possession of a laser pen on school property. The code also strictly regulates school dances and student dress.

In this way, the net is widened to formally regulate a variety of behaviors, including child's play and dress (Morris 2005). This in effect collapses the line between dangerous and annoying behaviors; students who pose a danger to others are equated with those who challenge authority through dress or bring a hockey stick to school so they can play with their friends, and the same zero-tolerance approach is applied.

Normal social interaction is also regulated. For example, the teacher who knows a student well is not allowed to let her enter a school dance if she does not provide an authenticated form of identification, and a minimum of two police must supplement supervision by teachers and parents at dances (SRB Code of Behavior, C). All visitors are subject to a policy based on suspicion. At both schools, visitors, including parents, are required to "report immediately to the office to identify themselves and their purpose for being on school property" (D.3). Accordingly, informal social relationships are restructured to conform to a set of rules that ostensibly promote safety. However, this may come at the expense of what individuals come to know about each other through their social interactions and their ability to develop relationships based on trust.

This devaluing or lack of trust in informal social relationships is reiterated in the Alleged Harassment Policies (P.053.HR; PR.543.HR). A zero-tolerance approach is adopted to ensure that all members of the school community are "free of harassment and abuse" (P.053.HR, s. 1). The prohibition captures a range of behaviors: from sexual harassment and hate, to "embarrassing or harmful references to an individual's intellectual or physical capacities or appearance" (s. 2.1(d)) and "condescending or patronizing behavior which undermines self-respect" (2.2(d)). Informal resolution is disallowed (s. 3.4) and formal investigations, with written records of interviews with parties and witnesses (PR.543.HR, s. 4.1(d)), a decision in writing on the part of the Superintendant of Schools (s. 4.2(a)), and an appeal process (s. 4.4), are mandatory. The Alleged Harassment Policy expressly states that it "is not intended to interfere with normal social interaction between people employed by the Board" (P.053.HR, s. 3.6), but makes no such claims regarding student-teacher or student-student relationships.

The Alleged Harassment/Abuse of a Student by a Student Procedure (PR.544.HR) mirrors the provisions of the other harassment policies, with three differences. First, there is no appeal process for a decision taken by the principal. Second, the procedure explicitly sets out "initial steps" a student "may" take when being harassed by another student. These steps include confiding in: another student, a peer support group, a teacher, the principal, the vice-principal, or a parent or guardian. Peer support groups and teachers are required to inform the principal. Parents are "expected" to inform the principal. Accordingly, an appeal to help from the people within the community by the student will initiate a formal process of investigation and possible punishment, predicated on a wide-spread duty to report. The only exception is when the student confides in another student; in those circumstances, the other student "*should* offer support and *may* encourage" the student to report the incident (emphasis added).

Third, police involvement is mandated in a number of ways. Principals are required to inform all students of the existence of a hotline, and to report any critical incidents to the police regardless of the student's age (PR.533.SCO, s. 2.2). Moreover, a duty is imposed on the principal to inform victims of support services available through the school, the board, and the police service, in effect embedding police within both the disciplinary process and the rebuilding of personal and community cohesion. This is an inherent contradiction within leadership and social control roles, clearly seen in the community policing movement.

When bullying prevention programs were formally mandated by the board in 2008, the language of intervention began to depart from the zero-tolerance mantra that dominated the policies passed at the time of Columbine. For example, the Bullying Prevention and Intervention Policy (P.123.SCO) expressly incorporates progressive discipline principles (P.124.SCO; see also PR.660.SCO) that are to be "applied within a framework that shifts the focus from one that is solely punitive to one that is both corrective and supportive" (s. 2.0). This approach seeks to create a "safe learning and teaching environment" (s. 3.1) through the adoption of restorative justice practices (PR.660.SCO, s. 2). Interestingly, the document does not mention the police, except perhaps indirectly when it reiterates the need to "strengthen community partnerships/linkages to promote positive student behavior" (P.124.SCO, s. 1(d)).

The same shift in language is seen in the School Board Code of Conduct, also issued in 2008. Although safety is still the key motivator for policy development, the discourse has broadened to include as a policy objective the promotion of positive personal and community development (P.125.SCO, s. 3(b)). The role of the police is also less apparent, and only becomes visible for those "fewer students" who benefit from "supports" such as suspension, expulsion and the "involvement" of the police officer working in the school (see the appendix to this chapter).

Given the growth of evidence between 1998 and 2008 that zero-tolerance policies are ineffective (Skiba 2008) and have had a negative impact on students' privacy and civil rights (Addington 2008), one could argue that it is not surprising that the board is in some ways moving away from the language of punishment and criminality (although the link between evidence and policy is rarely direct). However, despite the shift toward a softer discourse of "supports," restorative justice, and community development, the zero-tolerance approach remains intact, and the new policies continue to be tied to the post-Columbine concern with bullying as a precursor to random acts of violence by students. Not only are the earlier policies still in force and effect, but many of the elements introduced in them, such as mandatory reporting and increased supervision, reappear in the policies enacted in 2008. Bullying has simply been added to the list of unacceptable behaviors (P.123.SCO, s. 1.1(e)). In this sense, the

2008 policies reflect the ongoing tendency to widen the zero-tolerance net (Morris 2005), as once again relatively innocuous behaviors are collapsed into a class of violent crimes that cannot be tolerated.

Perhaps more importantly, security continues to be framed within the context of rules, surveillance, and an escalating set of punishments, and school response is built on early prevention and intervention. Accordingly, it is necessary to regulate a large range of "normal" social behaviors, such as respect, honesty, and integrity, because students can only "work to their full potential" (s. 4.3(a)) when their social interactions with each other are controlled by formal mechanisms that clearly articulate which behaviors will not be tolerated. From this perspective, schools are no longer potentially unsafe solely because of school shooters, but because all students may be bullies in disguise.

Safety in Practice: Some Ethnographic Observations

Although there is a growing body of research on zero-tolerance policies, "very little is known about the subjective experience of school actors—especially students—living within, navigating, and appropriating everyday surveillance" (Monahan and Torres 2010, p. 14) in the post-Columbine school. The following section examines changes in practices and beliefs about school violence and security exhibited by students, teachers, and school administrators in Briargreen and SRB from the late 1990s to date. We hope to provide some insight into the unintended consequences these policies have had for the children they seek to protect. We also examine how these practices draw on broader beliefs about fear and safety, especially in the context of children and youths.

Our analysis draws on ethnographic data collected by coauthor Steeves through observation and participation as a school volunteer and parent. From 1992 to 2004, Steeves was actively involved with the Briargreen School Council and in that capacity interacted with the school principal on a monthly basis on a number of issues, including school safety and bullying. She also volunteered in a number of capacities, tutoring students in the classroom, leading the school choir, working in the library, and assisting with multiple field trips. As such, she was working in the school at least one day per week from 1996 to 2001, which provided her with an opportunity to converse with students and teachers without interviewing them formally.

Our discussion is divided to address four questions: (1) Who is the problem? (2) What is the problem? (3) Where does the problem occur? and (4) How do control agents respond to the problem? For ease of reading, personal pronouns are used when describing Steeves's observations and experiences.

Who Is the Problem?

Ostensibly, zero-tolerance policies are intended to regulate the behavior of students who are likely to participate in "truly dangerous and criminal behavior" (Dunbar and Villarruel 2004). However, our experience within the school system indicates that the definition of the person being regulated has been widened to include parents and families as well as students, and that being labeled "unsafe" may have serious repercussions.

For example, when our daughter was in first grade, she told us that we would no longer be allowed to send her to her room because, if we did, she would call the hotline and the police would come and punish us for being "mean" to her. Pursuant to board policy, the teacher had explained that when parents are "bad," children can call the hotline for "help." From our six-year-old's perspective, the school's instructions offered a new resource for asserting her interests. We explained to her that such reporting was only for serious offenses. But the incident nicely illustrates how, in an admirable attempt to protect children at risk, the private sphere of the home can be opened up to scrutiny by the school with insufficient thought to how children will interpret the information or how this might alter family dynamics. Moreover, the extreme cases where child abuse has come to the attention of the authorities and protective action has not been taken suggest that often the problem is not that the state is unaware but that it does not act on the knowledge it has.

The same dynamic can be seen in the classroom; writing assignments in particular can be a means of opening up the private sphere of the student and the family. For example, our children have been asked to write about their use of drugs and alcohol, and their "most shameful" actions. These assignments are crafted as confessional; the students are encouraged to reveal personal details to the school as an institution. When our children have questioned these assignments, a few teachers have indicated their discomfort with the school's interest in their students' personal lives. However, rather than changing the assignments, they told the children to "just make something up."

More typically, teachers treat these assignments as routine curricular requirements, with interesting consequences. In a health unit on eating disorders and family violence, for example, one class of girls was asked to write letters of apology to their bodies for "abusing" them. When our daughter asked what was she to do since she does not abuse her body and has a happy family life, the teacher smiled and said, "Come on, be honest." The girl's experience of nonabuse was accordingly problematized and seen as inauthentic, and the confessional nature of the assignment implicitly framed the school as worthy of intimate trust and the family as a source of pathology and violence. From this perspective, the school shooter behind zero-tolerance policies recedes and every child and every family becomes a potential source of danger.

What Is the Problem?

Since the late 1990s, the definition of what is considered "unsafe" has changed considerably, and often in ways that defy common sense (Staderab 2006). Board policies target a variety of behaviors, many of which are closely aligned with problems caused by school shootings (such as weapons offenses, police intervention in cases of school violence, and bullying). However, in practice, a growing number of interactions that were previously considered to be within the range of normal behavior have fallen within the purview of increasingly restrictive technologies of control (Morris 2005); some have been hard-engineered into the school environment and others have been imposed on student behavior.

Children's play is the foremost example; whereas it was previously largely a matter of personal choices and private interactions, it has increasingly been regulated by the schools. For example, Briargreen's playground equipment was replaced twice, to control behavior that had been redefined as "dangerous." The first time was to reduce the risk of a child falling off the structure into the sand below. The children complained because the new structure was less fun, but they still had swings, slides, and the zipline, a fifteen-foot wire with a handle approximately four feet off the ground. The next year, the school board replaced the new equipment with an even lower structure. The slides were enclosed and the plastic made them difficult to slide on. A number of swings were replaced with swings with child guards, which made them difficult for the older children to play on. A special playground was built for the kindergarten students, who were segregated from the older children by a wire fence to "reduce bullying." This was particularly disturbing to siblings and friends accustomed to playing together on the playground. The zipline survived, although older children and younger children were not allowed to use it at the same time, which made it difficult for the younger children who, up until then, had relied on the assistance of the older children to reach the handle. The changes accordingly limited the children's opportunities for both large muscle play and cooperative interaction.

Playground trees were also altered to control the children's behavior and make it easier to place them under surveillance. In 2002, the favorite climbing tree was cut down because it posed a danger. Two years later, the lower branches of all of the pines were removed to make the children visible at all times. Trees lining the street were identified as particularly risky because they offered protection for a stranger bent on child abduction.

New controls were also brought to the school's sports equipment. The principal sold the field hockey equipment because hockey was "dangerous." Baseballs, baseball bats, and footballs were forbidden because they were "weapons." To fill the gap, the parent-teacher council purchased plastic and foam floor hockey sticks with foam balls as pucks, but their use was abandoned because the equipment made it impossible for the children to play the game.

In addition to these kinds of resource bans, a number of controls were put into place to regulate the games children were allowed to play. Some, like tag, were banned outright because they were "contact sports." In other instances, the activity was allowed but modified in order to soften its rough edges. For example, after one of our children was hit in the eye by a badminton birdie (but not injured), the students were told that they were no longer allowed to play the game unless they wore goggles.

Boys in fifth and sixth grade had a particularly difficult time with the lack of activity at recess. Since they had nothing to do, they would roam around and bother the girls or the younger children, and the number of fights increased. Parents and teachers complained about an increase in misbehavior in class, often citing as the cause the inability of the boys to run around and play during recess. When one of my daughters complained, her teacher told her the boys were a "roving band of juvenile delinquents."

Teachers would also appeal to safety concerns to stop annoying but otherwise normal behavior. For example, Canadian schoolchildren celebrate Remembrance Day by wearing red poppies that are attached to their shirts with straight pins. One sixth grader who joked with a friend about poking him with the pin was suspended for a day for "threatening with a weapon." Snowball fights and fort building are a staple of Canadian child's play. After snowball throwing was banned because it was too dangerous, one sixth grader was given detention and threatened with suspension for playfully throwing a handful of snow into the air and crying, "It's snowing!" Again, safety concerns were used to justify the detention. A five-year-old child walking down the hall was told by a distraught teacher to take her hands out of her pocket or else she might "fall and die."

Rather than making the students fearful, these kinds of interactions are taken as proof that adults are overly controlling for no apparent reason. Their authority is therefore seen as irrelevant. For example, "gang clothing" was banned at SRB and students were no longer allowed to wear bandannas or hoods even though there were no gangs at this suburban school. The boys made a game of it. When the vice principal would walk by, one of them would throw up a friend's hood, so the friend would be put on the school's "hoodie list" and receive detention for gang-like behavior. A girl was also given detention for wearing a sweater even though the temperature in the hall was in the 50s (Fahrenheit) because the sweater was deemed to be a coat and therefore part of the "gang colors" prohibition. From the students' perspective, this absolutist approach to rules enforcement underlined the administration's ineffectualness, because adults could not properly discern when a problem such as gang involvement was actually present.

Most, if not all, of the students we talked to indicated that the constant monitoring of their behavior, even though they were simply going about their business, created a sense of disillusionment. As Weiss reports in her study of student resistance to school surveillance, "Students in these schools experience first-hand what it is to be monitored, contained, and harassed, all in the name of safety and protection, and they are deeply aware that the persistent advancement of surveillance measures inside their schools has ill-intended consequences" (Weiss 2010, p. 214). This results in a "cumulative effect of claustrophobia in the lived experience of the student" (p. 215).

Over time, it has become increasingly difficult to challenge these kinds of rules. Although zero-tolerance policies were, at least in part, motivated by the ways in which "tragedies of school shootings become shared media and cultural spectacles, instigating moral panics that overshadow any cold, objective assessment of risk"

(Monahan 2006), that intolerance to risk has grown to encompass an ever-widening conception of what constitutes a danger, and children's movements, play, and autonomy have been increasingly curtailed.

Where Does the Problem Occur?

Most of the time, safety rules are restricted to the school's borders; and children gladly leave the school yard to play road hockey or tag or participate in snowball fights. However, as noted above, a number of board policies extend the jurisdiction of zero-tolerance rules beyond the school yard. This creates a liminal space between school and public space in which the behavior of students—and parents—is sometimes subjected to both informal and formal regulation.

Because of the liminal nature of the boundary, it is often difficult for children to navigate the transfer from the regulated nature of school space to the relative autonomy of public space. For example, one Halloween, a boy in tenth grade was leaving the school wearing a costume he had worn throughout the schoolday. Just as he was walking out the door to the school, he put up his hood because it was cold outside. The vice principal gave him detention. When the boy complained that he was in the process of leaving the building, the vice principal told him, in all seriousness, that it was crucial that the administration be able to identify all students at all times in order to keep them safe and that hoods interfere with that. The boy was wearing a mask that completely covered his face at the time.

In addition, it is often difficult to discern when regulation will be extended beyond the school and when it will not be. As part of the SRB's graduating class's celebrations each year, a large number of students gather at local parks on the last night of school to drink and commit acts of vandalism. The event is known as Tequila Sunrise. The community has routinely protested and asked the police to intervene but the event has continued and been ignored by the school. In 2007, students participating in the event were drinking in the basement of a partially completed house in the area and lost control of a fire they had built. The building was completely destroyed. The next year, students returned to the same house during Tequila Sunrise and it was again burned to the ground. Interestingly, SRB refused to take part in the investigation of the fires and some teachers continued to encourage students to attend the event because, in the words of one teacher, it was "just good clean fun."

How Do Control Agents Respond to the Problem?

The ambivalence shown toward Tequila Sunrise demonstrates the frequent gap between administrative policy and implementation. It is noteworthy that, at the same time that zero-tolerance rules constrain young people's behavior to protect them from dangers, in practice the same young people are often given a high degree of license regarding behaviors that have been identified as unsafe. For example, on a number of occasions, students who were found drunk at school dances were suspended only to be immediately reinstated as soon as their parents complained to the board. One such student had been taken to the hospital during the dance for alcohol poisoning; the next week, his parents drove him to Tequila Sunrise because they felt it was unsafe for him to walk to the park in the dark. Similarly, many teachers chose not to challenge students who swore at them in class because—in spite of zero-tolerance punishments—they believed "there's nothing [we] can do"; teachers who did discipline students for swearing often lamented the lack of parental support for their actions.

Although parents often appeared willing to sacrifice their children's autonomy to ensure their safety, many were equally unwilling to let the school discipline their children. In effect, rules were accepted as a way to protect a child but rejected as a way of holding a child accountable for transgressive action. This creates a complex set of conflicting pressures on teachers and administrators seeking to implement board policy.

School practice departed from policy in another significant respect. In spite of the central role given to the police in board policies, student interaction with the police, in general, and the SRO in particular, was typically limited to the annual safety assembly. Students did, however, rebel against the criminal justice–style restrictions placed on them, and frequently complained that the school administration treated them like criminals. Many practices associated with the police, such as administering breathalyzer tests to students before allowing them to attend school dances, were undertaken by the school administration, and from the students' perspective, they were routinely presumed to be guilty of a variety of infractions. Students felt this was condescending and did not reflect the fact that they were capable of making responsible decisions. They also complained that adults did not trust them to behave in reasonable ways or to learn from their mistakes.

The board reliance on students informing on their peers also failed to materialize much in practice. On one occasion, when a boy in eleventh grade threw eggs at his younger brother as a practical joke, the school reported the incident to the police and asked students to identify the offender so charges could be brought. The students refused to cooperate, believing that the school was overreacting and that punishment was unwarranted. By refusing to inform on their peers, students were able to neutralize the school's control.

At the same time, students complained that the new safety regime was particularly ineffective when they did need adult assistance to deal with conflict. When one boy, known as a bully, beat up a classmate in 1996, he was suspended for three days, after which the behavior was not repeated. His fellow students saw the suspension as fair. When his younger brother did the same thing three years later, the new principal brought the two boys into her office and told them to exchange telephone numbers so they could "work it out with words." The children concluded that the antibullying program was a joke because they were no longer allowed to use the words "stupid" and "dumb," but the bullies could get your phone number and harass you at home as well as at school. In effect, the safety rules made it difficult for them to deal with aggressive behavior on the part of their peers because they could no longer use shaming or ostracism to constrain the offender, or to call others—or be called by others—to account when their behavior was hurtful or socially inappropriate.

However, one element of the zero-tolerance approach introduced in the post-Columbine panic over school violence has continued to thrive: the reliance on early identification and intervention. Since each student is framed as a potential risk, there have been ongoing attempts to collect information about all students in order to assess the need for intervention on an individual basis. In a particularly controversial move, the board initiated a student survey in 2011 that asked every student from kindergarten to twelfth grade to provide information about his or her "ethnicity, socioeconomics, gender, sexual orientation, student engagement, sense of belonging, school climate, student health, extracurricular activities and special accommodations" (Ottawa-Carleton District School Board 2011). This was done so that specific children could be tracked over time and the school could intervene to manage problems.

However, the general ethos of early identification and intervention can easily go awry. Our son's experience on his first day of kindergarten offers a prime example. He was wrongly put on a school bus even though he tearfully tried to explain that he was "a walker" and that his parents were coming to get him. When we complained that our five-year-old son was forced onto a bus that could have dropped him off in an area that was completely unknown to him if we had not located the bus before it reached its destination, the teacher insisted that a school board psychologist assess him because he was "violent" and did not "respond well to authority." Even though her actions ostensibly created a safety risk, her request reframed the incident by fitting it within the board's goals of prevention and protection. This brought a new problem to us as parents. We needed to thwart a system that would "identify" our child in order to "intervene." We were successful, but here we see how the formal system of labeling embedded in board policies comes to be used for ends unrelated to safety: the teacher was trying to avoid a reprimand in her employment record and we were concerned about an unwarranted negative notation in our son's permanent school record.

Accordingly, the practice of zero tolerance is a complex one. It both captures and regulates an overly wide range of behaviors and fails to effectively respond to student concerns about security. It also reshapes the relationships between students and teachers to conform to a model that asserts that safety and security must be externally imposed through rules, surveillance, and punishment, rather than through commonly agreed practices and behaviors (Chesler, Crowfoot, and Bryant 1979). In this sense, "rather than provide an orderly basis for *education,* rules are part of the technology of *social control*" (p. 500, emphasis in original). The result is a school climate that weakens bonds of trust, detracts from students' sense of competency to handle their own problems, and leaves students feeling that adults are ineffectual at responding to safety risks.

Conclusion

Although immediate fears about school shootings have receded since 1998, the post-Columbine notion that security can be obtained through the imposition of rules, surveillance, and punishment has continued to reshape the relationships between students, teachers, administrators, and parents. Safety concerns have become dominant, and are implicitly prioritized over rival ideas about how to provide an orderly foundation for education, such as trust, mutuality, discretion, and transparency (see, e.g., Chesler, Crowfoot, and Bryant 1979).

The technologies of social control that have been imposed in the school reflect an intolerance of any perceived harm, no matter how small or insignificant, and the net has widened to capture behaviors and activities that were previously considered normal. Both hard and soft measures of control have limited children's opportunities for large muscle play, creativity, and social interaction, and have led to a sense of claustrophobia and frustration on the part of many students. However, this intolerance of risk may also have unintended consequences for children's educational experiences and moral development.

Hope (2010) suggests that fears over safety cause many schools to "overblock" or unreasonably limit students' educational experiences. Because of this, "some frustrated students may be forced to seek alternative sites of learning or, worse, start to withdraw from certain educational processes" (p. 242). Cameron and Sheppard (2006) warn that zero-tolerance regimes treat students as "untrustworthy and incompetent, suggesting to them that they are best off following directions and conforming to expectation. This may have a diminishing effect on students' developing autonomy and responsibility, as well as their capacities for independent thought" (p. 19).

In like vein, Bergin and Bergin (1999) suggest that discipline centered on compliance may work against the development of self-control and the internalization of community values. On the other hand, Morris notes that overly restrictive rules may "inadvertently [transform] the expression of youth identity, encompassing relatively innocuous stylistic rebelliousness, into a mode of subversive opposition" (Morris 2005, p. 43). Although this may lead to either complicity or disengagement from school, it is also possible that subversive resistance "may actually reflect sophisticated social skills on the child's part . . . [that] mark the child's emerging ability to balance autonomy with social responsibility in a socially acceptable form" (pp. 198–199).

Further research is needed to more fully understand the range of effects post-Columbine disciplinary regimes have on students' education and development. Current policies should also be reassessed to determine the extent to which they flood the system with complaints and escalate incidents which could be resolved through informal social mechanisms as they often were traditionally. Certainly, the tendency to import formal criminal justice practices into schools has been heavily critiqued in the literature. Giroux, for example, argues that children are "increasingly isolated, treated with suspicion, and subjected to diminished rights to privacy and personal liberties"

(Giroux 2003, p. 553), creating a "generation of suspects" (p. 554). Cornell (2003) argues that this could be corrected by a return to case-by-case assessment of student threats by administrators who can place the incident into a broader context and apply "good judgment" rather than draconian punishments. Caplan (2003) suggests that administrators should consider the context and meaning of students' actions and exercise their discretion to make individualized determinations about appropriate consequences.

However, discretion and judgment do not occur in a vacuum. Since the current regime sees any child as a potential source of danger, it has become imperative to invade the private sphere of the child and the family to identify risks for the purposes of intervention. Accordingly, the borders between school and police, school and family, and public and private have increasingly blurred, and a growing range of behaviors, on the part of students and parents alike, have been brought into the regulatory net through formal and informal mechanisms of surveillance.

Although child safety is a laudable goal, the lack of specificity in the post-Columbine safety regime leaves vast room for interpretation on the part of students and control agents. As noted, the regime has had unintended, and often ironic, consequences, reflecting a world of imperfect choices and trade-offs. Better policy requires an awareness of the ways in which well-intentioned rules may help in some ways and harm in others.

Appendix

Ottawa-Carleton District School Board Policies

Alleged Harassment/Abuse of a Student by a Student, PR.544.HR. (1998, August).
Alleged Harassment of a Student Procedure, PR.543.HR. (1998, August).
Alleged Harassment Policy, P.053.HR. (1998, August).
Bullying Prevention and Intervention Policy, P.123.SCO. (2008, May).
Bullying Prevention and Intervention Procedure, PR.659.SCO. (2008, May).
Guidelines for Dealing with Reports of Strangers Approaching Students Policy, P.042.SCO. (1998, May 15).

Guidelines for Dealing with Reports of Strangers Approaching Students Procedure, R.532.SCO. (1998, May 15).

Police Involvement in Schools Policy, P.043.SCO. (1998, August).

Police Involvement in Schools Procedure, PR.533.SCO. (1998, August).

Progressive Discipline and Promoting Positive Student Behavior Policy, P.124.SCO. (2008, May).

Progressive Discipline and Promoting Positive Student Behavior Procedure, PR.660.SCO. (2008, May).

Safe School Policy, P.032.SCO. (2001, September 4).

Safe School Procedure, PR521.SCO. (1998, May 15).

School Board Code of Conduct Policy, P.125.SCO. (2008, May).

Video Surveillance Policy, P.047.FAC. (2007, June).

Weapons Policy, P.036.SCO. (1998, May 15).

Weapons Procedure, PR.525.SCO. (1998, May 15).

School and Provincial Codes of Conduct

Briargreen Public School. Our Student's Pledge. Expectations and Routines. Retrieved from http://briargreenps.ocdsb.ca/index.php?id=20.

Ontario Ministry of Education. Code of Conduct. Retrieved from http://www.edu.gov.on.ca/eng/safeschools/code.html.

Sir Robert Borden High School. Code of Behavior. Retrieved from http://www.sirrobertbordenhs.ocdsb.ca/index.php?id=30.

8

Racial Implications of School Discipline and Climate

Kelly Welch and Allison Ann Payne

As most modern urban public schools continue to be guided by a crime control model (Simon 2007), embraced in part as a response to highly visible instances of student violence (Muschert and Peguero 2010), schools are increasingly adopting prisonlike practices (Ferguson 2000; Fine et al. 2004; Giroux 2003; Noguera 2008; Parenti 2000; Staples 2000; Wacquant 2001; Watts and Erevelles 2004). "School prisonization" is manifested in myriad ways (Hirschfield 2008), including surveillance and security measures such as detectors to keep weapons off school grounds (Beger 2002; Brooks, Schiraldi, and Ziedenberg 2000; Mawson et al. 2002) and locked or monitored doors and gates to stop both unauthorized individuals from coming on campus and students from leaving (DeVoe et al. 2005; Gottfredson and Gottfredson 2001). Additionally, many schools have implemented policies requiring student identification badges (Beger 2002; Brooks et al. 2000) and uniforms or dress codes (Gottfredson and Gottfredson 2001; Watts and Erevelles 2004). Hallways are generally supervised by school staff and administrators (DeVoe et al. 2005), and many schools hire uniformed security guards or law enforcement officers to carry out this task (Beger 2002; Giroux 2003; Kupchik and Ellis 2008; Watts and Erevelles 2004). Many schools also install security cameras (DeVoe et al. 2005; Watts and Erevelles 2004), perform regular locker searches, require students to carry clear book bags (Brooks et al. 2000; DeVoe et al. 2005; Gottfredson and Gottfredson 2001), and use drug-sniffing dogs to facilitate enhanced monitoring of student behavior (Giroux 2003; Gottfredson and Gottfredson 2001). Ironically, even with the proliferation of these practices, parents and school boards have continued to call for stricter measures of control (Brooks et al. 2000) to manage the fear and anxiety surrounding school violence in what has been termed the "Columbine Effect" (Muschert and Peguero 2010).

In addition to the tightening of school security, the intensification of student disciplinary policy has led to the trend of criminalizing students. Student discipline in American schools has grown increasingly severe, as evidenced by greater use of exclusionary punishments like expulsion, suspension, and in-school suspension, as well as the implementation of strictly enforced zero-tolerance policies (Gottfredson and Gottfredson 2001; Kupchik and Ellis 2008). Moreover, students found in violation of rules are frequently punished by schools aiming to reduce school-based delinquency in a manner that is somewhat analogous to the treatment of criminals by the criminal justice system (Fantz 2008; Giroux 2003; Kupchik and Monahan 2006; Mawson et al. 2002; Noguera 2003b; Tredway, Brill, and Hernandez 2007). A clear example of this is how the actions of school troublemakers are often described with criminal justice language (Tredway et al. 2007), such as referring to students as "suspects" or "repeat offenders," who are then involved in "investigations," "interrogations," and "searches" by dogs or school resource officers (SROs). Students may then be involved in "line-ups" and school "courts" before being punished by detentions, suspensions, and expulsions, which have been likened to the banishment of incarceration or execution, albeit only until those students relocate to a different school or school system. In addition, zero-tolerance policies operate much like mandatory minimum criminal-sentencing statutes that offer no forgiveness after predetermined violations. Further, delinquency that occurs on school grounds is more often referred to formal law enforcement rather than being addressed internally (Beger 2002). A consequence of these changes in student discipline is that schools are becoming less oriented to creating a positive educational environment and more like prisons in that their populations are subject to risk assessment, surveillance, and punishment that produces an adverse environment (Ferguson 2000; Fine et al. 2004; Giroux 2003; Parenti 2000; Staples 2000; Watts and Erevelles 2004).

One might assume that these trends are a response to more instances of school violence. However, evidence suggests that this intensification of student discipline is not actually associated with increases in student delinquency and misbehavior (Kupchik and Monahan 2006; Skiba and Peterson 1999). In fact, these changes in school punitiveness have occurred despite a documented decline in student delinquency, student drug use, violent victimization in schools, and school-related deaths (Beger 2002; Brooks et al. 2000; DeVoe et al. 2005; Dinkes, Cataldi, and Lin-Kelly 2007). Notwithstanding the widespread use of these punitive disciplinary practices, the Columbine Effect (Muschert and Peguero 2010) is causing community endorsements of increasingly restrictive disciplinary measures that have resulted in students feeling less safe and more aware of violations in schools that implement these school practices (Brooks et al. 2000).

One might not be surprised to learn that harsh disciplinary practices are not applied equally in response to student violations (Vavrus and Cole 2002), and that black students are more likely than white students to be subjected to stricter treatment and harsher punishment. Coupled with the fear of school-based violence that characterizes the Columbine Effect, criminal stereotypes of black students may exacerbate that impulse to intensify school discipline, particularly for minorities. This is another trend that mirrors patterns in the US criminal justice system: criminal justice institutions have not only become increasingly punitive despite decreasing crime rates (Austin and Irwin 2001; Currie 1998), but have also produced a dramatic racial disparity in who is punished in the criminal justice system relative to representations in the larger national population (Nichols 2004; Noguera 2003a; Skiba 2001; Wacquant 2001).[1]

Racial Threat and the Intensification of Student Punishment

There have been a number of attempts to explain this apparent disparity between levels of school delinquency and the severity of school discipline policies, as well as the racial disparity of discipline. While the range of potential influences on school discipline that have been assessed in prior research is broad, a limited amount of research has examined the possibility that the proportion of black students in schools is partially responsible for some degree of the punitiveness of student disciplinary policies implemented by many schools nationwide (Payne and Welch 2010; Welch and Payne 2010). Specifically, these studies have found that racial threat is associated with harsh approaches to school discipline.

The racial threat hypothesis is a macro-level theory, which conjectures that a greater ratio of blacks will intensify public punitiveness. This support for punitive criminal justice responses is predicted to be a result of inherent economic and political competition presented by a growing minority population (Blalock 1967), as well as a perceived criminal threat posed by a growing number of blacks (Crawford, Chiricos, and Kleck 1998; Liska 1992) that are driven by stereotypes linking race with crime (Welch 2007). Studies typically operationalize racial threat by the racial composition of place (Behrens, Uggen, and Manza 2003; Demuth and Steffensmeier 2004; Mosher 2001; Smith and Holmes 2003) and show strong support for this explanation for increased social control, indicating that racial composition is related to resources allocated to law enforcement (Chamlin 1989), rates of arrest (Mosher 2001) and of incarceration (Jacobs and Kleban 2003), resources and size of corrections (Jacobs and Helms 1999), and executions (Baumer, Messner, and Rosenfeld 2003), among a myriad other criminal justice outcomes.

While the effects of racial threat are predominately tested in criminal justice contexts (Demuth and Steffensmeier 2004; Holmes 2000; Keen and Jacobs 2009), the fact that school discipline as a process has become so similar in many ways to criminal punishment suggests that the application of this perspective in schools is not inappropriate. In fact, tests for effects of racial threat in schools have found that the racial composition of students in schools influences the types of disciplinary policies implemented (Welch and Payne 2010). Specifically, schools with a greater proportion of black students use more punitive approaches, more zero-tolerance policies, and fewer mild responses (Payne and Welch 2010; Welch and Payne 2010). In addition, schools responding to student misbehavior with one type of discipline tend to use other types of responses as well (Payne and Welch 2010). Clearly, the intensification of school punishment that is impacting our youths is most profoundly affecting those students enrolled in predominantly minority institutions. And, presumably, this means that minority students are bearing the brunt of this harsh treatment. Neither the strict discipline increasingly used in schools nor the racially disparate nature with which that discipline is sanctioned seem particularly conducive to a positive and productive school environment.

School Climate: Communal School Organization and Student Bonding

One consequence of school-based racial threat and its influence on student discipline is the troubling climate within schools, linking the macro-level threat processes with the meso-level school climate

(Henry 2009). Further, it is also likely that these effects diminish the capacity for students—especially those attending schools with pro-portionately more black students as well as the black students them-selves—to feel connected with their schools, a micro-level outcome that produces several distinct disadvantages for those youths. Puni-tive responses to misbehavior often create a climate of fear and re-sentment, resulting in negative attitudes toward school common among students where harsh discipline is used (Nichols 2004; Schi-raldi and Zeidenberg 2001). There is a strong chance that this will lead to students feeling as though they do not belong in their schools, which, in turn, may decrease learning and increase the likelihood of engaging in deviant and delinquent behavior (Payne 2008; Payne, Gottfredson, and Gottfredson 2003).

Indeed, research demonstrates a definite relationship between school climate and general school disorder. In one of the earliest school-level studies on school social organization, Gottfredson and Gottfredson (1985) found that in schools in which teachers and administrators had low levels of cooperation, teachers had punitive attitudes, rules were perceived by students as neither fair nor firmly enforced, students were not compelled by conventional rules and laws governing behavior, and there was more teacher victimization. These results were found even as community and student demo-graphic characteristics were taken into account. Corroborating these findings, it has also been found that teachers in disorderly schools tend to have lower morale and poor perceptions of school adminis-tration (Gottfredson 1987; Gottfredson et al. 2005). Furthermore, teacher satisfaction and commitment are associated with lower stu-dent dropout rates, fewer disciplinary problems, and higher atten-dance rates (Ostroff 1992). In addition, schools that have a system of shared values and expectations and that experience meaningful social interactions also have less disorder, as do schools in which the stu-dents have a high sense of belonging (Duke 1989).

Communal school organization, a more specific perspective of school climate, refers to the organization of schools as communities (Lee, Bryk, and Smith 1992), as indicated by supportive relationships between and among members of the school, a common set of goals and norms, and a sense of collaboration and individual involvement. Schools that are communally organized have more positive student attitudes, better teacher morale, and less student deviance (Gottfred-son 2001). A school that has a strong sense of community is one in which "members know, care about, and support one another, have common goals and sense of shared purpose, and to which they actively contribute and feel personally committed" (Solomon et al. 1997, p. 236). A communally organized school emphasizes informal social relations, common norms and experiences, and collaboration and participation; by contrast, more bureaucratic schools emphasize formal organization, technical knowledge, and regulation and standardization (Lee, Bryk, and Smith 1992; Rowan 1990).

Communal schools meet the needs of both teachers and students who, therefore, become bonded with other school community members, committed to the school's mission and goals, and are then more likely to internalize school norms and rules (Battistich et al. 1995; Payne 2008; Payne, Gottfredson, and Gottfredson 2003). Essentially, because the relationships that develop among members in a communal school are more caring and supportive and because the planning and decisionmaking that occur in a communal school are influenced by all members, individuals in a communal school develop a strong sense of belonging and a common set of goals.

The importance of different aspects of the communal school concept has been conclusively demonstrated without necessarily identifying the school as a community (Bryk and Driscoll 1988; Rutter and Maughan 2002; Solomon et al. 1997). For instance, a common purpose and a set of shared values among the teachers and administrators have been highlighted as key elements of many successful schools (Grant and Capell 1983; Rutter et al. 1979). Further, school environments that promote supportive relationships between teachers and students can protect those students from high-risk behavior (Werner and Smith 1992; Zimmerman and Arunkumar 1994), as well as offering other advantages for students (McLaughlin 1990). In addition, a collaborative school culture, in which teachers share responsibility and commitment to the students and the school, is more effective for both student achievement and prosocial behavior than the individualistic culture that characterizes most schools (Fullan and Hargreaves 1996).

Other research has illustrated the benefits of the overall communal school organization model (Bryk and Driscoll 1989; Gottfredson 2001; Payne 2008, 2009; Payne, Gottfredson, and Gottfredson 2003). Teachers in communally organized schools experience better morale and satisfaction as well as fewer absences and less victimization (Battistich and Solomon 1997; Bird and Little 1986; Bryk and Driscoll 1989; Little 1985; Newmann, Rutter, and Smith 1989; Payne

2008, 2009; Payne, Gottfredson, and Gottfredson 2003). In addition, all students in communally organized schools demonstrate less delinquency, misbehavior, fear, victimization, and dropping out, and have greater empathy, school bonding, and academic interest, motivation, and achievement (Battistich et al. 1995; Battistich and Hom 1997; Bryk and Driscoll 1989; Payne 2008; Payne, Gottfredson, and Gottfredson 2003; Phaneuf 2006; Solomon et al. 1992; Stewart 2003), regardless of their race or ethnicity (Payne, Gottfredson, and Kruttschnitt 2009).

Hirschi's (1969) social control theory provides a link between communal school organization and school disorder: students in a communally organized school appear to be more bonded to the school. The supportive relationships, common norms and goals, and greater involvement and participation found in communally organized schools theoretically increase the likelihood that students will become more bonded to their school, and thus less likely to misbehave (Payne 2008; Payne, Gottfredson, and Gottfredson 2003). As the members of the school create a community, the climate becomes warmer, more inclusive, and participatory. The students' feelings of belonging and attachment then increase, as do their school commitment and their levels of belief in and internalization of school norms and values. They feel they belong to the school and are valued and accepted (Payne, Gottfredson, and Gottfredson 2003).

This is key for schools because students who are well integrated in school are not only more likely to have a positive learning experience, but are also less likely to be deviant. Those who have more positive attachments, who have invested greater effort into school, who are involved in more school activities, and who believe in the rules of the school are less likely to engage in antisocial behavior (Welsh, Greene, and Jenkins 1999). Indeed, much research supports the finding of low school bonding leading to student misbehavior (Cernkovich and Giordano 1992; Gottfredson, Wilson, and Najaka 2002; Hirschi 1969; Jenkins 1997; Krohn and Massey 1980; Liska and Reed 1985; Payne 2008, 2009; Payne, Gottfredson, and Gottfredson 2003; Welsh, Greene, and Jenkins 1999), with most research suggesting similar relationships for minority and white students (Payne, Gottfredson, and Kruttschnitt 2009). In addition, the few studies that have specifically tested the mediated relationship between communal school organization, student bonding, and school disorder are supportive of this proposed link (Payne 2008; Payne, Gottfredson, and Gottfredson 2003; Wilson 2004). Essentially, students who attend communally organized schools are more bonded to school, which, in turn, causes them to be less deviant.

Clearly, communal schools have powerful consequences for both teachers and students. Schools that are communally organized generally have more effective teachers who enjoy their jobs more and have more positive perceptions of the school in general (Gottfredson 2001). These schools also have students who are more bonded to both their teachers and to their school's norms and who exhibit higher academic achievement and less deviant behavior (Gottfredson 2001). It has also been demonstrated that student bonding is an important concept for student achievement and delinquency: students who are more attached to teachers, more committed to school, and have stronger belief in school norms will display higher academic achievement and less deviant behavior (Welsh, Greene, and Jenkins 1999).

Punitive Discipline, Race, and School Climate

But what happens to the school community and subsequent student bonding when harsh discipline and zero-tolerance policies are implemented? It has been suggested that this type of punitive response to misbehavior "exacts a heavy toll on students, teachers, and the entire school community" (Noguera 1995, p. 189; Watts and Erevelles 2004), such that "the students' trust in the school and in their fellow students, and their ability to learn effectively, are undermined" (Henry 2009, p. 1258). Harsh discipline, particularly exclusionary practices such as suspension and expulsion, have clear negative consequences, including school failure, grade retention, negativity toward school, and a greater likelihood of dropping out (Nichols 2004; Schiraldi and Zeidenberg 2001; Skiba and Peterson 1999, 2000). In fact, severe responses to misbehavior seem to actually increase the probability that sanctioned students will engage in delinquency both at school (Schiraldi and Zeidenberg 2001) and in the greater community (Foney and Cunningham 2002; Nichols 2004). This failure of harsh discipline is largely due to its reliance on a free will view of behavior as a result of choice based on a rational consideration of costs and benefits. The behavioral reality of conditional free will or even limited rationality is far more likely, suggesting that a "range of individual, situational, environmental, structural, and cultural factors shape and channel available behavioral choices" (Henry 2009, p. 1247). Current disciplinary practices, however, do not take these multilevel factors into account.

Based on the conclusions of Welch and Payne (2010), racially disparate punitive disciplinary practices can have even more salient consequences for schools and their students. Along these lines, schools with a greater proportion of minority students are also less likely to be communally organized (Bryk and Driscoll 1989; Payne 2008, 2012; Payne, Gottfredson, and Gottfredson 2003) and have students who are less bonded to school (Payne, Gottfredson, and Gottfredson 2003; Payne 2008). The fact that the implementation of communally organized schools is also influenced by racial composition may further disadvantage the students—many of whom are black—in educational settings where harsh discipline is already favored.

However, recent research suggests that, although larger and more racially diverse schools may have more difficulty creating a school community, once this community is created in these schools, it actually has a greater protective impact on school disorder (Payne 2012). That is, communal school organization reduces school disorder more in racially heterogeneous schools than in racially homogeneous schools. Thus, even though it is less likely for racially heterogeneous schools to develop a strong community, those schools that do develop these communities are more likely to see even greater reductions in disorder. In other words, it appears that the strength of communal school organization can actually buffer any effect that racial heterogeneity has on school disorder by focusing on the communal aspects of the school (Payne 2012). The communal school organization that is achieved in these schools is actually stronger as a result of members of the community working together to overcome the structural factors that may be obstacles to the creation of this community. This process would lead to more collaborative and supportive relationships and to a more supported and integrated set of common norms and goals. This stronger school community would then lead to greater student bonding and have a stronger protective impact on school disorder. However, while this outcome offers distinct advantages for white and minority students attending heterogeneous schools that have organized communally, the implementation of punitive disciplinary policies is sure to operate as a considerable obstacle to developing this type of school climate in the first place.

Restorative Justice in Schools

Given both the negative consequences of harsh student punishment on individual students and on the overall school climate, along with the subsequent increases in misbehavior and disorder seen in non–communally organized schools, it is clear that schools need to reconsider their responses to student misbehavior. Morrison (2003, 2005) and others offer an alternative to such punitive discipline by arguing for the use of restorative justice practices in schools. One of the many methods used to address student misbehavior in schools, restorative justice is a relatively recent and innovative technique that focuses heavily on relationship building and repairing the harm caused by school violence (Ashworth et al. 2008; Cameron and Thorsborne 1999, 2001; Chmelynski 2005; McCluskey et al. 2008; Morrison 2003, 2005; Morrison, Blood, and Thorsborne 2005; Shaw 2007; Wearmouth, McKinney, and Glynn 2007).

Originally applied to the criminal justice system (Sherman 2003), restorative justice interventions have attempted to repair the harm caused by criminal offenses while preventing further crimes from occurring; this is generally accomplished through conferences that seek to produce reconciliation between offenders, victims, and community members (Sherman 2003). The importance of communication between offenders, victims, and the community affected by the harmful act is also emphasized (Macready 2009), as is resolution to the offense that allows the victim to feel closure and requires the offender to take responsibility for the harmful actions (Karp and Breslin 2001; Macready 2009), without rejecting the whole person. Allowing the offender to discuss and be accountable for the harm caused is an important part of restorative practices that can aid in reducing the recurrence of such behavior (Braithwaite et al. 2001). Communication between the victim and offender allows the offender to see how this behavior harms others (Morrison 2005) and also enables the two parties and their supporters to make joint decisions on how to repair the damage (Chmelynski 2005). Results of randomized controlled trials of restorative conferences show lower levels of recidivism, particularly in the case of violent offenses (Sherman 2003).

Restorative justice practices were first implemented within schools in Australia in 1994, and studies since then have illustrated the effectiveness of restorative justice conferences as a response to student misbehavior (Blood and Thorsborne 2005; Queensland Department of Education 1996; Youth Justice Board 2005). Completely contrary to the disciplinary practice of student exclusion, restorative approaches in schools focus on relationships, shifting from punishment and isolation to reconciliation and community (Morrison et al. 2005). Some have even argued that restorative justice is best applied to the school context because of the nature of relationships in these institutions, where students see each other day after day and encounters can turn dangerous if not adequately managed (Morrison, Blood, and Thorsborne 2005). Thus, Bazemore and Schiff (2010) propose that a restorative justice approach to discipline, combined with a focus on routine activities (Eck 1994; Felson 1993) and communal school organization (Gottfredson 2001; Payne, Gottfredson, and Gottfredson 2003), offers a model of inclusionary dialogue that repairs harm and creates a whole-school environment of supportive relationships, accountability, and peacemaking values.

Within the school-based restorative justice model, misbehavior is viewed as a violation of a relationship, either with teachers, administrators, or other students (Drewery 2004; Morrison 2003). In order to restore the harm of such a violation, the offending student and the individual whose trust was violated must reconcile and the relationship must be mended. The importance of building and maintaining positive relationships, especially between members of a school community, is continually stressed (Thorsborne and Cameron 2001).

One of the advantages that restorative practices possess over traditional punishment is the ability to create specialized solutions to each situation; these solutions work to repair the harm and allow victimized students or school staff to receive closure, and they are manageable for the delinquent student to fulfill (Wachtel 2001). Specific procedures that fulfill school-based restorative objectives include student conferences and peer mediation, which can lead to outcomes such as restitution, in which the offending student is required to repay the school or a victim for damages or harm done, or complete community service (Fields 2003; Wachtel and McCold 2001). As expected, restorative procedures are generally preferred by students over the traditional practices of detention, suspension, and expulsion. These restorative techniques have had high satisfaction rates in schools and hold much promise for reducing school violence (Drewery 2004; Fields 2003; O'Dea and Loewen 1999).

Restorative justice proponents caution that the implementation of a full restorative model of discipline will require a fundamental shift in thinking, one that addresses not just school discipline and student delinquency but the entire school climate and community as well (Bazemore and Schiff 2010; Cremin 2010; Morrison 2010). This shift from "authoritarian and punitive to democratic and responsive" (Bazemore and Schiff 2010, p. 8; Morrison 2002) must take into account the complicated nature of education as an institution, acknowledging schools' focus not just on safety but, of course, on teaching and learning as well (Cremin 2010). Thus, in order for restorative practices to be successful, schools must fully change how they conceptualize discipline, viewing it not as a function of a student's ability to follow a set of rules but rather as a student's capacity to consider how his or her behavior is impacting the greater school community (Morrison, Blood, and Thorsborne 2005). In this way, a shift from the view of human action as a purely rational choice to one that recognizes the multilevel factors that influence this choice is required (Henry 2009), moving from an individually focused model of behavior to a socially interconnected one (Morrison 2010).

In order to maximize its success, schools and districts must realize that restorative justice is not simply a set of behavioral modification techniques or a way to reduce conflict between students and a community, but rather a whole community philosophy that must be adopted at all levels of the educational institution (Braithwaite et al. 2001; Calhoun and Daniels 2008; Thorsborne and Cameron 2001; Chmelynski 2005; Fields 2003; Hopkins 2002; Karp and Breslin 2001; Morrison, Blood, and Thorsborne 2005; Shaw 2007; Watchel 1999). Wearmouth, McKinney, and Glynn (2007) argue that restorative justice should be a community-wide effort and will be effective in schools only if other groups reach out and support the approach. Indeed, most research suggests that in order for the restorative policies to be sustained in schools and to continually produce positive results, the entire school population must adopt the philosophy and not just implement one program in one classroom or in one level of administration (Braithwaite et al. 2001; Calhoun and Daniels 2008; Thorsborne and Cameron 2001; Chmelynski 2005; Fields 2003; Hopkins 2002; Karp and Breslin 2001; Morrison, Blood, and Thorsborne 2005; Shaw 2007; Watchel 1999). In fact, for these changes to be most successful, the shift to a philosophy of engagement over control is needed at the cultural and structural levels, not just at the student and school level. Changes at the local micro- and meso-levels must also be supported by changes in the wider macro-level (Henry 2009), such that the restorative philosophy is reflected throughout society.

Conclusion

Although previous research testing the influence of racial threat in schools has shown that schools with a greater percentage of black students are less apt to implement mild disciplinary techniques in favor of harsher ones (Payne and Welch 2010; Welch and Payne 2010), a switch from a punitive view of discipline to a restorative justice philosophy and its application through related processes seems necessary for a decrease in school disorder as well as a less racially disparate educational system. It is likely that the use of restorative approaches to misbehavior will mitigate much of the negativity produced in racially heterogeneous schools. Further, it is unlikely that restorative discipline will unfairly benefit white students only, since this type of student justice is more frequently prevalent in communally organized schools, and these schools are simply less apt to adopt prejudicial policies. Black students may not only experience fewer school sanctioned punitive punishments, but they may also encounter fewer of the many detrimental side-effects of such punishments, including decreased learning, grade retention, dropping out, and delinquency. Thus, the Columbine Effect may be mitigated by the use of restorative disciplinary techniques.

Transforming to a restorative philosophy would enable schools to emphasize social engagement over social control (Morrison 2010). This could lead to a reduction in the use of exclusionary discipline, the reintegration of "problem" students, and the creation of a true school community. Implementing such a philosophy would enhance school efforts to become more communally organized, thereby leading students to become more bonded to school, which, in turn, decreases the likelihood those students will misbehave. These changes would then decrease the level of school disorder and allow schools to focus on their ultimate academic mission in a manner that is equal for students of all racial backgrounds. Despite the need for this challenging shift in disciplinary orientation, indeed *because* of its transformative nature, restorative justice remains a promising approach to school discipline.

Note

1. Although the US population is 72.4 percent white, 12.6 percent black, and 16.3 percent Hispanic (US Census Bureau 2011), among those who are imprisoned, only 34.2 percent are white, while 38.2 percent are black and 20.7 percent are Hispanic (US Department of Justice 2010).

9

Violence Prevention and Intervention

Jun Sung Hong, Dorothy L. Espelage,
Christopher J. Ferguson, and Paula Allen-Meares

The Columbine tragedy was among the most talked-about school shooting incidents. Over 26,000 pages of police documents were exhibited to the public, countless pages of lawsuits filled the courthouses, a plethora of news stories packed the news archives, and dozens of books on this case were published (Kass 2010). The Cable News Network (CNN) coverage of victim Rachel Joy Scott's funeral shortly after the shootings was also one of the most watched events, surpassing the funeral of Diana, Princess of Wales, in 1997 (Nimmo and Scott 2000). In the weeks, months, and years that followed, questions were repeatedly raised about the shooters, what provoked the shootings, and what measures need to be taken to prevent "another Columbine."

Many efforts were made to prevent another devastating tragedy. Within the past decade, school districts have endeavored to keep students safe by profiling potential shooters; implementing antibullying, school safety, and zero-tolerance policies; increasing security measures; and foiling planned attacks (Calefati 2009). The tragedy also prompted swift and aggressive responses from federal, state, and local lawmakers. Government funding was provided for metal detectors, security cameras, and emergency-response plans, along with putting police officers and school resource officers (SROs) in school districts and training for students to handle bullying and resolve peer conflicts (Simon 2007). The issue of gun safety was also raised, as then-president Bill Clinton called on the Congress to pass a legislation mandating child safety locks for gun owners.

Despite these efforts, however, over sixty high-profile shootings have occurred in school districts nationwide since Columbine, and of these, the most notable was the Virginia Tech massacre in 2007, which eclipsed Columbine as one of America's deadliest school shootings. Moreover, there were multiple copycat school shootings that followed, such as the California Santana High School shootings in 2001, where a fifteen-year-old shooter threatened to "pull a Columbine" days before the shootings, which left two students dead and fifteen others seriously injured. Considering these events that followed the Columbine shooting, it is time to reexamine efforts made within the past decade to prevent school shootings tragedy. A serious question remains: What has been done since Columbine and where do we go from here?

The focus of this chapter is to examine school and youth violence programs and policies since Columbine, within the context of the ecological systems levels: micro-, meso-, exo-, and macrosystems. We first argue that school shooting events are multilevel phenomenon, and then discuss existing programs and policies within the ecological context. We finally suggest ways in which youths and school violence can be addressed to enhance school safety in America's school districts.

Columbine as a Multilevel Phenomenon

Scholars studying school violence and school shootings have recognized the importance of a multidisciplinary and multilevel approach to explicating factors underlying aggressive and violent behaviors in school (Fast 2008; Garbarino 1999; Henry 2009; Hong et al. 2011; Newman 2004; Tonso 2002; Verlinden, Hersen, and Thomas 2000). Social scientists have argued that a variety of factors may contribute to school shootings, and thus, no single factor is sufficient to explain such events (Muschert 2007b). Such incidents may emerge from individual, community, and social and cultural contexts (Muschert 2007b). Henry (2009) also asserts that "school violence is a broad phenomenon with multiple manifest forms that together compose a continuum of violence" (p. 1250). The author further notes that the problem with examining school violence and school shootings is that researchers categorize it into types and subtypes of violence in attempts to explain each as fragmented parts, without understanding the cumulative interrelations and interaction among them (Henry 2009). Factors that are associated with the shooting event are both proximate (e.g., deviant peer affiliation) and distal (e.g., gun control laws).

An Ecological Analysis of Post-Columbine Efforts at School Violence Prevention

In the aftermath of the Columbine shootings, researchers (e.g., Fast 2008; Henry 2009; Hong et al. 2011; Leary et al. 2003; Mulvey and Cauffman 2001; Verlinden, Hersen, and Thomas 2000; Weisbrot 2008; Wike and Fraser 2009) have focused considerable attention on efforts to investigate the etiology of school shootings in order to effectively prevent violence and homicides in the schoolyards. A recent examination of the risk factors for Columbine conducted by Hong and colleagues (2011) found that the shooting incident involved a constellation of factors at multiple levels of the social ecology, and the ecological framework is highly appropriate for understanding these factors. Factors identified in this study included residential mobility (chrono), socially constructed masculinity and gun "control" measures (macro), media exposure to violence (exo), teacher-peer relationship (meso), and parenting and peer influences (micro). The authors also noted that "the levels of [the ecological] systems interact with each other to influence individual behavior, and school shooting incidents might be artifacts of these interactions" (p. 865). They concluded that effective means to prevent school violence necessitate integrative and holistic approaches—the ecological systems theory.

Astor, Pitner, and Duncan (1996) argue that the ecological systems theory is an invaluable assessment tool for school counselors and social workers in assisting teachers and school officials frame appropriate questions and generate effective school-based responses to violence. The ecological systems theory can facilitate our understanding of the complexities surrounding school violence and the implementation of school violence prevention and intervention. Bronfenbrenner (1976) conceptualized the social environment as an interactive set of systems, which are conceived as the major dynamic shaping the context in which the individual experiences social reality (Garbarino and Bronfenbrenner 1976). The individual is a part of the various levels of the environment, which consists of the micro-, meso-, exo-, and macrosystems, and development reflects the influence of these environmental systems. Although various development theories emphasize the nature and nurture interaction in child development, the ecological system theory explicates the individual's environment both in terms of its quality and context, and changes or conflict in one layer ripple through other layer (Paquette and Ryan 2001). Moreover, as the individual develops, the interactions within these layers become more complex. Therefore, it is imperative that school violence interventions need to consider the multilevel ecological environment in which youths and their schools are situated (Espelage and Swearer 2003, 2004, 2011) rather than simply identifying factors that contribute to violence.

As Kerns and Prinz (2002) argue, interventions that do not target the multiple environments are less likely to be effective than those that comprehensively target the social ecology. This is critical, as reflected in the number of federal agencies that emphasize the importance of efficacy and effectiveness in evidence-based practices (Nickerson and Brock 2011). Thus, the effectiveness of school violence prevention and intervention programs and policies need to be understood within the context of the social-ecological framework (Espelage and Swearer 2003, 2004, 2011).

Microsystem

The microsystem represents the first level of the social-ecological theory of child development, which is composed of individuals and others with whom the individual has interactions (e.g., parents, peers, and teachers), across different settings (e.g., home, school). Given the direct effect of the microsystems on youths' attitudes and behaviors, a number of antiviolence prevention and intervention programs in schools have directed interventions at conflicts among peers and bullying, and understanding and promoting positive school climates (Breunlin et al. 2002; Heydenberk and Heydenberk 2007; Heydenberk, Heydenberk and Tzenova, 2006).

Peer Conflicts and Bullying

Peers are often influential players among children and adolescents' microsystem, which involves children interacting with, socializing with, and influencing one another (Rodkin and Hodges 2003). Adolescence, in particular, is a period in which there is a crucial need for friendships and peer support, as adolescents look to their peers more than caregivers to form their attitudes and behaviors (Ayyash-Abdo 2002). Considering that negative peer relations and previous peer victimization have been documented as major risk factors for over half of the school shootings cases (US Department of Health and Human Services 2001), a major focus has been on implementing bullying prevention and peer conflict resolution programs (Garbarino 2004). Additionally, shortly after the Columbine tragedy, many state legislatures adopted legal mandates requiring that all K–12 schools implement antibullying policies or prevention programs to address this problem (Limber and Small 2003). Most recently, several federal agencies have also joined efforts to address the issues and problems of bullying in schools. Six federal departments hosted a Bullying Prevention Summit, which was aimed to mobilize interest, advocacy, and input from multiple stakeholders and partners (Bryn 2011). The underlying goal of these programs and policies was to ensure that all students feel safe and valued and that there are negative consequences to bullying and peer victimization (Espelage and Swearer 2003).

In response to the Columbine tragedy and growing public fear of school safety, a number of bullying prevention and intervention programs have been implemented in school districts. The Blueprints for Violence Prevention of the Center for the Study and Prevention of Violence at the University of Colorado reviewed 600 bullying and youth violence prevention programs. Of these, eleven programs met the scientific standards of efficacy, and eighteen programs have been evaluated as "promising" (Blueprint for Violence Prevention 2002–2004). Several meta-analyses conducted within six years found that schools continue to use punitive approaches (also called zero tolerance) to bullying, including suspension and expulsion. Other popular approaches to bullying prevention are programs that provide students with information about bullying, consequences of bullying, and the importance of being a defender for targeted peers (Hong and Espelage 2012). One such program is the Olweus Bullying Prevention Program, a Norwegian-based program, which targets ecological factors associated with bullying and school problems. The core components of the Olweus Bullying Prevention Program are implemented at the individual, classroom, and school levels. The program consists of parental involvement, intervention with victims and perpetrators of bullying, school-wide rules against bullying, school staff meetings, and training for school staff members. Results, however, have been mixed. Some researchers found that the program has been effective in reducing bullying and peer victimization and in fostering a proso-cial school environment (see Limber et al. 2004). Others found that the program had mixed positive effects on preventing or reducing bullying and peer victimization in American schools (Bauer, Lozano, and Rivara 2006).

School Climate

Confronted by increasing incidents of violence in schools in the aftermath of the Columbine shootings, teachers, parents, and school officials have called for increased attention to school safety initia-tives and asked to make school environments safer. In response, many schools have implemented punitive measures that would sus-pend or expel potentially at-risk students, rather than working to fos-ter a sense of safety and belonging (Mulvey and Cauffman 2001). At the same time, numerous prevention programs directed at teaching students various attitudes, knowledge, and skills to effectively con-front peer conflicts and reduce their involvement in violence have been implemented in school districts nationwide, which has become a part of the national agenda (Farrell et al. 2001; Twemlow et al. 2001). School-based violence prevention and intervention programs have traditionally targeted developmental processes for risk factors, as empirical evidence suggests that violent behavior in schools occurs along a developmental continuum. Thus, several early preven-tion programs have been developed, which focused on altering at-risk developmental trajectories for youth violence, such as the Good Behavior Game (GBG) and Linking the Interests of Families and Teachers (LIFT; Flannery et al. 2003).

Although a multitude of school violence prevention programs have been developed in an effort to combat crime, violence, and homicides in the schoolyards, relatively few have been systematically evaluated (Farrell et al. 2001; Twemlow et al. 2001). As a conse-quence, there have been limited data to inform decision-makers about which specific strategies are effective with certain populations and under what conditions. As a result, school and community leaders, and policy makers have been falsely convinced that they are address-ing the problem when the resources committed to such efforts can be better used to develop and implement more effective programs (Far-rell et al. 2001).

Nonetheless, researchers consistently suggest that promoting a healthy school climate by fostering students' sense of belonging and school connectedness is more effective in reducing school violence and crime than implementing punitive disciplinary measures (Brookmeyer, Fanti, and Henrich 2006; Loukas, Suzuki, and Horton 2006; McNeely, Nonnemaker, and Blum 2002; Nettles, Mucheran, and Jones 2000). School climate can be defined as the feelings that students and school staff have about their school environment over a period of time (Peterson and Skiba 2001). *School climate, teacher support,* and *student engagement* are terms that have frequently been employed by researchers over the years (Blum 2005). Bonding to school represents an important area in promoting a positive school climate, which has been shown to increase positive development and buffer the effects of risks, such as problem behaviors (Catalano et al. 2004). Intervention programs that promote school connectedness have increasingly been recognized as effective in reducing risk factors and in enhancing protective factors for elementary school–age children's health and problem behaviors (Catalano et al. 2004; McNeely, Nonnemaker, and Blum 2002).

In recent years, a number of programs that target school climate and school connectedness for elementary school–age children have been examined for efficacy, such as Healthy Kids Mentoring Programs (King et al. 2002) and Raising Healthy Children (Catalano et al. 2004). These programs are designed to enhance children's sense of connectedness to their school climate through classroom instruction and management (e.g., cooperative learning), child skill development (e.g., cognitive and social skills training), and parent intervention. They have reportedly been effective in enhancing positive development of children in the school settings.

For postsecondary students, creating more personalized educational environments, particularly ones that encourages teacher-student rapport, has been found to be effective. One example is the First Things First (FTF; Quint et al. 2005), an education reform initiative, which collaborates with the Institute for Research and Reform in Education to improve students' academic performance. FTF is designed to: (1) strengthen relationships among students, school staff members, and families; (2) improve teaching and learning in every classroom; and (3) reallocate budget, staff, and time to achieve the abovementioned goals through restructuring schools into small learning communities (Klem and Connell 2004). To our knowledge, however, fewer programs that promote school connectedness among postsecondary students have been empirically evaluated for efficacy or effectiveness. This is surprising considering that older students are less likely to be attached to school, compared to younger students (e.g., McNeely, Nonnemaker, and Blum 2002), and school connectedness has been a powerful predictor of health and academic outcomes among middle and high school students (Whitlock 2006).

We should also note that school-based programs that aim to change the individual in lieu of focusing on school climate and policies can be ineffective or counterproductive. As argued by Welsh (2000), programs that attempt to increase children's school effort, promote positive associations, and demonstrate the importance of obeying school rules may also be critical for reducing school disorder and violence in school. A positive school climate can be maintained by conscious efforts of students, parents, teachers, school administrators, and community groups; this requires multilevel assessments of school disorder made by utilizing multiple measures of school climate and school violence. Such assessment necessitates detailed examination of interpersonal, situational, and institutional factors, which can facilitate guidance of appropriate, effective prevention and intervention strategies (Welsh 2000).

Mesosystem

The mesosystem represents the second level of the ecological theory of child development, which is defined as interrelationships between two or more microsystems in which the individual is situated (e.g., home and school). Experiences in one microsystems level or direct interactions can influence another (Bronfenbrenner 1976). An example of a mesosystem is the interrelations between the home and school, such as parents' involvement in the child's school. A child's family is the most critical component of the proximal social level of influence, as parents can influence or inhibit risks for violence (Reese et al. 2000; Tolan and Guerra 1994). However, parents are not normally present on the school grounds when school problems occur, and most family influences in school problems are indirect (Swearer and Doll 2001). Regardless, parental involvement in their children's school is crucial as it conveys to children the value of education, provides them with additional social support, and maintains continuity between home and school influences (Epstein and Lee 1995). Moreover, research findings also indicate that parental involvement promotes a healthy and consistent learning environment (e.g., Sheridan, Warnes, and Dowd 2004), and fosters a sense of safety in school (Hong and Eamon 2012; Sheldon and Epstein 2002).

Recognizing that partnerships among students, schools, families, and community are fundamental to the success of school violence prevention efforts, school counselors are becoming more aware of the need for family-school therapeutic alliances (Hudson, Windham, and Hooper 2005; Sandu and Aspey 2000). The US surgeon general concludes that the most effective approaches to violence reduction take a comprehensive approach by fostering parental and family involvement (US Department of Health and Human Services 2001). The rationale underlying family involvement in violence prevention efforts is that families have the most direct influence on their children's attitudes, behaviors, and social functioning, and families spend the most time with students outside the school context.

Reese and colleagues (2000) highlighted several types of family-involved violence prevention programs in recent years, which include home visits (a primary prevention program that consists of home nurse visits to at-risk pregnant women). Functional family therapy is a prevention program in which the goal is to prevent the continuation of maladaptive youth behaviors through engagement, motivation, behavior change, and generalization (Alexander and Robbins 2010). Multisystemic therapy is also a tertiary program, which targets youth criminal activity and other delinquent behaviors through individualized treatment of youths within a comprehensive approach (Huey et al. 2000). Moreover, given the demonstrated effectiveness of family-involved prevention programs, such programs have been increasingly emphasized by federal government agencies in recent years. Such agencies include the Center for Disease Control and Prevention and the Office of Juvenile Justice and Delinquency Prevention, which subsidize programs for youth violence prevention that emphasize family involvement in violence prevention efforts (Reese et al. 2000).

Hudson, Windham, and Hooper (2005) also outlined some notable family-school prevention and intervention models, such as the Seattle Social Development Project, Preventive Intervention, and the Olweus Bullying Prevention Program. The Seattle Social Development Project targets both family and school environments through family involvement in efforts at school violence prevention by combining parent and teacher training in areas ranging from communication skills to appropriate use of discipline. The Preventive Intervention reinforces communication between students, teachers, and parents to foster appropriate student behavior. And the Olweus Bullying Prevention Program seeks to change the social climate of the school while intervening with individual students and their parents to reduce negative peer interactions (see Hong 2009).

Although family-school partnerships are apparently a viable and essential method of enhancing students' academic and social lives, and reducing violence, they are also often met with formidable challenges. To illustrate, there is a major disconnect between family and school—two primary socializing agents for positive educational outcomes. As argued by Christenson (2004), such a disconnect between the two agents may be due to extreme social and physical distance between teachers and families, limited resources for implementing such programs, and challenges involving all families in prevention efforts. Moreover, school policies and practices are not always aligned with such a notion (Christenson 2004).

Exosystem

The exosystem comprises the third level of the ecological framework, which includes combinations among two or more forms of social interaction or setting, one of which does not directly influence the individual. There has been some debate about the influence of such distal influences on violence, with some scholars concluding that variables at this level are too distal to have much influence on violent behavior (Ferguson and Beaver 2009) and others arguing that their effects are an essential dynamic to the overall production of school violence as they permeate cultural and structural relations (Henry 2009). Indeed, indirect interactions or settings can influence the processes within the direct setting where the individual is situated (Bronfenbrenner 1976). Mass media is one example of effects on local situations from the exosystem. Concerns over media violence heightened shortly after the Columbine and subsequent school shootings. After the Columbine shooting, then-president Clinton called on the Federal Trade Commission (FTC) to investigate whether movies, music, and the video and computer game industries marketed violent content to children and adolescents. The FTC concluded that violent entertainment was being marketed to children (US Federal Trade Commission 2000).

Some professional organizations concluded that media violence pose significant harmful effects on children (American Academy of Pediatrics 2000; American Psychological Association 2005). However, these reviews were often heavily influenced by scholars deeply invested in theories that media could be harmful. Subsequently, numerous errors have been found in these position statements (Block and Crain 2007; Ferguson 2009; Freedman 2002; Savage 2004). Independent reviews by the US government (US Department of Health and Human Services 2001; US Secret Service and US Department of Education 2002) and Australian government (Australian Government Attorney General's Department 2010) have concluded that media violence effects are minimal. This appears consistent with recent research that has found little relation between media violence exposure and youth violence, particularly when other important variables are well controlled (Anderson et al. 2001; Ferguson 2011; Ybarra et al. 2008) or that violent media is associated with reduced aggression and increased prosocial behaviors (Ferguson and Garza 2011; Shibuya et al. 2008). Further, as violent content in the media has soared, youth and adult violence at all levels from assaults through rapes and homicides have declined in most industrialized nations to the lowest levels in forty years (van Dijk, van Kesteren, and Smit 2007). Finally, related to events such as Columbine, the US Secret Service report on such shooters indicated that such individuals may consume lower than average levels of violent media, not higher (US Secret Service and US Department of Education 2002). Thus, the association of violent media with youth violence generally or events such as that at Columbine are increasingly being ruled out by multiple forms of data.

An assumption was made that the Columbine shooters had been violent media aficionados and it was the exposure to violent media that might have explained their violence (Gauntlett 1995). In reality, most young males consume considerable amounts of violent media (as do many young females), thus this correlation was always an illusory one. Further, some young school shooters have been specifically found *not* to be consumers of much violent media (e.g., Virginia Tech Review Panel 2007), and the issue of violent media remains noticeably absent when older adults commit mass school homicides such as in the case of Amy Bishop (a biology professor apparently angered by not receiving tenure) in Alabama as well as a rash of mass school homicides in China during 2010, mainly committed by middle-aged men. Thus, the "link" between violent media and school shootings represented a natural societal demand for quick, easy answers, fueled sometimes by irresponsible comments by some politicians, scholars, and activists, rather than solid data. Nevertheless, the lack of robust evidence on media effects does not, in itself, rule out the importance of exosystem effects.

Macrosystem

Macrosystem, the fourth and final level of the ecological systems, is referred to as a "cultural blueprint," which may determine the social structures and activities in the immediate systems levels. The macrosystem level consists of organizational, social, cultural, and political contexts, which may determine the interactions within other system levels (Bronfenbrenner 1976). For instance, a number of school antiviolence policies, including control through surveillance, emergency management planning, gun control, and zero tolerance evolved in the aftermath of Columbine (see Muschert and Peguero 2010). These policies were developed to address the varying levels of violence in schools and to reduce psychological and symbolic harm (Henry 2009). Interestingly, school violence policies were based on the concept that restricting access to potential victims of violence can result in greater safety among all in school (Muschert and Peguero 2010). Although several school violence prevention policies emerged post-Columbine, we identified gun control policies and zero-tolerance measures as macrosystem level factors, as these received a considerable amount of public attention.

Gun Control

The issue of gun control has been widely debated among the president, Congress, private interest groups, and ordinary citizens in the aftermath of the shooting. There has been a major disagreement over whether there is a need for more gun laws or better enforcement of the existing gun laws. More than fifteen states passed gun control bills or dropped NRA-supported bills. California passed a sweeping reform, which limits firearms purchases to one per month, expands a 1998 assault weapons ban, and requires trigger locks on all guns sold. Maryland also implemented a "Smart Gun" law requiring outside trigger locks on guns sold in the state and built-in handgun locks (Danitz and Nagy 2000). At the federal level, Congress had been working on new gun control laws. Then-president Clinton proposed tougher gun control legislation, which included raising the legal age of firearms possession to twenty-one; parental liability for gun-related crimes committed by children; and closing a loophole on sales without background checks at gun shows. Subsequent to the Columbine shootings, the House of Representatives also passed a bill that would pay states to enforce a five-year prison sentence to anyone who commits a violent crime using firearms. However, there are no studies to date that empirically examined the effects of changes in gun control laws on school violence.

Zero Tolerance or Social Control?

No other school violence prevention policy has received as much attention as zero tolerance (Verdugo 2002). There has been a significant increase in the promulgation of zero-tolerance school policies since the passage of the Gun Free Schools Act by Congress in 1994. Zero tolerance had been designed to ensure school safety by increasing security measures and punishing both major and minor incidents in school to "send a message" that certain behaviors will not be tolerated (Skiba and Peterson 1999). The severity of school violence in the latter half of the 1990s has elevated zero tolerance from an issue of school-wide debate to one of nationwide urgency (Insley 2001; Skiba and Peterson 2000). The Columbine shooting was a renewed call for the use of tough, zero-tolerance policies concerning weapons in school (Ashford 2000), which heightened public perceptions of schools as unsafe and increased reliance on security devices in many school districts (Gaustad 1999; Schneider 2001). Almost all states complied with the federal statute by enacting this policy by 1995, and nine out of ten public schools reported zero-tolerance policies for firearms and weapons possession in the schoolyard by 1998 (Insley 2001). Nationally, public school districts nationwide spend $795 million on school security devices annually (Snell et al. 2002).

Researchers, however, have criticized the policy, arguing that such punitive approaches are not only ineffective but also potentially detrimental to students they intend to protect (Phaneuf 2009; Skiba and Peterson 2000). Skiba and Peterson (2000), for example, found that unfair and inconsistent application of this disciplinary measure has been common, as low-income and racial or ethnic minorities were most frequently targeted. Zero-tolerance policies can also negatively affect school climate by creating an atmosphere of fear or intimidation. Additionally, some researchers (see Greene 2005; Snell et al. 2002) found that there have been relatively few empirical evaluations of the efficacy of zero-tolerance policies and school security measures, while others reported that employing security measures appeared promising in mitigating school problems (e.g., bullying, racial tension, gangs; see Jennings et al. 2011).

Discussion

In this chapter, an ecological system theory was used as a framework to understand what is being done in schools and communities to reduce the risk factors associated with violence such as school shootings. Programs are being developed to address the different levels of the social ecology, including school prevention programs that emphasize behavioral management and bullying awareness, family-directed programs that attempt to curb aggression and misconduct broadly, and institutional shifts that require public schools and college campuses to improve school climates, intergroup relations, and community safety. But are we doing enough?

American youths are confronted with violence on a daily basis, in their families, their schools, and their communities. While we know that not any one of these environments has a direct effect on their decision to commit a school shooting, we do have theories to suggest that exposure to violence over many years and from different sources could place a children and adolescents at-risk for significant levels of violence. For instance, life course theory purports that youths who lack bonding to conventional people or institutions that value law-abiding behavior are prone to delinquent, deviant, and violent behavior (Sampson and Laub 1993). Social Learning theorists also propose that aggressive and violent behaviors are learned through exposure to deviant role models. Youths may model behaviors after the behavior of violent peers and find that their violent behavior is rewarded by group acceptance (Akers 1998). Since the Columbine shootings, increased attention to school safety can be documented in K–12 public schools and on college campuses. In recent years, there have been many attempts to provide guidance or assistance for schools in their efforts to establish and maintain effective school violence interventions and disciplinary systems (see Osher, Dwyer, and Jimerson 2006; Skiba et al. 2006). However, significant work still needs to be done to prevent violence from erupting in schools.

Although there is no realistic way to completely prevent all school shootings, more needs to be done, especially for those youths at particular risk for violence. Practitioners in school (i.e., school psychologists, school social workers, counselors) are in a unique position to influence school-wide policies and practices. Practitioners can assess ecological risk factors that may contribute to problem behaviors and develop individualized, classroom-based, and school-based prevention and intervention programs (Reinke and Herman

2002). Individualized targeted interventions need to be consistently evaluated for use with youths who are showing early signs of aggression or those that have compromised mental health. Considering that practitioners frequently consult with teachers at the classroom level, they can also educate teachers about how to assess factors that contribute to violent behaviors and develop classroom-based behavior support plans (Reinke and Herman 2002). Moreover, prevention efforts must consider how youths growing up in the United States are desensitized to violence and why some schools are unpleasant environments that support violence, such as school shootings. Because family-school collaboration has demonstrated positive youth outcomes, practitioners also need to actively target parents in their assessment plans and intervention strategies. They should educate parents on the negative outcomes associated with youths' problems with their peers and teachers and the importance of parental involvement in school.

We also recommend practitioners to utilize their consultation and group facilitation skills to assume a leadership role in creating safe school environments (Reinke and Herman 2002). They can collaborate with school officials in developing and implementing school-wide interventions that target multiple ecologies. Further, they can work with teachers and school officials to enforce appropriate disciplinary measures in the classroom and school settings for misconduct and school rule infractions (Hong and Eamon 2012). As researchers have warned, relying exclusively on punitive measures, such as zero-tolerance policies, may actually exacerbate the potential danger by inflaming at-risk and potentially dangerous students (Garbarino et al. 2002). A "whole school" intervention approach, which is predicated on the assumption that programs need to target the social ecology of the school environment rather than a particular individual, has been reported to be effective in a limited number of schools (Blueprint for Violence Prevention 2002–2004). However, additional research is needed to evaluate the efficacy of whole school programs.

In summary, intervention programs in American schools must aim to prevent and/or interrupt the dysfunction when the various ecological levels interact and cause the occurrence of school violence. The ecological framework provides the needed directions to further develop empirically validated remedial and preventative intervention programs that target the microsystem, mesosystem, exosystem, and macrosystem levels. After all, risk factors for school violence can be located in any one of these levels and be the consequence of dysfunctional interactions among them.

Part 3
Alternatives

10

Encouraging Positive Behavior

Jeffrey R. Sprague, Daniel W. Close,
and Hill M. Walker

Creating and maintaining a safe and healthy school environment, one in which children and youths can be free of fear and victimization from all forms of violence, remains a major concern in the United States, even though the most serious forms of violent juvenile crime (i.e., rape, sexual assault, robbery, aggravated assault, and homicide) rarely occur on school grounds (Dinkes, Cataldi, and Lin-Kelly 2007). School leaders, teachers, and parents face tremendous challenges in this regard and naturally seek access to the most reliable information and supports available for making schools safer and more conducive to the learning and healthy development of students. Since the mass school shootings of the 1990s profoundly shocked our society, school administrators have been under enormous pressures from parents, policymakers, legislators, the media and the larger society to make schools as safe as possible against such egregious acts. The gatekeepers of schooling have had little choice but to respond vigorously to these continuing pressures.

School shootings are considered acts of terrorism in many quarters and the US Office of Safe and Drug Free Schools has now become part of the Department of Homeland Security. Federally issued reports and annual profiles now regularly provide a detailed picture of school safety and school climate and highlight real and potential risks to school safety (Dinkes, Cataldi, and Lin-Kelly 2007; Vossekuil et al. 2002). However, as Henry (2009) and Muschert and Peguero (2010) have recently noted, the impact of the horrendous acts of violence on school campuses, as widely dramatized in the Columbine and Thurston High School shootings, has been to produce a climate of fear that has ushered in a new generation of school security measures and policies—many of which are considered overly punitive forms of social control.

This chapter discusses the topic of school violence response from the perspective of a social-ecological framework (Stokol 1996). Distal and proximal influences associated with school violence are described, and categories of risk that reduce school safety are identified. A well-established, effective, and broadly accepted social-ecological intervention, called School-Wide Positive Behavioral Intervention and Supports (SWPBIS), is described herein and has been implemented in over 16,000 US schools. We also discuss our agreement with Henry (2009) and Barak (2003) and their call for an integrated and interdisciplinary approach to addressing school violence and disagreement with the broad definition of violence adopted by Henry (2009), which he asserts should be the criterion for determining whether a violent act has been committed against an individual or group. We suggest that a focus on the more proximal as opposed to distal factors in Henry's (2009) conceptualization of school violence, combined with a careful analysis of risk and protective factors at the school and student levels, is a more feasible alternative for consideration by educators.

Efforts to improve school safety and reduce youth violence in general have been expressed in five major courses of action over the past two decades, each of which continues to shape and define critical issues regarding school safety (Sprague and Walker 2011). These five major trends, which now overlap and blend together, include (a) reducing violent juvenile crime, (b) responses to mass school shootings (the focus of this volume), (c) integration and implementation of universal prevention initiatives in schools, (d) interpretation of school violence as domestic terrorism following 9/11, and (e) initiatives to address child and youth mental health issues, with schools as the center of these intervention efforts (Blaber and Bershad 2011; Kutash, Duchnowski, and Lynn 2006).

Every school in the United States has been affected by the changed landscape of school safety and security over the past two decades. Electronic and mechanical approaches that involve the use of sophisticated technology to solve school security problems are now standard fare in many school settings, especially those serving urban areas (Green 1999). Unfortunately, many urban schools have been turned into fortress-like structures in the name of security using these measures. Crisis intervention planning and staff training for a potential school tragedy are now required elements in the operational procedures of many school districts and individual schools (Paine and Sprague 2002; Readiness and Emergency Management for Schools Technical Assistance Center 2011). Schools serving deteriorating urban communities and neighborhoods routinely employ public safety and school resource officers as part of the regular school staff, and this practice is spreading rapidly to suburban communities as well (Atkinson and Kipper 2000; National Association of School Resource Officers 2011). Violence prevention curricula and peer mediation strategies are used routinely to teach anger management and conflict-resolution skills to all students in thousands of schools, which reduces instructional time for core subject matter instruction. For example, the Second Step Violence Prevention Curriculum, developed by the Committee for Children (for further information see Committee for Children n.d.; see also Frey, Hirschstein, and Guzzo 2000), is currently used in more than 25,000 US schools. Schools at all grade levels have invested heavily in such social skills training and violence prevention curricula but research to date has not clearly established either the efficacy or effectiveness of such efforts (Detrich, Keyworth, and States 2008; US Institute of Medicine 2009; *Morbidity and Mortality Weekly Report* 2007).

School leaders and teachers are now open to preventive approaches that were given scant attention in the past. In addition, educators are pressured to profile at-risk students and to identify those considered most likely to commit an act of school violence, even though acceptable and valid methods for accomplishing this goal remain obscure. The risks to individual students who are targets of these efforts can be severe (Cornell and Sheras 2006). With the exception of attempts to profile potential school shooters, the *collective* impact of this prevention focus has generally been positive and has contributed to creating school ecologies that are more conducive to learning, achievement, and bonding to the schooling experience (Hawkins et al. 1999; Muschert and Peguero 2010).

Although most schools in the United States remain relatively safe places for children, youths, and the adults who teach and support them (Dinkes, Cataldi, and Lin-Kelly 2007), no school is immune from aggressive, antisocial forms of behavior and the potential for violence; and some schools do have serious, continuing problems with violence due to specialized circumstances of youth crime, neighborhood violence, student demographics, the influence of gangs, and so on.

The extent of this challenge obviously differs in intensity and frequency across schools, districts, and communities that vary significantly on a host of protective factors. It is well known that the onset and development of antisocial behavior patterns are associated with a variety of school, community, and family risk factors (Reid, Patterson, and Synder 2002; Sprague et al. 2002; Walker, Ramsey, and Gresham 2004). The challenge is to anticipate and identify these risks, to reduce their number and intensity to the extent possible, and to buffer their impact while recognizing that schools and educators can do very little, if anything, to address conditions of risk occurring outside the school setting.

Thousands of students today enter school with a history of exposure to multiple and overlapping risks, such as those noted here, in addition to poverty, divorce, and domestic violence (Felitti, Anda, and Nordenberg 1998). These risk factors negatively affect today's students in family, school, neighborhood, and community contexts. Their cumulative effect is to place vulnerable children and youths on a pathway to destructive outcomes that are often manifested in adolescence and young adulthood (e.g., drug and alcohol abuse, delinquency, violent acts, and criminal behavior). In the absence of offsetting protective factors or the ability to access key support services and structures in a timely manner, it is unlikely that these individuals will be able to get off this destructive path if it has not been accomplished by the end of the primary grades (Biglan, Wang, and Walberg 2003; Kauffman 1999). Rather, these individuals will likely require continued supports and services throughout their lives to reduce the ongoing harm they cause to themselves and others. However, in spite of such risk exposure, there is a very low probability that such marginalized students will commit acts of physical violence in school. Nevertheless, our society is required to build "host environments" in families, communities, and schools that simultaneously address these multilevel risk factors and systems of support and response (Zins and Ponte 1990; Zins et al. 2004).

Causal Influences in Accounting for School Violence

In the article, "School Violence Beyond Columbine: A Complex Problem in Need of an Interdisciplinary Analysis," Henry (2009) advocates for the integration of multiple perspectives and theories of crime causation to explain the phenomenon of school violence. Henry argues that many researchers and theorists have described the complex and interrelated set of influences or factors that operate on individual, school, community, and national levels and that form a continuum that, over time, he asserts, can coalesce in violent acts on the part of a small number of at-risk individuals. Henry (2009) utilizes Barak's (2003) theory of reciprocal violence to illustrate a series of multiple pathways to violence. These pathways include the cumulative influences of individual, institutional, and structural relations that span family, school, and society.

As educational researchers who have all worked extensively with schools, legislatures, and community agencies in addressing school violence, we agree with Henry (2009) and Barak (2003) and their call for an integrated and interdisciplinary approach to addressing school violence that moves beyond a discipline-specific interpretation of this phenomenon and its causal influences. This multidisciplinary approach has much to recommend it, as such an approach allows for consideration of a broad range of disparate, seemingly unrelated (to each other) risk factors (e.g., the mental health problems of marginalized students, the architectural design of school structures to enhance school security and surveillance, deviancy training in violent and aggressive forms of behavior that occurs when marginalized students are grouped together for instruction or therapeutic treatments, the contagion effect of media reporting of violent school events, and so on). However, we do not agree with the overly broad definition of violence adopted by Henry (2009, p. 1253), which he asserts should be the criterion for determining whether a violent act has been committed against an individual or group. He defines school violence as follows:

> Any acts, relationships, or processes that use power over others, exercised by whatever means, such as structural, social, physical, emotional, or psychological, in a school or school-related setting or through the organization of schooling and that harm another person or group of people by reducing them from what they are or by limiting them from becoming what they might become for any period of time.

Using this definition as a basis for policy or accepted practice in coping with *physical* acts of violence in school contexts would be unthinkable—a nightmare of epic proportions for responsible school administrators and other school staff. It is useful to speculate on the potential causes of school violence in broad terms and to consider the potential role, at a theoretical level, of such macro-level risk factors as poverty, culture, the characteristics and impacts of societal institutions, media violence, and so forth. However, converting these influences into workable policies that could be effectively implemented in schools seems, at present, a practical impossibility. Who decides, for example, what constitutes harm when it occurs, and who are the victims and the perpetrators? Even assuming that it were possible to reliably make such difficult discriminations, we are bereft of the evidence that links such harm to the perpetuation of physical violence, which remains the overarching concern regarding school violence by our society. Further, the motivation to seek out and address such harm and the resources required to do so would have to be a shared one with many sectors of society. Coordinating such efforts effectively would also likely be unrealistic.

We think a focus on the more proximal, as opposed to distal, factors in Henry's (2009) conceptualization of school violence, combined with a careful analysis of risk and protective factors, is a more feasible alternative for consideration by educators. Such proximal factors would include the mental health status of at-risk students (e.g., severe depression, bipolar disorder, paranoid schizophrenia), as well as their associating with antisocial peers, making verbal threats, being a target of severe harassment and bullying, having easy access to weapons, being socially isolated from peers, and so forth. In particular, we need to provide more careful monitoring and provide better supports to students who are marginalized in a mental health sense. Kip Kinkel of Thurston and both Klebold and Harris of Columbine all struggled with severe mental health problems and were off and on psychotropic medications for years. The emotional volatility of such students can be extreme, and often the line between suicide and homicide is quite thin.

Figure 10.1 provides an illustration of risks to school safety that operate at various levels of intensity depending on a school's population, location, and characteristics.

We have the ability to identify and catalog these risk factors to school safety and to address the proximal ones but also note the existence of distal ones (student poverty, juvenile and adult crime, child abuse, and so on). On the protective side of the ledger, we believe that one of the best steps schools can take is to create a positive school ecology and culture that teaches all students important values (being respectful of others, avoiding conflict in relationships, regulating and managing one's emotions, valuing academic achievement, etc.) and that fosters positive relationships with key social agents (teachers, peers, parents).

It is important for school personnel to take reasonable steps to secure the school commensurate with the level of risk that a careful assessment calls for. It is of at least equal importance to create positive school ecology and to provide the best supports possible for marginalized students with the dual aim of preventing the onset of anti-

Figure 10.1 Four Sources of Vulnerability to School Violence

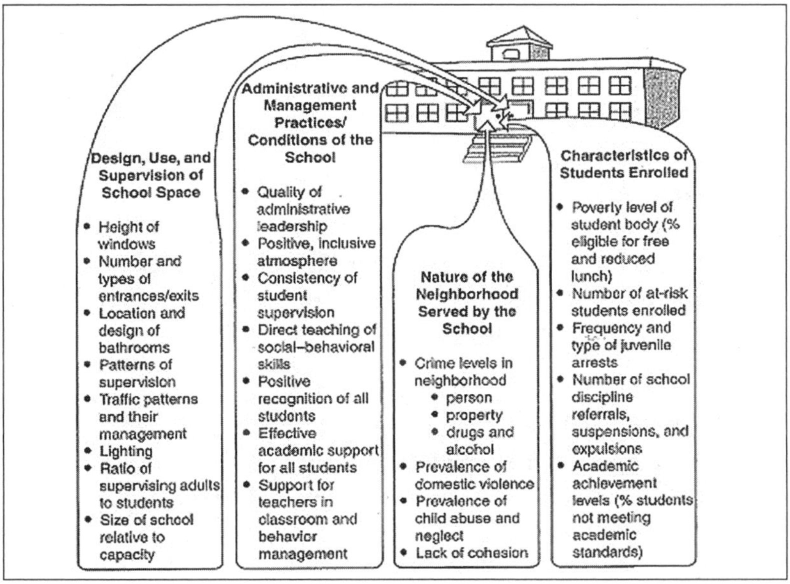

Administrative and Management Practices/ Conditions of the School

- Quality of administrative leadership
- Positive, inclusive atmosphere
- Consistency of student supervision
- Direct teaching of social–behavioral skills
- Positive recognition of all students
- Effective academic support for all students
- Support for teachers in classroom and behavior management

Design, Use, and Supervision of School Space

- Height of windows
- Number and types of entrances/exits
- Location and design of bathrooms
- Patterns of supervision
- Traffic patterns and their management
- Lighting
- Ratio of supervising adults to students
- Size of school relative to capacity

Nature of the Neighborhood Served by the School

- Crime levels in neighborhood
  - person
  - property
  - drugs and alcohol
- Prevalence of domestic violence
- Prevalence of child abuse and neglect
- Lack of cohesion

Characteristics of Students Enrolled

- Poverty level of student body (% eligible for free and reduced lunch)
- Number of at-risk students enrolled
- Frequency and type of juvenile arrests
- Number of school discipline referrals, suspensions, and expulsions
- Academic achievement levels (% students not meeting academic standards)

Source: Sprague and Walker (2005).

social and violent behavioral patterns, and reducing the harm they may cause to themselves or others.

The remainder of this chapter describes the School-Wide Positive Behavior Intervention and Supports (SWPBIS) systemic intervention. SWPBIS is based on a social-ecological theoretical framework that creates a positive school ecology (Bronfenbrenner 1979; Romer and Heller 1983), fosters positive social relationships and student achievement, teaches important values, and is focused on careful analysis of the interactions between school setting structural variables and student behavior (Sugai and Horner 2002). SWPBIS is that rarity of interventions that is both efficacious and highly accepted by participating school personnel.

School-Wide PBIS: Creating a School-Based Host Environment

Muschert and Peguero (2010) have recently conducted a systematic review of six school-based, antiviolence policies and practices along with the evidence base that supports each of them. They include (1) environmental design, (2) zero tolerance, (3) antibullying programs, (4) emergency management planning, (5) peer mediation, and (6) initiatives to influence school climate. These investigators find problems and deficits with each of these approaches with the exception of those approaches focusing on creating improved school climates in which positive school staff and student relationships are emphasized. We are strong advocates of such approaches and believe they offer one of the very best approaches for improving the safety and effectiveness of schools.

Long-term longitudinal research by Hawkins and his associates (Hawkins et al. 1999) provides additional support for approaches of this type, which are associated with increased bonding, engagement with and attachment to the schooling process, and the prevention of a series of health risk behaviors for at-risk students in adolescence. Their seminal study was based on schools serving high-risk neighborhoods in which at-risk students, teachers, and parents in the primary grades were all involved in a carefully coordinated and well-implemented ecological intervention. Over the long term, students exposed to this intervention showed lower levels than "usual care/treatment as usual" controls in such outcomes as violent juvenile crime, school behavior problems, teenage pregnancy, and drug and alcohol use, as well as higher achievement levels. Follow-up of this sample into adult life continued to reveal much better adjustment and quality-of-life outcomes for those exposed to this early intervention in the primary grades. This study also speaks to the power and efficacy of intervening as early as possible in the lives of at-risk children and youths and involvement of the social agents who are most important in their lives.

School personnel have long recognized the power and positive impact of their daily interactions with students. This factor has been expressed best in the national initiative to promote school-wide positive behavior interventions and supports (SWPBIS) (www.pbis.org 2013; see also Sugai and Horner 2002), funded by the US Office of Special Education Programs. As of 2011, more than 16,000 schools across the country have actively implemented SWPBIS (www.pbis.org 2013). These schools are reporting reductions in problem behavior, improved perceptions of school safety, and better academic outcomes (Bradshaw, Mitchell, and Leaf 2010; Horner et al. 2009). Although no direct empirical evidence (in the form of a randomized experiment) links SWPBIS implementation and reduced school violence, there is some evidence of an increased perception of student and staff safety in SWPBIS schools (Horner et al. 2009), and ample support for the multiple intervention components that make up SWPBIS (Gottfredson and Gottfredson 2002; Osher et al. 2010; Sugai and Horner 2010).

School-Wide Positive Behavior Interventions and Supports (SWPBIS; Simonsen, Sugai, and Negron 2008; Sprague and Golly 2005; Sugai and Horner 2010) is a comprehensive and proactive approach to behavior management in schools. SWPBIS is based on the assumption that actively teaching and acknowledging teacher and school, behavioral expectations can change the extent to which students expect appropriate behavior from themselves and each other. When consistent, positive expectations are established by all adults in a school, evidence clearly exists that the proportion of students with serious behavior problems will be reduced and the school's overall social climate will improve.

The procedures that define SWPBIS are organized around three main themes: (a) prevention, (b) multitiered support, and (c) database decisionmaking. Investing in the *prevention* of problem behavior involves (1) defining and teaching a set of positively stated behavioral expectations to students, teachers, and parents (e.g., be safe, respectful, responsible); (2) acknowledging and rewarding those behaviors (e.g., compliance to school rules, safe and respectful peer to peer interactions, and academic effort/engagement); (3) systematically supervising students in classrooms and common areas; and (4) establishing and implementing a consistent continuum of corrective consequences for problem behavior. Schools are encouraged to reduce the use of out-of-class referrals and out-of-school suspensions as a response to problem behavior. The goal is to establish a positive social climate, in which behavioral expectations for students are highly predictable, directly taught, consistently acknowledged, and actively monitored.

Multitiered support is provided beyond the universal level for those students at risk for, or engaging in, antisocial or problematic behavior and is based on a public health model of intervention (Sprague and Walker 2005). The greater an individual student's need for support, the more intense is the support provided. Within the SWPBIS approach, the emphasis has been on using the principles and procedures of applied behavior analysis as a foundation for defining the antecedents (environmental cues) and maintaining consequences for behavioral problems and also completing functional behavioral assessments to confirm these relationships (O'Neill et al.

1997). These assessments, in conjunction with person-centered planning processes (Eber et al. 2009), are used to design effective and efficient procedures for addressing patterns of unacceptable behavior that often prove intractable and unresponsive to ordinary behavior management procedures typically used by schools.

Data-based decisionmaking is a theme that is interwoven throughout SWPBIS, and builds on the assumption that staff members, family, and students will be most effective in the design and implementation of behavioral supports if they have access to regular, accurate information about the behavior of students. It is equally important to regularly assess adherence or fidelity to support plans, and to share those data with implementers. The value of data for decisionmaking is emphasized for both the design of initial support systems, and the ongoing assessment and adaptation of support strategies (Sugai and Horner 2010). The SWPBIS approach includes adoption of practical strategies for collecting, summarizing, reporting, and using behavioral and fidelity data on regular cycles.

The available evidence suggests that high fidelity and sustained use of SWPBIS practices can act as a protective measure in shielding at-risk children from antisocial behavioral outcomes, and prevent the onset of risk behavior in typically developing children (Bradshaw, Mitchell, and Leaf 2010; Horner et al. 2009). It is expected that effective and sustained implementation of SWPBIS will create a more responsive school climate that supports the twin goals of schooling for all children: *academic achievement* and *positive social development* (Sprague and Walker 2005; Walker, Ramsey, and Gresham 2004; Zins et al. 2004).

The challenge, then, with SWPBIS and school-based intervention approaches generally becomes how to give schools the capacity to adopt and sustain the processes, organizational structures, and systems that will enable them to carry out promising and proven interventions (Fixsen et al. 2007). Gottfredson and Gottfredson conducted the National Study of Delinquency Prevention in Schools—the first of its kind. They argue convincingly that the problem is not the availability of *efficacious* programs (i.e., those that work), but rather the problem is one of *effectiveness* (i.e., helping typical schools adopt and carry out proven interventions and approaches in a manner that allows their effectiveness to be demonstrated). It is likely, therefore, that the problem of overlapping or poorly implemented intervention approaches is affected by a lack of useful needs assessment and effectiveness information to guide the implementation process (Gottfredson 2001; Gottfredson, Gottfredson, and Czeh 2000).

Implementing School-Wide Positive Behavior Interventions and Supports: Key Practices

School-Wide Positive Behavior Interventions and Supports (SWPBIS) is a systems-based approach that promotes safe, healthy, and successful schools. Researchers at the University of Oregon (Sprague and Golly 2005; Sugai and Horner 2010; Walker et al. 1996; see also www.pbis.org) have tested the feasibility and efficacy of SWPBIS approaches in reducing school behavior problems and promoting a positive school climate. SWPBIS is a multisystem approach to addressing the problems posed by students displaying antisocial behaviors and coping with challenging forms of student behavior. The key practices of SWPBIS include:

- Providing clear definitions of expected appropriate, positive behaviors for students, parents, and staff members;
- Defining problem behaviors and their consequences for students, parents, and staff members;
- Delivering regularly scheduled instruction, reminders, and assistance to display positive social behaviors;
- Providing effective incentives and motivational systems to encourage students to behave differently;
- Encouraging staff members to commit to staying with the intervention over the long term and to monitor, support, coach, debrief, and provide booster lessons for students as necessary to maintain the achieved gains;
- Providing staff members ongoing training, feedback and coaching about effective implementation of the systems; and
- Adopting and using systems for measuring and monitoring the intervention's effectiveness.

The process for adopting and sustaining SWPBIS revolves around a school team typically composed of five to ten individuals that includes an administrator, representative faculty and staff members, and local family and community members. While it may seem ideal to train all school staff members all the time, it will rarely be feasible or sustainable to provide training at this level due to costs and logistical concerns. However, a representative group of adults, representing all school stakeholders (including students at the secondary level), can learn the key practices of SWPBIS and set goals for improvement in a written action plan. The stakeholders can then function as leaders or coaches as they inform their groups of the team activities (for example, at staff or area meetings) and give support and encouragement during the implementation process. Increasingly, district- and state-wide initiatives are supporting the dissemination of SWPBIS training and coaching systems (www.pbis.org 2013).

While participating in training, and after mastery of the basic material, it is recommended that SWPBIS teams (building administrator, representative teachers, and other stakeholders) meet approximately once per month to review training content as needed and to set up a regular process of reviewing and refining the school discipline plan (initial goals are developed during training) and other, school site–based activities. A format for these meetings is specified and each meeting should last between twenty and sixty minutes.

Set and promote school-wide expectations. A critical first task for the implementation team is to establish school-wide behavior rules for teaching processes related to student-teacher compliance, peer-to-peer interaction, academic achievement, and academic study skills. Using the general framework of "safety," "respect," and "responsibility" and directly teaching lessons throughout the year to establish and maintain the patterns of behavior associated with these personal qualities is highly recommended. In addition, posting the rules publicly in posters, school newsletters, local media, announcements, and assemblies throughout the school setting provide additional social marketing support.

Plans to recognize expected behavior and actively supervise students. The school will need to establish a consistent system of enforcement, monitoring, and positive reinforcement to enhance the effect of rule teaching and maintain patterns of desired student behavior. Reinforcement systems may include school-wide token economies in the form of "tickets" stating each school rule delivered by all adults in the building. These tokens are to be "backed up" with weekly drawings and rewards for the teachers as well. Each school should implement the procedures to fit within their school improvement plan and specific disciplinary needs.

Define and effectively correct problem behaviors and their consequences for students and staff members. As stated earlier, schools using excessive sanctions and forms of social control experience greater levels of vandalism and other forms of misbehavior (Mayer and Sulzer-Azaroff 1991; Skiba and Peterson 2003). Positive reinforcement is more effective than punishment as it does not result in the type of counteraggression and withdrawal (fight or flight) that punishment can produce and because it does not focus teachers' attention on detecting and correcting student rule violations.

Students should see rules being applied fairly. When they believe that rules are unevenly applied, students are more likely to resist them. Schools with clear rule and reward systems and business-like corrections and sanctions also experience fewer problems. These schools signal appropriate behavior for students and respond to misbehavior predictably. Students in such schools are clear about expected behavior and learn that there are consequences for misbehavior. When rules are consistent, students develop a respect for them, and internalize beliefs that the system of governance works effectively and fairly (Bryk and Driscoll 1988; Gottfredson and Gottfredson 2002).

Report and use data for problem solving and decisionmaking. The efficiency of team problem solving is enhanced by providing the SWPBIS team with data-based feedback regarding their implementation of basic SWPBIS practices and the impact of implementation on problem behavior as indexed by discipline referral, suspension, and expulsion patterns (Irvin et al. 2006). The goal is to use highly efficient data collection and reporting systems that allow teams to ask whether (1) they are implementing evidence-based, SWPBIS practices, and (2) the practices are having an effect on the behavior of students. Data on implementation of SWPBIS practices typically are collected, summarized, and reported quarterly, and data on student behavior are collected continuously and reported to the school team weekly, the school faculty monthly, and the school district annually. Irvin and colleagues (Irvin et al. 2004, 2006) provide an evaluation documenting the impact that regular access to student behavioral data has for SWPBIS school teams.

Examples of data collection and display tools for assessing implementation of SWPBIS can be found at https://www.pbisapps .org/Applications/Pages/PBIS-Assessment.aspx (Boland et al. 2006). Similarly, an example of a web-based information system designed to help school personnel to use office referral data to design schoolwide and individual student interventions is available at www.swis .org (May et al. 2000). It is anticipated that as data management systems become more common, an increasing array of data collection and reporting options will become available to schools to allow them to track and evaluate patterns of behavior at the individual student, classroom, and school level. These data may also be combined with student academic performance, attendance and other factors such as eligibility for free or reduced price lunch. A major focus for research on educational systems-change lies in the process and impact of providing teachers, administrators, families, and students with regular, accurate information for decisionmaking about the effects of their practices (Newton et al. 2009).

Implementing for Sustainability

Too often educational interventions, even efficacious interventions, have been implemented but not sustained (Fixsen et al. 2005). If SWPBIS is to result in educational change at a scale of practical relevance, schools adopting these procedures will need to sustain the practices for multiple years. An important feature of the SWPBIS approach is inclusion of formal strategies for improving the likelihood of such sustained implementation. These include (1) the development of training materials at each school that make it "easier" to implement from year to year, (2) the implementation of policies for using SWPBIS, and reporting student data, and (3) the training of district- or building-level "coaches" who are available to provide booster training for school teams, initial training for new faculty members, and help with problem solving around more intense challenges. The coaching role is designed to help a school team sustain effective practices through periodic perturbations in the staffing, organization, or fluctuation in student behavior (Mohr, Cuijpers, and Lehman 2011). The issue of sustaining educational innovation is not unique to SWPBIS, and remains a worthy focus for research.

Conclusion

Schools remain the ultimate setting for educating our children and youth and secondarily for socializing them to norms of civil behavior. The school, as an institution, is charged with educating all who walk through the schoolhouse door regardless of background, personal characteristics, or specific attributes. Schools are far more diverse today than they have ever been in our history. This fact represents an enormous challenge for educators in maximizing each student's educational potential within the context of group-oriented instruction and management.

Schools are profoundly affected by their students' personal beliefs, prior experiences, behavioral characteristics, family history, and the risk and protective factors to which they have been exposed. Students are the instrument by which schools are made more, or less, safe. Through their participation in the schooling process, they provide a direct route for the infusion into the school's ecology of all the risks (and protections) they have experienced through their respective socialization processes. Thus, as our society and its social and economic conditions change, so do our students and the schools they attend. In this sense, schools very much mirror the society they serve.

Schools and their staffs have been asked to assume enormous burdens in teaching and helping to socialize our children and youths, but this task becomes ever more daunting as we see the continuing declines in our collective quality of life and respect for institutional authority. Schools can do little about the tsunami of risks that many students now bring with them to school. Perhaps their best hope is to implement procedures and teach values, such as those described herein, that offer a degree of protection from these risks in terms of buffering and offsetting their negative effects. To do so will require parent, teacher, and community partnerships, which currently are in short supply but are essential for realizing the vision we have for safe, healthy, and effective schools.

11

Ecological, Peacemaking, and Feminist Considerations

Daniel Hillyard and M. Joan McDermott

There is no denying the tragedy of school rampage shootings like the one that occurred in Columbine High School. When evaluating the future risk of such events, we can weigh the magnitude of harm caused and the probability of the events recurring. The magnitude of harm caused is devastatingly high, while the probability of recurrence relative to the overall time that students are in schools is very low. While this low probability might be expected to assuage fear of school shootings, instead events like Columbine "exert strong leverage on the discourse about and responses to school violence" despite their rarity, and "the risk tolerance for these events is very low, if not nil" (Muschert and Peguero 2010, p. 118). Indeed, scholars who study rampage shootings and their impact on school antiviolence policy note that rather than a historical event, Columbine is discussed metaphorically as a "keyword for a complex set of emotions surrounding youth, fear, risk, and delinquency in 21st century America" (Muschert 2007a, p. 365).

Muschert and Peguero (2010) report that rampage shootings change the way we think about managing school violence and security, as the changes are highly associated with increased fear of future incidences of such violence. The result of such fear is the implementation of school antiviolence policies whose efficacy, studies show, is mixed at best (see Addington in this volume). What is significant to us, and what we focus on in this chapter, are scholarly assertions that "often, although certainly not always, such policies have been punitive, as opposed to restorative or aimed at mediation, in their efforts to control violence" (Muschert and Peguero 2010, p. 119).

We take stock of three startling research conclusions. First, what has been called the "New American school" institutionalizes school antiviolence policies wherein social control and fear become integral parts of students' lives (Hirschfield 2008; Kupchik and Monahan 2006; Muschert and Peguero 2010; Noguera 2003; Wacquant 2001). Second, this socialization, in what Wacquant (2001) labels "institutions of confinement," is not restricted to students' lives as students but rather portends that control, security, and restricted access are to be expected in adult life. Third, Kupchik and Monahan (2006, p. 628) conclude that fear-driven policies based on control, security, and restricted access "facilitate the criminalization of poor students in order to establish and maintain a criminal class to legitimate systems of inequality."

Given inconsistent and debatable research findings, we are involved in recent efforts to expand the theoretical framework used to assess whether fear-based policy structures produce unintended consequences (Henry 2009) and how these theoretical efforts may advance opportunities to predict whether, and how, alternative policy structures such as peacemaking and feminist perspectives may enhance our abilities to ameliorate not only school violence but also the unintended consequences of current fear-based policies (Muschert and Peguero 2010). We root our analysis in an integrated theoretical framework, following particularly the interdisciplinary analytical framework developed by Henry (2009). Henry (2009, p. 1248) advocates analyzing school violence as a multicausal, reciprocal process that spans "individuals and their interactive social processes" (micro-level analysis), "kinds of organization and their organizational processes" (meso-level analysis), and "kinds of structure, culture, and context" (macro-level analysis).

In the remainder of this chapter, we discuss how "get tough," retributive, and fear-driven school antiviolence policies are related to broad social structures and cultural values concerning crime, and how alternatives to getting tough seek to transform those structures and values. We link the punishment response to social inequality and discuss how both peacemaking and feminist perspectives seek to change "get tough" systems based on domination of some groups by others. We also discuss the punishment response in terms of its societal and individual consequences, and highlight the significance of transformation of the individual, as well as social transformation, to both feminism and transformative justice perspectives. We root our analysis in literatures on the criminalization of deviance and on overcriminalization (the limits of the criminal sanction). We start by exploring elements of the social structure and cultural values that have provided a backdrop for the post-Columbine policing of behavior in schools.

The Social Ecology of Getting Tough

Stigmatization, condemnation, segregation, retribution, and rehabilitation are the hallmarks of fear-based strategies to "combating" school violence. A "get tough" orientation reinforces the dominant standards of social control in a local school setting. In the context of school violence, to change the definition of violence, and policies for handling it, requires collective action. Thus, the study of school antiviolence policies reveals the links between violence, political action, and social change. More particularly, a social problems viewpoint looks at social meanings, or collective definitions of violence.

Schur (1980, p. 8) offers a view of deviance defining: "When people engage in organized political activity on deviance issues they are, in fact, intentionally trying to ensure that a particular balance of power will tip in their favor." The definition of school violence involves not only groups who wield the power to impose or extend violence definitions, and to see to it that others who deviate from favored moral stances are subjected to school-administered punishment, but also a process of stigmatization that implies social standing or acceptability for these groups. Three propositions can be derived from these observations. First, what is officially designated as violent is often a political decision. Second, official rules associated with official designations are tied to interest groups and power. Third, these definitional and rulemaking processes are a form of social control.

Henry (2009, p. 1262) concludes that in the wake of incidents of school violence, "although we can examine the psychological processes and situational explanations why students acted violently, we need to step outside of the microcontexts to explore the wider framing discourses of gender and power, masculinity and violence, and social class and race that produce social exclusion, victimization, anger, and rage."

Rooting our analysis in the criminalization of deviance literature parallels Henry's (2009) integrated theoretical approach. For we find within the deviance literature the observation that "more significant than the objective conditions of a putative social problem are the definitional activities of social actors who perceive and judge them as offensive and undesirable" (Hillyard 2007, p. 1098). These definitional activities include individual activists, interest groups, the media, and organized social movements; the tactics, power, and motivations of these social forces, entities, and actors; and the political opportunities and structural conditions that, in the context of defining school anti-violence as a problem, make possible the process of stigmatization that implies social standing to wield power to impose or extend violence definitions and impose school-administered punishment vis-à-vis students who deviate from favored moral stances. An interactive, multilevel approach entails combinations of these factors, as well as how they operate across time. Finally, more recent analytical expansion further accounts for the interrelationship between local context and societal- and cultural-level norm and system pressures in the content, timing, and implementation of newly adopted definitions and social control responses (Hillyard 2007).

Turning to retributive social control policy responses in terms of their societal and individual consequences, the extensive literature on overcriminalization spans the grand debate in political theory on the proper scope of state authority to criminalize behaviors whose primary objections are moral ones (Mill [1859] 1869; Stephen 1873), consequentialist concerns with legislating morality (Kadish 1967; Morris and Hawkings 1970; Packer 1968), and a recent focus on the injustice of punishing individuals subject to a criminal justice system experiencing explosive growth in questionable categories of offenses (Husak 2008). As we noted, numerous studies of school antiviolence policies have concluded that as surveillance cameras, metal detectors, police patrols, zero-tolerance policies, lockdowns, drug-sniffing dogs, and locker, backpack, and pat-down searches become the norm in elementary, middle, and high schools across the nation, students are being conditioned to expect that adult life portends restricted accesses, security, and control. The unintended consequences to society that are documented in the overcriminalization literature appear to be societal consequences that have trickled down from adult life to the lives of children. These include: heavy enforcement costs, including costs of police, courts, and incarceration; creation of thriving black markets that occasion commissions of other crimes and support for organized crime; enforcement efforts that entail serious breaches of privacy; general disrespect for law since it is widely known that most people are not being caught; and selective and arbitrary enforcement with attendant issues of discrimination based on class, race, sexual orientation, and so on. While criminology and criminal justice scholars frequently focus their discussions of overcriminalization on adult populations and adult offenses, there is evidence that our nation's youth and juvenile misbehaviors are being affected as well. For example, Chesney-Lind and Irwin (2008) offer the concept of "upcriming" as one result of the increasing social control on girls. They explain (2008, p. 148), "Upcriming refers to policies (like 'zero-tolerance' policies) that increase the severity of criminal penalties associated with particular offenses."

Thus far in this social ecological foundation for our analysis of the potential for social transformation under both feminism and transformative justice perspectives, we have discussed punitive responses to school violence in terms of *societal* consequences. Because feminism and transformative justice perspectives each highlight the significance of transformation of the individual, we complete our social ecological foundation with a few points regarding the *individual* consequences of the punishment response.

As mentioned earlier, the latest theoretical expansion in the overcriminalization literature focuses on effects of inflicting too much punishment on individuals, rather than on society. Legal philosopher Douglas Husak is a leader in this theoretical expansion. Husak (2008, p. 14) states:

> My central concern is that overcriminalization results in unjust punishments. The primary victims of this injustice are the persons who incur penal liability. That is, the main problem with overcriminalization derives from its impact on those who are punished, rather than for its effects on taxpayers, our culture of compliance, the rule of law, or society generally. Injustice is most glaring when defendants are sentenced for conduct that should not have given rise to criminal liability at all.

For purposes of operationalizing conduct that should not have given rise to criminal liability at all, Husak describes three categories of offenses: overlapping, ancillary, and risk prevention. For Husak, possession offenses are a prime example of overcriminalization that results in unjust punishment of individuals since they "typically overlap with those that proscribe use, are designed to prevent the risk of harm rather than the harm itself, and qualify as ancillary because possession is easier than use or acquisition to detect and prove" (2008, p. 44).

News stories are rife with examples of schoolchildren suspended, expelled, arrested, and even jailed for possession under zero-tolerance policies that test the bounds of sensible judgment. In a recent example, four boys were suspended for possessing oregano under a Virginia zero-tolerance policy that bans possession of *imitation* controlled substances. Other children have been punished for possession of Midol (for menstrual symptoms), Tylenol cough syrup, cough drops, mouthwash, and even medical necessities such as asthma inhalers— as these are common items defined as contraband under zero-tolerance, antidrug policies. In an infamous case of school action, which was ruled unconstitutional by the US Supreme Court, a thirteen-year-old girl was strip-searched based on vague allegations that she possessed two tablets of ibuprofen.

Such insensible actions by school authorities also occur with respect to zero-tolerance policies related to weapons possession. Often it is readily apparent that particular children are good citizens and high achievers, yet school officials aver that punishment of these children demonstrates fairness. In North Carolina, a standout high school student accidentally took her father's lunch box to school, and during a search of lunch boxes, school officials found a small paring knife to slice an apple packed in her father's lunch box. The young woman was charged criminally and suspended for the remainder of her senior year. In another case, police spotted a kitchen knife in the vehicle of a National Merit scholar who, a week before, had used the knife to open boxes at home and neglected to remove the knife from her car. The young woman was taken into custody during class, hand-cuffed, charged with a felony, and banned from attending her school graduation. In each of these instances the students' stories were undisputed, but school officials cited the need for fairness in administering their zero-tolerance policies.

Our point in raising these admittedly exceptional examples has been to demonstrate how retributive and fear-driven school antiviolence policies that change from valid concerns with preventing harm into definitions of offenses that are increasingly removed from actual harm, often result in the unjust punishment of individuals. We turn now to a consideration of alternative perspectives for developing school policies that seek to create environments that replace the social and individual injustices of overpunishment and inequality with nonviolent and nurturing strategies.

Peacemaking Criminology and Transformative Justice

We begin the discussion of alternatives to fear-based strategies by drawing on criminology as peacemaking, a body of thought and a movement that seeks to replace retributive, get tough, violent justice, with a nonviolent justice based on core concerns such as care, connectedness, community, and personal and social transformation. Pepinsky and Quinney's (1991) groundbreaking *Criminology as Peacemaking* included an array of essays from "long standing traditions of thought and action" (Pepinsky 1991b, p. 299). Pepinsky (1991b) points specifically to humanist, feminist, and critical contributions. More recently, adherents of peacemaking like Wozniak (2008c) have elaborated on the diverse perspectives that feed criminology as peacemaking. (See also Pepinsky 2000 and Caulfield 2000 for discussions of peacemaking in schools.)

We start with key concepts and principles in peacemaking criminology. Wozniak (2008b) identifies three principal themes: *connectedness*, *mindfulness*, and *caring*. Connectedness refers to the bonds we have with each other and with our environment. Mindfulness, or awareness, refers to a mind that is open to possibilities and does not cling to deeply ingrained concepts that shape our perceptions of reality. Clear comprehension of what is happening is a step toward the cultivation of inner peace and personal transformation. Caring is the perspective or mind-set from which we respond to individuals in our lives.

McDermott (1994, pp. 24–28) identifies the core ethical concerns of peacemaking criminology:

1. Without loving and compassionate individuals, we cannot achieve justice and peace.
2. We are tied to other human beings and also to the environment.
3. The nonviolent ethic is one of responsiveness (compassion, forgiveness, and love). From love and compassion flow understanding, service, and justice.
4. Responsiveness requires equality.

Note the identification of both personal and social transformation, and the themes of connectedness and caring. Also important, particularly if we are to reflect on the problems and injustices of such strategies as zero-tolerance policies in schools, is the concept of responsiveness, contributed by Pepinksy (1991a) in *The Geometry of Violence and Democracy*. Here Pepinsky views crime as *unresponsiveness*. *Responsiveness* means "that what one expects to achieve by one's actions (in common law parlance, one's 'intent') is modified continually to accommodate the experience and feelings of those affected by one's actions" (1991a, pp. 15–16). To be responsive is to be compassionate and to forgive. Responsiveness requires mutual respect on an individual level, and the elimination of social inequality on the societal level. Inequality supports and sustains violence; crime is caused by social structures and processes that differentiate among groups of people and associate those differences with evaluations of worth (Berger, Free, and Searles 2005, as cited in Wozniak 2008a).

What policy responses flow from these central concerns of peacemaking? How do concerns for care, connectedness, community, responsiveness, and so on, translate to policy guidelines and proposals for change? In terms of the specific issue of crime and other rule-violating behavior in schools, we begin to sketch this out in the last section of the paper. Here we identify some of the basic tenets of *justice* in a peacemaking framework. Certainly, the most basic tenet is *nonviolence*. In peacemaking perspectives, the criminal justice system in the United States is founded on violence. A punitive and retributive "war on crime" framework is contrasted with a system based on concerns such as care and connectedness. The peacemaking perspective looks to changes in individuals and changes in social processes and social structures. On the latter type of change, Quinney (2000, p. 205) contrasts positive peace and negative peace:

> Much of what is called "criminal justice" is a violent reaction to, or anticipation of, crime. The criminal justice system, with all its procedures, is a form of *negative peace*, its purpose being to deter or process acts of crime through threat and the application of force. Positive peace, on the other hand, is something more than the deterrence or punishment of crime. . . . *Positive peace* demands that attention be given to all those things, most of them structured in society, that cause crime. . . . Positive peace exists when the sources of crime—including poverty, inequality, racism, and alienation—are not present. (emphasis in original)

The ecological perspective and integrative theories are important, then, because solutions to crime from the peacemaking perspective are framed in matters of social justice and the elimination of social inequalities.

At the individual level, responses to specific offenders emphasize inclusion of the victim and the community. The intent is to heal both the offender and the victim, to mend the community, and to encourage the offender to accept responsibility. This is why there is so much attention in peacemaking criminology to things like mediation and conflict resolution, and to what are typically thought of as restorative justice programs.

More recently the concepts of social transformation and *transformative justice* have been used to describe justice processes in the peace tradition. Wozniak (2008c) provides a review of alternative conceptions of transformative justice. Most generally, transformative justice refers to efforts to involve a caring and inclusive community, efforts that entail both individual and social change in the development of this community. Wozniak (2008a) concludes there is no universally accepted definition of transformative justice.

Whitehead, Gillespie, and Braswell (2008) provide a thoughtful discussion of the future of peacemaking. Of particular concern are difficulties of translating broad peacemaking concerns to specific guidelines. Who would argue against the proposition that "humans should be mindful of one another and nature, care for fellow humans, and realize that all of us are interdependent and interconnected" (p. 235)? Their analysis provides several examples of conflicting choices that may in fact derive from the same principle of caretaking. At this stage in the development of criminology as peacemaking and transformative justice thinking, it may be easier to develop strategies that are consistent with basic tenets than it is to address specific, difficult choices.

Whitehead, Gillespie, and Braswell (2008) suggest that peacemaking efforts be examined at three levels: the social system, the cultural system, and the level of the personality. In this chapter we view the individual as embedded in an interpersonal and social context that spirals out from the intrapersonal to relationships and family, neighborhood, community and local institutions such as schools, society and its structures and culture, and to global phenomena.

Feminism, Peacemaking, Gender, and School Victimization

Just as there is no single peacemaking perspective, there is no single feminist perspective. What all feminists would agree on is that there is gender discrimination and that we should strive to eliminate it. Feminists depart in their views on the causes of discrimination and the solutions. Here we draw primarily on literature in feminist peacemaking, feminist ethics and ethic of care, multicultural feminism, and third-wave feminism.

As noted earlier, feminism and women's voices have made strong and lasting contributions to peacemaking and peacemaking criminology (Pepinsky 1991b). Warren and Cady (1996, p. 3) note:

> Feminism and peace share an important conceptual connection: Both are critical of, and committed to, the elimination of coercive power-over privilege systems of domination as a basis of interaction between individuals and groups. A feminist critique and development of any peace politics, therefore, ultimately is a critique of systems of unjustified domination.

It is because of feminist agreement on the elimination of oppression, and because of the recognition of multiple and interlocking systems of oppression (race/ethnicity, class, sexuality, nationality, religion, age, ability, body size, and so on), that the contemporary feminist movement has become a movement to eliminate all systems of unjustified domination.

Warren and Cady (1996) also point to the difference between negative peace and positive peace. Their notion of positive peace is close to our vision of social relations in schools and communities with reduced levels of violence, bullying, and other types of misbehavior in which individuals are harmed. While negative peace is the absence of war, "where order is imposed by outside domination" (p. 3): "Genuine peace ('positive peace') on the other hand, involves interaction between and among individuals and groups where such behavior is orderly from within, cooperative, and based on agreement. . . . ends are sought and accomplished through coalition, interactive, cooperative means." Note the similarity between their definition of positive peace and that offered by Quinney (2000).

An examination of the core concerns of feminist ethics or the ethic of care shows how ethical concerns of feminism are similar to those of peacemaking and how they can contribute to an alternative framework for addressing crime in schools. Drawing on works by Gilligan (1982), Noddings (1984), and others, McDermott (1994) identifies the central ethical concerns of feminist ethics:

1. Caring individuals are responsive to others' points of view.
2. We exist in a web of relationships.
3. Moral behavior and justice flow from caring and responsiveness. Moral judgments are contextual, although based on a universal ethic that it is wrong to hurt anyone and it is right to sustain human relationships.
4. Responsiveness requires equality.

These concerns echo peacemaking themes: responsiveness, caring, connectedness, and equality. McDermott writes that (1994, p. 33):

For feminists, ethical actions involve individuals who meet as equals. Human connectedness and interdependence assume a nonhierarchical model. Caring-for relationships, such as care for children or elderly parents, are not characterized by domination of the cared-for, but by respect and understanding of the other's needs. Power over another, or the desire to have power over another, will bring instability to a relationship. Like detachment, power entails the potential to do violence.

Thus, in the long term, solutions to problems like crime in schools will need to address issues of inequality at the macro-, meso-, and micro-levels.

Since the ethic of care, contrasted with the masculine ethic of justice, presumably derives from "feminine" or "maternal" caring, the ethic of care has been criticized, along with much cultural feminism, for being essentialist (McDermott 1994). However, the issue of essentialism—that there are firm and immutable differences among women—is really separate from the ethic of care. Gilligan, Noddings, and others (especially Ruddick 1989) associate the ethic of care with the role of caretaking. In our patriarchal society and culture the activity of caretaking has been traditionally devalued and assigned to women. Some feminist ethicists seek a moral theory that will bring together the justice and the care orientations (see, e.g., Harris 1991).

In their analysis of the intersection of peacemaking and third-wave feminism, Zimmerman, McDermott, and Gould (2009) discuss transformations on the intrapersonal, interpersonal, societal, and global levels. We turn now to this discussion because we believe that any attempt to suggest alternatives to retributive, get-tough justice, must include addressing issues of individual responsibility. This is what we are asking our schools to do—*to educate and to nurture caring children for responsive and responsible participation in a democratic society.* Zimmerman and colleagues begin by framing third-wave feminism as a movement that continues to advance the women's rights agenda of the second wave, although "third wave feminists tend to view themselves as departing from the second wave by being more inclusive, by operating in a different climate, by emphasizing personal narratives, responsible choices and individual-level political activism, and by being comfortable with the uncertainty of knowledge" (2009, p. 77).

According to Zimmerman and colleagues (2009, p. 78), the most critical aspect of feminism within third-wave thought is the power of choice, and "the focus is on empowering all people to make socially informed and world responsible choices." The authors describe the responsible actor as one who is empowered to more freely direct the course of his or her life and so to hold him- or herself accountable in situations, while at the same time holding others accountable for their choices.

Multicultural and multiracial feminism directs our attention to other issues relevant to finding solutions to the problem of crime in schools, for it is in this perspective that we grapple with the realization that not all women (or men) are alike, that individual lives are framed by a matrix of oppression, or what is often referred to as intersectionality, or the coming together of multiple systems of oppression. For example, there is ample evidence that school crime and rule-violating behavior is gendered and this gendered victimization is experienced differentially depending on one's position in other systems of inequality (race, class, etc.). Jody Miller's (2008) work provides extensive evidence of how gender, race, and class inequalities combine to expose young women in disadvantaged neighborhoods to victimization both in the neighborhood and in school. Chesney-Lind and Irwin's (2008) critical analysis of the media hype surrounding "bad girls" in and out of schools documents both gender discrimination in social control and race and class discrimination in the creation and enforcement of punishing school climates and disciplinary codes. Muschert and Peguero (2010, p. 137) conclude that the differential development and enforcement of school antiviolence policies and the associated discourse "have a longer history in urban areas within racial and ethnic minority and poor communities."

Feminism has much to offer for envisioning alternative policies and programs by the ethic of care and by way of reminding us of the importance of nurturing individual-level responsibility and freedom and striving to eliminate the sociocultural context of multiple oppressions. We turn now to a consideration of ways in which the ecological, peacemaking, and feminist perspectives suggest alternatives to punitive and fear-inducing social control strategies.

Principles for the Development of Alternative Policies

From this review we can distill two broad principles to guide intervention in problems of school crime and misbehavior: (1) strategies for intervention must occur on multiple levels, and (2) strategies for intervention should be guided by notions of care, concern, community, and equality, and driven by the broad goal of education that nurtures the development of individuals who grow in positive ways and are prepared for responsive and responsible participation in a democratic society.

Henry (2009) defines multiple levels of causation in school violence and argues for an interdisciplinary, integrative approach in theorizing about problems of school violence. We have shown that the ecological, peacemaking, and feminist perspectives also suggest this multilevel intervention, and that no one level has primacy because the levels are interactive and interwoven. Here we use the multiple levels identified by Henry (2009) in his discussion of theoretical integration and by Muschert and Peguero (2010) in their essay evaluating policies to address school violence in the multilevels defined by Henry. Thus, interventions can be conceived of as: Level 1 (Individual), Level 2 (Group), Level 3 (Institutional/Organizational), Level 4 (Communal/Neighborhood), and Level 5 (Societal/Cultural). We suggest that interventions at each of these levels be guided by concerns identified in peacemaking and feminist themes, although we do not present a detailed delineation of specific interventions here.

Noddings's (2002) work on caring and social policy provides a useful starting point. While peacemaking uses the term *responsiveness* and third-wave feminism links freedom and equality to *responsibility* in the sense of accountability, Noddings uses the term *response-ability* (similar to Pepinsky's definition of responsive) to suggest that we cultivate in youth the ability to respond appropriately and with care (2002, p. 166). Noddings argues that the starting point for developing response-able individuals (Level 1) is the home (Level 2), and she asks how far "we can extend the attitude of caring that is characteristic of the best homes into the larger social domain" (2002, p. 4). Noddings (2002) writes of caring in the "best homes," that is, homes that nurture caring individuals who develop in positive and socially acceptable ways. To explain the link between the development of "response-able" individuals and caring in best homes, and particularly relevant to a critique of punitive school policies, Noddings writes (2002, pp. 4–5):

> The best homes, I argue, *rarely use coercion*. . . . Similarly, the best homes seldom invoke the concept of negative desert (one who does something bad deserves something bad in return). . . . One of the most important guidelines . . . [i]s that no policy or rule should be established that makes it impossible for agents to respond positively to those over whom they may have some charge or control. (emphasis added)

Noddings provides a strong critique of zero-tolerance policies (Level 3) that is linked to the guideline of not having social policies that make it impossible to respond to individuals *as* individuals and in a positive way. Comparing zero-tolerance policies to mandatory sentencing laws, she notes (2002, pp. 231–232):

> It is one thing to say that "we" will not tolerate certain kinds of behavior; it is quite another to insist on uniform penalties for infractions that cannot be easily categorized. . . . Educators, like judges, need to exercise judgment. . . . Rigid rules are often justified in the name of impartiality. . . . Events that are similar on the surface involve very different selves, and therefore are really different events. (emphasis added)

Other critics of zero-tolerance policies have provided evidence of absurdity in the application of these so-called "impartial" policies, *policies that result in unjust treatment of individuals* (Husak 2008). In a review of antiviolence policies, Chesney-Lind and Irwin (2008, p. 146) note that while some behaviors identified as violating various zero-tolerance school policies may be reasonably related to school crime (like wearing gang attire), others are not (like wearing outrageous hair styles, having too many body piercings, or carrying fingernail clippers or plastic knives to school).

By limiting discretion, zero-tolerance policies prohibit teachers and administrators from exercising response-ability, in the sense that they are unable to respond positively to individuals. Even sympathetic and understanding school officials need to follow the rules. These policies also absolve administrators of responsibility (accountability), because, given the written rules to fall back on, there is no need to take individual-level responsibility for their decisionmaking.

The model of school crime prevention that has potential, according to Muschert and Peguero (2010) is the one that addresses issues of school climate (Level 3). Like authors in the peacemaking tradition, many of these programs seek to build healthy relations and to develop a sense of community in schools. What we would suggest is that the social climate of schools emphasize caring relationships, the connectedness of individuals to each other and the world, equality (which we will discuss further), and the nurturing of response-able individuals who develop and grow in positive ways.

In our view, school climate issues are intertwined with problems created by some of the very strategies designed to combat school violence and misbehavior. In peacemaking terms, we are creating *violent* environments, (maybe) safer, but certainly not healthy ones. Thus we raise the question of fear and what fear does to the potential for the positive growth and development that should be occurring in school environments. As noted earlier, Muschert and Peguero (2010, p. 138) note a "prisonlike feel" of the "New American school." A peacemaking criminologist would contend that "violence breeds violence" and that the very nature of these prison-schools fosters rule violating behavior, especially to the extent that prisonlike schools are found more often in poor, urban neighborhoods with high proportions of racial and ethnic minorities.

Noddings (2002) writes about the need to shelter and protect children in homes and the delicate parental act of balancing care and protection with wanting the child to retain trust in the world. She writes (2002, p. 177): "All good homes try to keep children safe from harm, but the best homes try to reduce their children's fears and to maintain their faith in human beings." This balancing act—protecting children but not elevating fear—is difficult for parents in many specific situations, such as instructing children on interaction with strangers. This is precisely the balancing act faced by schools in the twenty-first century—how to balance protection of children, with the harm to the school learning and social environments caused by elevated levels of fear and "prisonlike" conditions.

Finally, we address the peacemaking and feminist concern of equality. A peaceable community is one that embraces equality and the elimination of oppression, whether that community is the home, a school, or some broader social unit. The elimination of inequality is a goal that can be addressed at multiple levels of causation. At Level 5 (Societal/Cultural), efforts are directed at eliminating social structural inequalities based on race, class, gender, and so on, and at transforming cultural values that contribute to the perpetuation of violence. For example, American society is one that sexualizes women at a young age, valorizes an ideal masculinity that reinforces the domination of men over women, and provides social and cultural support for violence. We cannot expect to eliminate violence against girls and women in this patriarchal social structure and culture. At Level 3 (Institutional/Organizational), much can be done within schools to address issues of inequality—such as reforming hiring practices; sexual harassment policies; school recognition of lesbian, gay, bisexual, transgendered, questioning alliance (LGBTQA) student groups; and efforts to promote cultural understanding and dialogue. At Level 2 (Group) families and at Level 3 (Organizational/Institutional), parents and schools can encourage interaction in which children are taught to meet other individuals *as* individuals, and not as members of groups defined as less worthy. Finally, at Level 1 (Individual), students should be encouraged to understand that we cannot expect a society free of inequality if our own attitudes and behaviors contribute to sustaining oppression.

The broad social changes and individual transformations suggested in this section will not be easily implemented or politically popular, and we are wary of unwittingly reinforcing suspicion that principled restrictions on the scope of school violence policies are hopeless. We nevertheless embrace the goal of a nonviolent and just society. Borrowing a few words from this volume's editors, a multilevel analysis of the causes of school violence driven by core concerns of peacemaking and gender dynamics within school environments contributes to the potential for a new comprehensive direction in school antiviolence policy.

12

Diagnosing and Preventing School Shootings

Douglas Kellner

After the sixth anniversary of the Virginia Tech shootings and the fourteenth anniversary of the Columbine tragedy, we still need to better understand and address how a wide range of school shootings have multiple causes and must be engaged by a diverse range of responses. While the motivations for the shootings may vary, they have in common crises in masculinities in which young men use guns and violence to create ultramasculine identities in producing a media spectacle that generates fame and celebrity for the shooters.

School shootings and domestic terrorism have been proliferating on a global level in the 2000s, as in recent years there have been rampage shootings in Finland, Germany, Greece, Brazil, and other countries as well as the United States. Although there may be national differences, in all cases the shootings feature young men in crisis who explode with rage, using guns and violence to resolve their crises and creating a media spectacle and celebrity through their deadly actions. Media coverage of the phenomenon rarely, if ever, roots rampage killing in male rage and crises of masculinity, and fails to see how the violence is a pathological form of resolving crises in masculinity, in which men in crisis use the media to gain celebrity and to overcome feelings of powerlessness and alienation. The media and academic discussions also largely tend to ignore the connection between hypermasculinity and guns, and thus fail to see how rampage shootings are a form of men and guns running amok.

By "crises in masculinity," I refer to a dominant societal connection between masculinity and being a "tough guy," assuming what Jackson Katz (2006) describes as a "tough guise," a mask or façade of violent assertiveness, covering over vulnerabilities. The crisis erupted in outbreaks of violence and societal murder, as men acted out rage, which took extremely violent forms such as political assassinations, serial and mass murders, and school and workplace shootings.

Crises in masculinities are grounded in deteriorating socioeconomic possibilities for men and are aggravated by our current economic troubles. They are also produced in part by a media that repeatedly shows violence as a way of solving problems. Explosions of male rage and rampage shootings are also connected to the escalation of war and militarism in the United States from the long nightmare of Vietnam through the military interventions of the Bush-Cheney administration in Afghanistan and Iraq, as well as to accelerating social violence in the media and society at large.

To be sure, there is a tradition of social scientists and activists who have explored the connections between crime, violence, and masculinity. In *Masculinities and Crime* (1993) and other writings, James Messerschmidt explores the link between masculine socialization and the overwhelming prevalence of male perpetration of crime—including violent crime. Emphasizing the social construction of gender, class, race, and crime, Messerschmidt stresses how these factors are interrelated, and that men learn violent behavior both as a means of "doing masculinity," and to assert dominance over women and other men, behavior that socially reproduces structures of capitalism and patriarchy.

Messerschmidt and Connell (2005) critically interrogate the concept of "hegemonic masculinity," whereby dominant models of an assertive—and sometimes violent—masculinity are constructed that reinforce gendered hierarchies among men and reinforce men's power over women. Hegemonic masculinity is the dominant form of masculinity in a culture at a specific period, and in the United States over the past century, hegemonic masculinity has been associated with military heroism, corporate power, sports achievement, action-adventure movie stars, and being tough, aggressive, and macho, ideals reproduced in corporate, political, military, sports, and gun culture, as well as Hollywood film, video games, men's magazines and other forms of media culture, and sites like the frat house, locker room, board room, male-dominated workplaces, bars, and hangouts where men aggregate.

In *The Macho Paradox* (2006), Jackson Katz explores how this conception of violent masculinity helps produce violence against women. Calling upon men to question such behavior and to seek alternative masculinities, Katz challenges men to confront violence against women and to struggle against it. All of these scholars share a critical relation to dominant conceptions of a hegemonic hyper and violent masculinity and all search for alternative modes of masculinity, a project that I share.

In this chapter, I argue that school shooters, and other indiscriminate gun killers, share male rage, attempt to resolve a crisis of masculinity through violent behavior, exhibit a fetishism of guns or weapons, and resolve their crises through violence orchestrated as a media spectacle. Yet there are many causes to the rise of school violence and events like the Columbine and Virginia Tech school shootings (Kellner 2008), so I do not want to advocate a reductive causal approach. Complex historical events like the Iraq invasion (see Kellner 2005), or the Virginia Tech and Columbine shootings, require a multiperspectivist vision and interpretation of key factors that constitute the constellation from which events can be interpreted, explained, and better understood. Thus addressing the causes of problems like societal violence and school shootings involves a range of apparently disparate things such as critique of male socialization and construction of ultra-masculine male identities, the prevalence of gun culture and militarism, and a media culture that promotes violence and retribution, while circulating and sensationalizing media spectacle and a culture of celebrity. Such a constellation helps construct the identities, values, and behavior that help incite individuals to use violence to resolve their crises of masculinity through creation of an ultra-masculine identity and media spectacle through gun violence.

Accordingly, solutions that I suggest to the problems of school violence and shootings range from more robust and rational gun laws, to better school and workplace security with stronger mental health institutions and better communication between legal, medical, and school administrations, to the reconstruction of masculinity and the reconstruction of education for democracy (Kellner 2008). In addition, we must consider examining better ways of addressing crime and violence than prisons and capital punishment, draconian measures aimed increasingly today at youths and people of color. Today our schools are like prisons, while in a better society schools would become centers of learning and self-developing, while prisons could also be centers of learning, rehabilitation, and job training and not punitive and dangerous schools for crime and violence (see Davis and Mendietta 2005).

In this chapter, I will suggest some proposals to deal with the escalating problem of school violence and school shooting and will argue for the importance of critical theory and radical pedagogy that propose new modes of conflict resolution and ways of dealing with bullying and violence that emerge in schools. While classic Frankfurt School research tended to decenter gender, today critical theory needs to discern crises in masculinities producing growing societal violence and aggression. In focusing on growing violence in society I am taking up a theme from Herbert Marcuse, but from the perspective of gender and crises in masculinities. Yet in discussing the reconstruction of masculinities and education, I will draw on ideas from Marcuse and the Frankfurt School, Freire and critical pedagogy, and Ivan Illich and John Dewey.

Guns in the United States, School Shootings, and Media Spectacle

To grasp the magnitude of societal violence and school shooting requires a critical theory of society focusing on problems of the present age. Escalating gun violence in schools and other sectors of society today in the United States is a national scandal and serious social problem. The United States has been experiencing epidemic levels of gun violence annually. According to the US Centers for Disease Control and Prevention, firearm violence claims over 30,000 lives a year, and for every person who dies from a gunshot wound, two others are wounded, meaning that every year there are more than 100,000 Americans who become victims of gun violence.[1] Gun ownership is rampant in the United States and gun violence is epidemic. According to an article published after the April 2012 Oikos University school shooting in Oakland:

- The United States has 90 guns for every 100 citizens, making it the most heavily armed society in the world.
- U.S. citizens own 270 million of the world's 875 million known firearms, according to the Small Arms Survey 2007 by the Geneva-based Graduate Institute of International Studies.
- About 4.5 million of the 8 million new guns manufactured worldwide each year are purchased in the United States, the report said.[2]

The massacre at Virginia Tech in 2007 was the twenty-fifth school shooting on an American campus since the Columbine school shootings in 1999. That figure represents more than half the number of shootings at schools across the world in the same time span.[3] Deadly school shootings at a wide range of schools have claimed over 400 student and faculty lives since Columbine. As publicists for a new edition of Lieberman's *The Shooting Game* pointed out (2006): "In March and April of 2006, 16 deadly Columbine-style plots were hatched by over 25 students arrested across the U.S.A. from the heartland up to North Pole, Alaska. As the fall semester began, there were more deadly shootings in Montreal, Colorado, Wisconsin and even a tiny Amish school in Pennsylvania."[4]

As I write in spring 2012, there have already been several well-publicized school shootings in the United States this year. On February 10, 2012, in Walpole, New Hampshire, a fourteen-year-old student shot himself in front of seventy fellow students; on February 27 at Chardon High School in Ohio, a former classmate opened fire, killing three students and injuring six, with the shooter telling police after his arrest that he had randomly picked students as victims; on March 6, 2012 in Jacksonville, Florida, Shane Schumerth, a twenty-eight-year-old teacher at Episcopal High School, returned to the campus after being fired, and shot and killed the headmistress, Dale Regan, with an assault rifle; and on April 2, 2012 in Oakland, California, One Goh, a forty-three-year-old Korean American former student, shot down seven people and wounded several other at Oikos University, a Christian school populated by mostly Korean and Korean Americans.[5]

My studies of school shootings in the past decades suggests that many school shooters have orchestrated shootings as media spectacles to dramatize personal grievances or to lash out against supposed tormentors, thus gaining their short bursts of celebrity and fame. In the case of the Virginia Tech shootings, it was clear that the alienated student and frustrated writer Seung-hui Cho carried out "The Virginia Tech Massacre," in which he was star, director, and producer. His multimedia dossier revealed that he was imitating images from films and carrying out a vengeance drama in the tradition of the Columbine School shooters, whom he cited as "martyrs."

The following year, in the February 14, 2008, shootings at Northern Illinois University, a former student, Steven Kazmierczak leaped from behind the curtain onto a stage in a large lecture hall. Armed with a barrage of weapons and dressed in black, he began randomly shooting students in a geology class, killing five before shooting himself. While his motivations were never made clear, it is apparent that he was obviously creating a highly theatrical spectacle of violence in the tradition of the Columbine and Virginia Tech shootings.

My notion of media spectacle builds on French theorist Guy Debord's concept of the society of spectacle, but differs significantly from Debord's concept. For Debord, spectacle "unifies and explains a great diversity of apparent phenomena" (Debord [1967] 1970, Thesis 10). Debord's conception, first developed in the 1960s, continues to circulate through the Internet and other academic and subcultural sites today. It describes a media and consumer society, organized around the production and consumption of images, commodities, and staged events.

For Debord, "spectacle" constituted the overarching concept to describe the media and consumer society, including the packaging, promotion, and display of commodities and the production and effects of all media. Using the term "media spectacle," I am largely focusing on various forms of technologically constructed media productions that are produced and disseminated through the so-called mass media, ranging from radio and television to the Internet and latest wireless gadgets. Every medium, from music to television, from news to advertising, has multiple forms of spectacle, involving such things in the realm of music as the classical music spectacle, the opera spectacle, the rock spectacle, and over the last decades, the hip hop spectacle. The forms and circulation of the spectacle evolve over time and multiply with new technological developments.

On my account, there are many levels and categories of media spectacle (Kellner 2003a). Some media spectacles, like Dayan and Katz's media events (1992), are recurrent phenomena of media culture that celebrate dominant values and institutions, as well as its modes of conflict resolution. They include media extravaganzas like the Oscars and Emmys, or sports events like the Super Bowl or World Cup, which celebrate basic values of competition and winning. Politics is increasingly mediated by media spectacle. Political conflicts, campaigns, and those attention-grabbing occurrences that we call "news" have all been subjected to the logic of spectacle and tabloidization in the era of the media sensationalism, infotainment, political scandal and contestation, seemingly unending cultural war, and the phenomenon of Terror War, which characterized the post-9/11 epoch (see Kellner 2003b).

Spectacles of terror, like the 9/11 attacks on the Twin Towers and Pentagon, differ significantly from spectacles that celebrate or reproduce the existing society, as in Guy Debord's "society of the spectacle," or the "media events" analyzed by Dayan and Katz (1992), which describe how political systems exploited televised live, ceremonial, and preplanned events. Spectacles of terror are highly disruptive events carried out by oppositional groups or individuals who are carrying out politics or war by other means. Like the media and consumer spectacles described by Debord, spectacles of terror reduce individuals to passive objects, manipulated by existing institutions and figures. However, the spectacles of terror produce fear, which terrorists hope will demoralize the objects of their attack, but which is often manipulated by conservative groups, like the Bush-Cheney administration, to push through right-wing agendas, cut back on civil liberties, and militarize the society.

I argue that what domestic terrorists like Timothy McVeigh, who was responsible for the Oklahoma City bombings; the Columbine shooters Eric Harris and Dylan Klebold; and the Virginia Tech Massacre shooter Seung-Hui Cho have in common is that the perpetrators created media spectacle to act out their grievances and in so doing achieved celebrity (Kellner 2008). This no doubt promoted copy-cat shootings, now on a global level. Indeed, school shootings can be seen as a form of terrorism, although there are often significant differences. Certain forms of terrorism have specific political objectives, while school shootings are more grounded in individual grievances or crises. Both, however, use violence to obtain goals and aim at media spectacle to get publicity for their actions and in some cases celebrity. Both are obviously forms of terror and use violence to generate fear and destruction. And in most cases, terrorism and school shootings are carried out by men, and many of these school shooters and domestic terrorists used guns and violence to resolve a crisis of masculinity through creating a media spectacle (Kellner 2008).

My cultural studies approach to guns and school shootings reads events like school shootings in their sociohistorical context and uses a critical theory of society to help situate, interpret, and trace the effects of certain texts, artifacts, or events.[6] Critical theory is historical theory, contextualizing its object in its historical matrix, and so I felt the need to ground my studies of guns and school shootings in the contemporary moment in the context of the history of guns in the United States and controversies over guns and their regulation. In 2000, Michael A. Bellesiles published *Arming America: The Origins of a National Gun Culture* with the prestigious Alfred Knopf publishers. It was garnished with an impressive array of reviews and won the Bancroft Award as the best historical study of the year. The book, however, was highly controversial and provoked a firestorm of critique. Right-wing gun advocates and their academic minions ferociously attacked Bellesiles's scholarship. It turns out he made mistakes, among other things, in his sample and interpretation of probate records that resulted in him underestimating the number of guns privately held in colonial America. With the ensuing scandal and fierce attacks, Bellesiles was stripped of the Bancroft prize and eventually lost his job at Emory University.[7]

Bellesiles's history describes the origins of a national gun culture and the ways that the gun became central to American life and concepts of masculinity. He seems to have underestimated the extent of early colonial gun culture and gun culture after the Revolution, but convincingly depicts the explosion of gun culture at the time of the Civil War, with the mass production of guns and the manufacture and marketing of guns in the post–Civil War period. He also convincingly reproduces the debates over guns at the time of the Constitutional Convention, when Federalists fought for a centralized federal government with a controlled standing army, while anti-Federalists supported state militias (Bellesiles 2000, p. 208). As Bellesiles argued, "The Constitutional Convention hammered out a document full of compromise and barely obtained concessions. On one point at least there was no disagreement: Congress should arm the militia" (2000, p. 213). Bellesiles sets out the debates on whether the militia should remain under the direct control of the states or federal government, whether or not to have a standing army, and what gun rights should be included. The result was the Second Amendment to the Bill of Rights, which held that "a well regulated Militia, being necessary to the security of a free State, the right of the People to keep and bear Arms, shall not be infringed" (2000, p. 217).

The context of the Second Amendment suggests an original intent to bestow the right to bear arms within the confines of a militia, itself to be regulated by the federal government, as in the phrase "*well regulated* Militia" in the Second Amendment (my emphasis). Some have argued that until the last few decades, the Second Amendment was largely read as supporting gun rights within militias, but not in terms of individual rights to bear firearms. But recently, accordingly to legal scholars and commentators, the Second Amendment has been interpreted by law professors, the courts, and the public to provide individual gun ownership rights to citizens, though controversies over the meaning of the Second Amendment continue until this day.[8]

I fear that initially Bellesiles and his impressive array of reviewers wanted to believe that gun culture was not so deeply entrenched in American history and that an earlier period could be pointed to as an ideal to emulate, whereas the problem of guns and violence may be more deeply rooted and intractable than liberals want to acknowledge. Both Bellesiles (2000) and Cramer (2006) emphasize the tremendous violence of the Indian wars that continued into the nineteenth century, the ferocity of the Civil War, and the eventual triumph of gun culture in the United States. Both Bellesiles and Cramer also point out how the federal government from the beginning regulated gun ownership and use, preventing, at different times, gun ownership by blacks, indentured servants, Indians, and other stigmatized groups. Together the books present a national history of gun culture that has bequeathed serious problems to the present age.

Building on these studies, Winkler argues in *Gunfight* (2011) that Americans have had the right to bear arms from the beginning of the Republic, but that there is also a long tradition of gun control. Recognizing that the Second Amendment, with its talk of militias, is "maddeningly ambiguous," Winkler argues that a balance between gun control and gun rights has marked US history until the current era, when gun rights groups dominate the discourse. Winkler points out that the National Rifle Association (NRA) strongly supported gun control until the 1970s, and that even the Ku Klux Klan started off as a gun control group—wanting to keep guns out of the hands of newly freed African American slaves.

Winkler opens by claiming that both "gun grabbers" and "gun nuts" pursue extremist objectives, either wanting to abolish gun ownership completely, or resisting even minimal gun control.[9] Winkler follows a 2011 Supreme Court ruling, *District of Columbia v. Heller*, that expands Second Amendment constitutional interpretation to move from a right to bear arms within militias to private gun ownership rights, and documents the fierce battles still going on between gun rights and gun control proponents, recognizing that the gun rights forces backed by the NRA have the upper hand.

Obviously, properly understanding the role of guns and gun culture in the epidemic of school shootings requires taking seriously the need for gun control and reforming of laws concerning access to firearms. Yet since I believe that school shootings have multiple causes, there need to be multiple solutions, which ultimately involve a restructuring of school and society, including new concepts of masculinity, better mental health facilities and treatment in schools and society, better gun control, and a curriculum in schools that involves peaceful conflict resolution, courses in nonviolence and peace studies, and teaching compassion and empathy while attempting to overcome or diminish societal alienation.

Yet, clearly, more rational policies about access to guns are one of the solutions to the problem. It is heartening that groups of people appalled by the Virginia Tech shootings have been campaigning to close gun show loopholes where people can purchase firearms without adequate background checks (as did a girlfriend of one of the underage Columbine shooters). But ABC's *20/20*, on April 10, 2009, broadcast a segment showing young men buying scores of weapons on the floor of a gun show, and even in the parking lot, without showing any identity or having any security check, so this loophole involving gun shows in many states is glaring.

Likewise a *60 Minutes* report on April 12, 2009, showed the startling increase in gun sales and increase in NRA membership after Obama's election in 2008, as if gun enthusiasts feared that the government was suddenly going to pull their rifles from their "cold dead hands."[10]

Barbara Kopple's 2011 HBO documentary *Gun Fight* also demonstrates how easy it is to purchase guns without background checks at gun shows from private owners, or to use a "straw purchaser," someone who can easily pass a background check to buy guns for those excluded because of age, mental health issues, or a criminal background, as did a friend of the Columbine shooters who bought guns for them at a gun show (Cullen 2009, pp. 90, 122).

We also need to examine the role of the Internet as a source of ammunition and firearms, where anyone can assume a virtual identity and purchase lethal weapons and ammo; it is perhaps not coincidental that the Virginia Tech and Northern Illinois University shooters both bought weapons used in their shootings from the same on-line business.[11] On the political front, however, neither Democrats nor Republicans want to address the issue of gun control, which was a dead issue throughout the Obama administration and was unlikely to be addressed during the 2012 election year.[12]

Indeed, the problem of escalating gun violence and random shootings is a larger problem than gun control alone. With discernible and accelerating alienation, frustration, anger, and even rage in the schools, universities, workplaces, public spaces, and communities of contemporary US society, we clearly need better mental health facilities and monitoring of troubled individuals. Yet we also need the monitoring of institutions like schools and the provision of mental health facilities to ensure that people are receiving adequate treatment and we are not breeding a generation of killers, with men and guns running amok.

Schools and universities, for example, have been scrambling to ensure that they have in place counseling and monitoring programs to deal with troubled students, as well as safety plans concerning how to deal with violence and crises. Schools should be assessed concerning how well they are caring for their students and providing a secure learning environment. After the Columbine shootings, there were strong demands for more student safety in schools, but often this led to increased surveillance, metal detectors, and harassment of students, which in many cases increased student alienation and may increase the possibility of violence, requiring serious assessment of how well violence prevention programs have (or have not) worked in schools (see Muschert 2007b).[13]

To be sure, in an era of war and growing poverty, there is likely to be increased societal violence, so that problems of random and targeted shootings will no doubt be a problem that we will face in the years to come. It is important, however, to address the issue of a crisis of masculinity, social alienation, and eruptions of societal violence and not use simplistic categories like mental health (e.g., "he's just crazy") to explain the issue, since mental illness is a complex phenomenon that has a variety of causes and expressions. It is also important not to blame scapegoats like the Internet, media, prescription drugs, or any one factor that may well contribute to the problem of rampage shooting but is not the underlying cause. Rather, we need to see the seriousness of the problems of school and rampage shootings and come up with an array of responses that will produce a more productive and humane society.

Beyond the Culture of Male Violence and Rage

In the rest of the chapter, I argue that dealing with problems of school and societal violence will require reconstruction of male identities and critique of masculinist socialization and identities, as well as changing gun laws and effecting stricter gun control. Unfortunately, the media and some gun cultures, gang culture, sports, and military culture consider ultramacho men an ideal, producing societal problems from violence against women to gang murder (see Katz 2006). As Katz urges, young men have to renounce these ideals and behavior and construct alternative notions of masculinity. As Katz (2006, p. 270) concludes, reconstructing masculinity and overcoming aggressive and violent macho behavior and values provides a vision of manhood that does not depend on putting down others in order to lift itself up. When a man stands up for social justice, non-violence, and basic human rights—for women as much as for men—he is acting in the best traditions of our civilization. That makes him not only a better man, but a better human being.

Major sources of violence in US society include cultures of violence caused by poverty; masculinist military, sports, and gun culture; ultramasculine behavior in the corporate and political world; high school bullying and fighting; and general societal violence reproduced by media and in the family and everyday life, and in prisons, which are schools for violence. In any of these cases, an ultra-violent masculinity can explode and produce societal violence, and until we have new conceptions of what it means to be a man that include intelligence, independence, sensitivity, and the renunciation of bullying and violence, societal violence will no doubt increase.

Lee Hirsch's film *Bully* (2011) has called attention to the phenomenon of bullying in schools, and it shows intense bullying taking place on school buses, playgrounds, classrooms, and neighborhoods. Focusing on five victims of bullying from various regions in the United States, two of whom committed suicide, Hirsch's film puts on display shocking physical mistreatment of high school students by their peers. In an allegorical mode, the wildly popular film *The Hunger Games* (2012) also presents a stark view of a dystopic world in which only the strongest survive and violence is valorized as the key to survival, although this time the hero is a young woman.

Sports culture is another major part of the construction of American masculinity that can take violent forms. In most of the high school shootings of the 1990s, "jocks" (high school athletes) tormented young teenage boys, who took revenge in asserting a hyper-violent masculinity and went on shooting rampages. Larkin (2007, p. 205) provides a detailed analysis of "Football and Toxic High School Environments," focusing on Columbine. He describes how sports played a primary role in the school environment, how jocks were celebrities, and how they systematically abused outsiders and marginal youths like Columbine shooters Eric Harris and Dylan Klebold.

The "pattern of sports domination of high schools," Larkin suggests, "is apparently the norm in America" (2007, p. 206). Larkin notes how football "has become incorporated into a hypermasculin-ized subculture that emphasizes physical aggression, domination, sexism, and the celebration of victory. He notes that more "than in any other sport, defeat in football is associated with being physically dominated and humiliated" (2007, p. 208). Further, it is associated with militarism as George Carlin, among others, has noted in his comedy routine:

> In football the object is for the quarterback, also known as the field general, to be on target with his aerial assault, riddling the defence by hitting his receivers with deadly accuracy in spite of the blitz, even if he has to use the shotgun. With short bullet passes and long bombs, he marches his troops into enemy territory, balancing this aerial assault with a sustained ground attack that punches holes in the forward wall of the enemy's defensive line.
>
> In baseball the object is to go home! And to be safe! (cited in Larkin 2007, p. 208)

Larkin argues that football culture has "corrupted many high schools," including Columbine, where "the culture of hypermasculinity reigned supreme" (2007, p. 209). Hence, Larkin concludes that "if we wish to reduce violence in high schools, we have to de-emphasize the power of sports and change the culture of hypermasculinity. Football players cannot be lords of the hallways, bullying their peers with impunity, sometimes encouraged by coaches with adolescent mentalities" (p. 210).

Hypermasculinity in sports is often a cauldron of homophobia, and many of the school shooters were taunted about their sexuality and responded ultimately with a berserk affirmation of compensatory violence. Yet hypermasculinity is found throughout sports, military, gun, gang, and other male subcultures, as well as the corporate and political world, often starting in the family with male socialization by the father, and it is reproduced and validated constantly in films, television programs, and other forms of media culture.

Obviously, media culture is full of violence and, according to the case studies in Chapter 3 in *Guys and Guns Amok,* full of violent masculinity. Timothy McVeigh, the two Columbine shooters, and many other school shooters were allegedly deeply influenced by violent media culture. Yet, while media images of violence and specific books, films, TV shows, or artefacts of media culture may provide scripts for violent masculinity that young men act out, it is the broader culture of militarism, gun culture, extreme sports, ultraviolent video and computer games, subcultures of bullying and violence, and the rewarding of ultramasculinity in the corporate and political worlds that are major factors in constructing a hegemonic violent masculinities. Media culture itself obviously contributes to this ideal of macho masculinity, but it is, however, a contested terrain between different conceptions of masculinity and femininity, and between liberal, conservative, and more radical representations and discourses (Kellner 1995).

After dramatic school shootings and incidents of youth violence, there are usually attempts to scapegoat media culture. After the Virginia Tech shootings, the Federal Communications Commission (FCC) issued a report in late April 2007 on "violent television programming and its impact on children" that calls for expanding governmental oversight on broadcast television, but also extending content regulation to cable and satellite channels for the first time and banning some shows from time slots where children might be watching. FCC commissioner Jonathan S. Adelstein, who was in favor of the measures, did not hesitate to evoke the Virginia Tech shootings, saying the call was made "particularly in light of the spasm of unconscionable violence at Virginia Tech, but just as importantly in light of the excessive violent crime that daily affects our nation, there is a basis for appropriate federal action to curb violence in the media."[14]

In a *Los Angeles Times* op-ed piece, Nick Gillespie, editor of *Reason,* noted that the report itself indicated that there was no causal relation between watching TV violence and committing violent acts. Further, Gillespie argued that given the steady drop in incidents of juvenile violence over the last twelve years, reaching a low not seen since at least the 1970s, it is inappropriate to demonize media culture for acts of societal violence. Yet, in my view, the proliferation of media culture and spectacle requires renewed calls for critical media literacy so that people can intelligently analyze and interpret the media and see how they are vehicles for representations of race, class, gender, sexuality, power, and violence.

In the wake of the Columbine shootings, fierce criticism and scapegoating of media and youth culture erupted. Oddly, there was less finger-pointing at these targets after the Virginia Tech Massacre—perhaps because the Korean and Asian films on which Cho modeled his photos and videos were largely unknown in the United States, and perhaps because conservatives prefer to target jihadists or liberals as nefarious influences on Cho (Kellner 2008, ch. 1). I want to avoid, however, the extremes of demonizing media and youth culture and of asserting that it is mere entertainment without serious social influence. There is no question but that the media nurture fantasies and influence behaviors, sometimes sick and vile ones, and to survive in our culture requires that we are able to critically analyze and dissect media culture and not let it gain power over us. Critical media literacy empowers individuals over media so that they can produce critical and analytical distance from media messages and images. This provides protection from media manipulation and avoids letting the most destructive images of media gain power over us. It also enables more critical, healthy, and active relations with our culture. Media culture will not disappear, and it is simply a question of how we will deal with it and if we can develop an adequate pedagogy of critical media literacy to empower our youth.

Unfortunately, there are few media literacy courses offered in schools in the United States from kindergarten through high school. Many other countries, such as Canada, Australia, and England, have such programs (see Kellner and Share 2007). In the next section, I will suggest that to design schools for the new millennium that meet the challenges posed by student alienation and violence and that provide skills that students need for a high-tech economy requires a democratic reconstruction of education.

I argue that to address problems of societal violence raised in these studies requires a reconstruction of education and society, and what Marcuse referred to as "a revolution in values" and a "new sensibility."[15] The revolution in values involves breaking with values of competition, aggression, greed, and self-interest and cultivating values of equality, peace, harmony, and community. Such a revolution of values "would also make for a new morality, for new relations between the sexes and generations, for a new relation between man and nature" (2001, p. 198). Harbingers of the revolution in values, Marcuse argued, are found in "a widespread rebellion against the domineering values, of virility, heroism and force, invoking the images of society which may bring about the end of violence" (p. 198).

The "new sensibility," in turn, would cultivate needs for beauty, love, connections with nature and other people, and more democratic and egalitarian social relations. Marcuse believes that without a change in the sensibility, there can be no real social change, and that education, art, and the humanities can help cultivate the conditions for a new sensibility. Underlying the theory of the new sensibility is a concept of the active role of the senses in the constitution of experience that rejects the Kantian and other philosophical devaluations of the senses as passive, merely receptive. For Marcuse, our senses are shaped and molded by society, yet constitute in turn our primary experience of the world and provide both imagination and reason with its material. He believes that the senses are currently socially constrained and mutilated and argues that only an emancipation of the senses and a new sensibility can produce liberating social change.

Ultimately, addressing the problem of societal violence requires a democratic reconstruction of education and society, new pedagogical practices, new social relations, values, and forms of learning. In the following section, I want to sketch out aspects of a democratic reconstruction grounded in key ideas of John Dewey, Paulo Freire, Ivan Illich, and Herbert Marcuse.

New Literacies, Democratization, and the Reconstruction of Education

To begin, we need to recognize a systemic crisis of education in the United States in which there is a disconnect between youths' lives and what they are taught in school. Already in 1964, Marshall McLuhan recognized the discrepancy between youths raised on a fast-paced and multimodal media culture and the linear, book- and test-oriented education of the time, where youths sit in a classroom all day. Since then there has been a proliferation of new media and technologies, but education has been retreating to ever more conservative and pedantic goals, most egregiously during the Bush-Cheney era and its deceptively named "No Child Left Behind" program, which is really a front for "teaching for testing." In this policy, which has been strongly resisted by many states and local school districts, incredible amounts of time are wasted preparing students for tests, while teachers and schools are basically rated according to their test results.[16]

Reconstructing education will involve an expansion of print literacy to a multiplicity of literacies. An expanded multimedia literacy and pedagogy should teach how to read and critically dissect newspapers, film, TV, radio, popular music, the Internet, and other media of news, information, and culture to enable students to become active and engaged democratic citizens. While 1960s cultural studies by the Birmingham school in England included a focus on critically analyzing newspapers, TV news and information programs, and the images of politics, much cultural studies of the past decades has focused on media entertainment, consumption, and audience response to specific media programs (see Kellner 1995). This enterprise is valuable and important, but it should not replace or marginalize taking on the system of media news and information as well. A comprehensive cultural studies will interrogate news and entertainment, journalism and information sourcing, and should include media studies as well as textual studies and audience reception studies in part of a reconstruction of education in which critical media literacy is taught from kindergarten through college (see Kellner 1995, 1998; Kellner and Share 2007).

Critical media literacy needs to engage the "politics of representation," which subjects images and discourses of race, gender, sexuality, class, and other features to scrutiny and analysis, involving a critique of violent masculinity, sexism, racism, classism, homophobia, and other hurtful forms of representation. Critical media literacy also positively valorizes more progressive representations of gender, race, class, and sexuality, and notes how many cultural texts are ambiguous and contradictory in their representations.

The Internet and multimedia computer technologies and cultural forms are dramatically transforming the circulation of information, images, and various modes of culture, and the younger generation needs to gain multifaceted technological skills to survive in the high-tech information society. In this situation, students should learn both how to use media and computer culture to do research and gather information, as well as to perceive it as a cultural terrain that contains texts, spectacles, games, and interactive media, which require a form of critical computer literacy. Youth subcultural forms range from 'zines or websites that feature an ever-expanding range of video, music, or multimedia texts to sites of political information and organization.[17]

Moreover, since the 1999 Seattle anticorporate globalization demonstrations, youths have been using the Internet to inform and debate each other, organize oppositional movements, and generate alternative forms of politics and culture.[18] After using the Internet to successfully organize a wide range of anticorporate globalization demonstrations in Seattle, Washington, Prague, Toronto, and elsewhere, young people played an active role in organizing massive demonstrations against the Bush-Cheney administration invasion of Iraq, creating the basis for a oppositional antiwar and peace movement as the Bush-Cheney administration threatened an era of perpetual war in the new millennium. Obviously, it is youth that fights and dies in wars that often primarily serve the interests of corrupt economic and political elites. Today's youth is becoming aware that its survival is at stake and that thus it is necessary to become informed and organized on the crucial issues of war, peace, and the future of democracy and the global economy.

Likewise, groups are organizing to save endangered species; to fight genetically engineered food; to debate cloning and stem cell research; to advance animal rights; to join struggles over environmental causes like climate change, global warming, and sustainability; and to work for creating a healthier diet and alternative medical systems. The Internet is a virtual treasury of alternative information and cultural forms, with young people playing key roles in developing the technology and oppositional culture and using it for creative pedagogical and political purposes. Alternative sites of information and discussion on every conceivable topic can be found on the Internet, including important topics like human rights or environmental education that are often neglected in public schools.

In 2011, youth used new media and social networking in the Arab Uprisings, which led to the overthrow of governments in Tunisia, Egypt, and Libya, with turmoil continuing through the Middle East. The same year, dramatic demonstrations throughout Europe used new media during the Europe debt crisis, and Occupy Wall Street morphed into Occupy Everywhere movements throughout the world, as youths carried out the most sustained political uprisings since the student revolts and antiwar and other movements of 1968 (Kellner 2012).

Consequently, at present, technoliteracies involve not merely technical skills and knowledge, but also the ability to scan information, to interact with a variety of cultural forms and groups, and to intervene in a creative manner within the emergent social and political culture. Whereas youths are excluded for the most part from the dominant media culture, new multimedia culture and social networking form a discursive and political location in which youths can intervene, producing their own websites and personal pages, engaging in discussion groups, linking with others who share their interests, and generating multimedia for cultural dissemination and a diversity of cultural and political projects. New media and social networking enable individuals to actively participate in the production of culture, ranging from discussion of public issues to creation of their own cultural forms, enabling those who had been previously excluded from cultural production and mainstream politics to participate in the creation of culture and sociopolitical activism.

Educated and empowered youth may be able to overcome the alienation and disempowerment evident in the school shooters discussed in this study. A postmodern pedagogy requires developing critical forms of print, media, computer, and multiple forms of technoliteracy, all of which are of crucial importance in the technoculture of the present and fast-approaching future (Kahn and Kellner 2006; Kellner and Share 2007), and may help enable youth to play a constructive role in the production of the future. Indeed, contemporary culture is marked by a proliferation of image machines that generate a panorama of print, sound, environmental, and diverse aesthetic artefacts within which we wander, trying to make our way through this forest of symbols. And so we need to begin learning how to read these images, these fascinating and seductive cultural forms whose massive impact on our lives we have only begun to understand. Surely, education should attend to the multimedia culture and teach how to read images and narratives as part of media, computer, and technoculture literacy, as well as to use new media and technologies to provide a voice, educate, mobilize for social change, and construct a democratic future.[19]

Such an effort would be linked to a revitalized critical pedagogy that attempts to empower individuals so that they can analyze and criticize the emerging technoculture, as well as participate in producing its cultural and political forums and sites. More than ever, we need philosophical reflection on the ends and purposes of educational technology, and on what we are doing and trying to achieve with it in our educational practices and institutions. In this situation, it may be instructive to return to John Dewey and see the connections between education, technology, and democracy; the need for the reconstruction of education and society; and the value of experimental pedagogy to seek solutions to the problems of education in the present day. A progressive reconstruction of education will urge that it be done in the interests of democratization, ensuring access to information and communication technologies for all, thereby helping to overcome the so-called digital divide and divisions of the haves and have-nots so that education is placed in the service of democracy and social justice (Dewey, [1916] 1997; Freire 1972, 1998) in light of Illich's (1970, 1971, 1973) critiques of the limitations and challenges of education in postindustrial societies. Yet, we should be more aware than Dewey, Freire, and Illich of the obduracy of the divisions of class, gender, and race, and so work self-consciously for multicultural democracy and education. This task suggests that we valorize difference and cultural specificity, as well as equality and shared universal Deweyean values such as freedom, equality, individualism, and participation.

A major challenge for education today is thus to promote computer and media literacy to empower students and citizens to use a wide range of technologies to enhance their lives and create a better culture and society. In particular, this involves developing Internet projects that articulate with important cultural and political struggles in the contemporary world, developing pedagogies whereby students work together transmitting their technical knowledge to other students and their teachers, and teachers and students work together in developing relevant educational material, projects, and pedagogies in the experimental Deweyean and Freirean mode.

Teachers and students, then, need to develop new pedagogies and modes of learning for new information and multimedia environments. This should involve a democratization and reconstruction of education such as was envisaged by Dewey, Freire, Illich, and Marcuse, in which education is seen as a dialogical, democraticizing, and experimental practice. New information technologies acting along the lines of Illich's conceptions of "webs of learning" and "tools for conviviality" (1971, 1973) encourage the sort of experimental and collaborative projects proposed by Dewey, and can also involve the more dialogical and nonauthoritarian relations between students and teachers that Freire envisaged. In this respect, the re-visioning of education involves the recognition that teachers can learn from students and that often students are ahead of their teachers in a variety of technological literacies and technical abilities. Many of us have learned much of what we know of computers and new media and technologies from our students. We should also recognize the extent to which young people helped to invent the Internet and have grown up in a culture in which they may have readily cultivated technological skills from an early age.[20] Peer-to-peer communication among young people is thus often a highly sophisticated development, and democratic pedagogies should build on and enhance these resources and practices.

One of the challenges of contemporary education is to overcome the separation between students' experiences, subjectivities, and interests, which are rooted in the new multimedia technoculture, and the classroom situations, which are grounded in print culture, traditional learning methods, and disciplines (Luke and Luke 2002). The disconnect can be addressed, however, by more actively and collaboratively bringing students into interactive classrooms, or learning situations, in which they are able to transmit their skills and knowledges to fellow students and teachers alike. Such a democratic and interactive reconstruction of education thus provides the resources for a democratic social reconstruction, and it cultivates the new skills and literacies needed for the global media economy. So far, arguments for restructuring education mostly come from the hi-tech and corporate sectors, which are primarily interested in new media and literacies for the workforce and capitalist profit. But reconstruction can serve the interests of democratization as well as the elite corporate few. Following Dewey, we should accordingly militate for education that aims at producing democratic citizens, even as it provides skills for the workplace and for social and cultural life.

Further, schools can teach nonviolent conflict resolution and media literacy courses that are critical of the ultraviolent images of masculinity circulating in the mainstream media, and that offer alternative images. Young men and women, in turn, need to construct healthier conceptions of masculinity and femininity and see the destructive effects of violence. There have been educational interventions that address hypermasculinity, violence against women, and homophobia, and that provide alternatives to a hegemonic violent masculinity. For example, since 1993 author and activist Jackson Katz and his colleagues have been implementing the Mentors in Violence Prevention (MVP) program, which trains high school, college, and professional athletes and other student leaders to speak out and oppose violence against women, gay-bashing, and other forms of domestic and sexual violence. Featuring interactive workshops and training sessions in single-sex and mixed-gender settings, as well as public lectures, MVP has been expanded throughout North America to deal with men's violence in many arenas, from the corporation to the political arena, police, and intelligence agencies, and other institutional arenas where men's violence is a problem.[21]

This is not to say that masculinity per se, or the traits associated with it, is all bad. There are times when being strong, independent, self-reliant, and even aggressive can serve positive goals and resist oppression and injustice. A post-gendered human being would share traits now associated with women and men, so that women could exhibit the positive traits associated with men and men could be more loving, caring, emotional, vulnerable, and other traits associated with women. Gender itself should be deconstructed, and while we should fight gender oppression and inequality, there are reasons to question gender itself in a more emancipated and democratic world, in which individuals create their own personalities and lives out of the potential found traditionally in men and women.

Toward a New Radical Pedagogy

The radical pedagogy that I envisage, which will guide a democratic reconstruction of the present age, will combine the work of Herbert

Marcuse and the Frankfurt School with that of a wide range of critical educators. Marcuse and the Frankfurt School both provide a framework to criticize education within the context of a one-dimensional society and offer alternative pedagogical perspectives and a "re-schooling of society" (see the studies in Kellner et al. 2009).

Similarly to Marcuse, both Paulo Freire and Ivan Illich saw that a glaring problem with contemporary educational institutions was that they have become fixed in monomodal instruction, with homogenized lesson plans, curricula, and pedagogy, and that they neglect to address challenging political, cultural, and ecological problems. The development of convivial tools and radically democratic pedagogies can enable teachers and students to break with these models and engage in a form of Deweyean experimental education. The reconstruction of education can help to create subjects better able to negotiate the complexities of emergent modes of everyday life, labor, and culture, as contemporary life becomes ever more multifaceted and dangerous. Supportive, dialogical, and interactive social relations in critical learning situations can promote cooperation, democracy, and positive social values, as well as fulfill needs for communication, esteem, and politicized learning. Whereas modern mass education has tended to see life in a linear fashion based on print models and has developed pedagogies that have divided experience into discrete moments and behavioral bits, critical pedagogies produce skills that enable individuals to better navigate and synthesize the multiple realms and challenges of contemporary life. Deweyean education focused on problem solving, goal-seeking projects, and the courage to be experimental, while Freire developed critical problem-posing pedagogies of the oppressed aiming at social justice and progressive social transformation, while Illich offered oppositional conceptions of education and alternatives to oppressive institutions. It is exactly this sort of critical spirit and vision, which calls for the reconstruction of education along with society, that can help produce more radicalized pedagogies, tools for social and ecological justice, and utopian possibilities for a better world.

A democratic reconstruction of education will involve producing democratic citizens and empowering the next generation for democracy. Moreover, as Freire reminds us (1972 and 1998), critical pedagogy comprises the skills of both reading the word and reading the world. Hence, multiple literacies include not only media and computer literacies, but a diverse range of social and cultural literacies, ranging from ecoliteracy (e.g., understanding the body and environment), to economic and financial literacy to a variety of other competencies that enable us to live well in our social worlds. Education, at its best, provides the symbolic and cultural capital that empowers people to survive and prosper in an increasingly complex and changing world and the resources to produce a more cooperative, democratic, egalitarian, and just society.[22]

Overcoming the alienation of students and youth is, of course, a utopian dream, but in the light of growing societal violence, domestic terrorism, and school shootings, such a reconstruction of education and society is necessary to help produce a life worthy of human beings.

Notes

1. See National Center for Injury Prevention and Control, US Centers for Disease Control and Prevention, *Web-Based Injury Statistics Query and Reporting System (WISQARS) Injury Mortality Reports, 1999–2009, for National, Regional, and States* (Sept. 2011) at http://www.lcav.org/statistics-polling/gun _violence_statistics.asp (accessed on April 4, 2012). A useful website collects statistics on gun violence, including murders, suicides, domestic violence, gun accidents, gun victims according to age and race, and other factors at http://www .lcav.org/statistics-polling/gun_violence_statistics.asp (accessed on April 4, 2012).

2. The first statistic is from Reuters News Service; for the remainder, see "US shooting suspect was teased," *PressTV*, April 6, 2012, at http://www.presstv.ir/usdetail/234881.html (accessed on April 17, 2012).

3. See "A time line of recent worldwide school shootings" at http://www.infoplease.com/ipa/A0777958.html (accessed on April 4, 2012).

4. The quote can be found at http://www.goodreads.com/book/show/1901337 .The_Shooting_Game (accessed on April 5, 2012).

5. "A Time Line," at http://www.infoplease.com/ipa/A0777958.html (accessed on April 4, 2012).

6. On my approach to cultural studies and critical theory, see Kellner and Durham (2012) and Hammer and Kellner (2009).

7. For a balanced and informed account of the Bellesiles controversy, see Wiener (2004). For Winkler's account of the promotion and limitations of Bellesiles' scholarship, see Winkler (2011), pp. 22–31.

8. See Adam Liptak, "A liberal case for the individual right to own guns helps sway the federal judiciary," *New York Times*, May 7, 2007, p. A18. Liptak notes that "there used to be an almost complete scholarly and judicial consensus that the Second Amendment protects only a collective right of the states to maintain militias. That consensus no longer exists—thanks largely to the work over the last 20 years of several leading liberal law professors, who have come to embrace the view that the Second Amendment protects an individual right to own guns." Liptak suggests that opinions over the last two decades by liberal law professors helped produce a decision whereby a federal appeals court struck down in March 2007 a gun control law on Second Amendment grounds. Adam Winkler (2011), whom I discuss later, documents how the militia argument for

interpreting the Second Amendment and gun rights has been replaced by interpreting the Second Amendment in terms of private gun ownership.

9. Interestingly, Barbara Kopple's HBO documentary *Gun Fight* (2011), with the same title and year of release as Winkler's book, has quite a different take on the debate between gun control and gun rights forces in the United States. While Winkler presents the two camps as extremist and diametrically opposed, Kopple's film shows gun control forces who are extremely reasonable, especially major figures in the Brady Center gun control camp, who are shown as moderate. In the film *Gun Fight,* they insist that they are simply advocating that the gun show loopholes where individuals can buy guns from private dealers at gun shows without any background check, registration, or paper trail would be closed. By contrast, Winkler presents the Brady group as extreme "gun grabbers," whose goal is banning and seizing all guns (p. 35), a position at odds with their portrayal in Kopple's *Gun Fight.* It thus appears that Winkler's attempt to brand gun control advocates as unabashedly absolutist in a desire to ban guns completely is problematic.

10. On the April *60 Minutes* report see http://www.cbsnews.com/stories/2009/04/09/60minutes/main4931769.shtml (accessed on April 15, 2012). See also, "Gun Sales: Will The 'Loophole' Close?," *CBS News*, July 26, 2009, at http://www.cbsnews.com/2100-18560_162-4931769.html (accessed on April 15, 2012).

11. See "Gun dealer sold to both Va. Tech, NIU shooters," *USA Today*, February 16, 2008, at http://www.usatoday.com/news/nation/2008-02-16-gundealer-niu-vatech-shooters_N.htm (accessed on April 16, 2012). Interestingly, Eric Thompson's company, TGSCOM Inc., which sold Cho and Kazmierczak weapons through his website www.thegunsource.com, offered customers weapons at cost for two weeks to help citizens get the weapons they needed for their own self-defense; see "Owner of Web-based Firearms Company that Sold to Virginia Tech and NIU Shooters to Forgo Profits to Help Prevent Future Loss of Life," April 25, 2008, *TGSCOM Inc.* at http://www.thegunsource.com/Article.aspx?aKey=Guns_at_Cost (accessed on April 16, 2012).

12. On the failure of Obama and other leaders of the Democratic Party to address gun control during the 2008 presidential election, see Derrick Z. Jackson, "Missing on gun control," *Boston Globe*, February 19, 2008 at http://www.boston.com/bostonglobe/editorial_opinion/oped/articles/2008/02/19/missing_on_gun_control/ (accessed on April 4, 2012). Adam Winkler recently claimed that "few presidents have shown as little interest in gun control as Barack Obama. . . . It's as if 'avoid gun control at all costs' has become a plank in the Democratic Party platform." Cited in Mitchell Landsberg, "NRA is restless despite clout. The group is so worried about Obama that it is willing to ignore Romney's past," *Los Angeles Times*, April 13, 2012: AA7. The Obama administration and Congress also failed to pass gun control legislation after the shock of the murder of twenty young students and six teachers in the Newtown massacre in December 2012. See "The Sandy Hook slaughter and copy cat killers in a media celebrity society: Analyses and plans for action," *Logos*, 12, no. 1, winter 2013 at http://logosjournal.com/2013/kellner/ (accessed March 25, 2013).

13. This volume contains articles examining the need, appropriateness, and efficacy of school antiviolence policies; see Parts 2 and 3.

14. Cited in Nick Gillespie, "The FCC's not mommy and daddy," *Los Angeles Times*, May 2, 2007: A23.

15. See Herbert Marcuse, "A Revolution in Values," in Marcuse (2001), and on the new sensibility, see my introduction to the volume of collected papers of Marcuse on *Art and Liberation* (2006).

16. This misplaced pedagogy of teaching for testing did not just originate with the Bush administration, but has long been a feature of pedagogically challenged schools; see Janet Ewell, "Test-takers, not students," *Los Angeles Times,* May 26, 2007: A19. For some compelling criticism of Bush administration "No Child Left Behind" policies, see the dossier "Correcting Schools," *The Nation,* May 21, 2007, pp. 11–21.

17. See Jones (2002) and Kahn and Kellner (2005). Some good sites that exhibit youth voices, participation, and politics include http://www.moveon.org; http://www.raisethefist.com; http://www.tao.com; and the youth blog site at http://www.Bloghop.com/topics.htm?numblogs=14566&cacheid=1044419966.3 569 (accessed on May 14, 2007). Since the boom of Facebook and social networking, youth sites and productions on YouTube, Twitter, and other new media forms are exploding exponentially

18. See Best and Kellner (2001) and Kahn and Kellner (2005).

19. There is neither space nor context in this article to express the downsides of new media, social networking, and the growing power of technology in this society. For serious reservations concerning these phenomena, see Morozov (2011). To counter negative effects that new technologies and social media may produce, I am arguing that a critical pedagogy that delineates how to use new technologies constructively to enhance education and democracy and that warns against its limitations and problematic aspects is necessary.

20. For instance, Mosaic, Netscape, and the first browsers were invented by young computer users, as were many of the first websites, listservs, chat rooms, and so on. A "hacker culture" emerged that was initially conceptualized as reconfiguring and improving the design, implementation, and use of computer systems, before the term became synonymous with theft and mischief, such as setting loose worms and viruses. On youth and Internet subcultures, see Kahn and Kellner (2003).

21. Information, publications, films, and other material on the Mentors in Violence Program can be found at http://www.jacksonkatz.com/ (accessed April 4, 2012). There is also a book *Violence Goes to College: The Authoritative Guide to Prevention and Intervention* (Nicoletti, Spencer-Thomas, and Bollinger 2001) assembled by a group that has yearly conferences on university violence in a multiplicity of forms and develops violence prevention strategies. Available online at http://books.google.com/books/about/Violence_Goes_to_College.html?id =T_ClourcxRwC (accessed on April 4, 2012).

22. For my further perspectives on developing a critical theory of education and reconstructing education, see Kellner (2004, 2006).

Part 4
Conclusion

13

Conclusion:
School Safety and Society

Stuart Henry, Nicole L. Bracy,
Glenn W. Muschert, and Anthony A. Peguero

> The merging of school and penal system has speeded the collapse of the progressive project of education and tilted the administration of schools toward a highly authoritarian and mechanistic model. This model collapses all the normal /expected /predictable vulnerabilities of youth into variations of the categories of criminal violence. This transformation is especially problematic since when the generally preferred "solution"—the tight policing of everyone—fails, as it inevitably will, the response is to shift responsibility onto everyone but the incumbent regime, primarily through such emotionally satisfying, but substantively empty, slogans as "accountability" and "zero tolerance." (Simon 2007, p. 9)

The chapters in Parts 1 and 2 of this book argue that the current cluster of school antiviolence policies not only fail to effectively prevent school violence, but they also transform schools from their potential of being nurturing sites of education and learning to sites of distrust, suspicion, fear, and symbolic aggression. We have seen how the formation of school antiviolence policy is based on the social construction of school violence through distorted media images and the fear of risk. The Columbine Effect became the exemplar for a set of policies that have had little effect on the problem of school violence in its most pervasive forms, but have had far-ranging negative effects on schools and the educational environment. In the thesis of presented in *Governing Through Crime,* Simon (2007) argues that the human subject "as victim" was elevated in importance and the governing priority became protection through tough, zero-tolerance policies of crime control. Applying this perspective to education, we are now seeing "Schooling Through Crime," whereby education and the environment for the care and nurturance of children is framed and mediated through the lens of crime control. In the previous chapters we have seen the transformative effects on the school personnel as they implement fear-driven policies that satiate a desire for safe and secure schools in a climate of uncertainty, searching for control amid the social vertigo of late modernity (Young 2007b). We have seen how school violence is used to justify control of behavior that has nothing to do with crime, but everything to do with alienation, resistance, and the existing distribution of power. We have seen how moral and political issues about schooling are depoliticized as urgent matters of control for safety, just as medicalization had made antisocial behavior a sickness some thirty years earlier (Conrad 1980; Searight and McLaren 1998). We have also seen how the community of schooling has succumbed to the formality of the control as, for example, school resource officers (SROs) increasingly arrest those who violate school rules, and as school administrators use courts and juvenile justice interventions instead of having conversations with parents and peers, as happens in schools that have not adopted SROs (Rich-Shea and Fox in this volume). In a reversal of Black's (1976) *Behavior of Law,* we have seen how, in this zero-tolerance environment, the more specialized functions of policing (symbolizing formal law) supplant traditional mechanisms of informal social control, in an increasing spiral of professional protection, dehumanized surveillance, and entry screening.

The contributors to Part 3 of this volume, however, highlighted alternative developments that counterpose this trend. While it is possible to envisage a variety of different approaches, the chapters presented here focus on the importance of taking an ecological approach that embodies antiviolence policies using restorative justice practices in a climate of peacemaking, rather than the more prevalent environment of conflict-sustaining control. Thus, we have seen how unacceptable behavior, rather than resulting in suspension and expulsion, can provide an opportunity for community building, settlement-directed discussion, peer mediation, and school-community dialog, all designed to restore the peace for the victim, the offender, and their community. Under these alternative models, school violence is seen as a preventable event in a process that involves active learning and collaborative problem solving, rather than one of exclusion, isolation, and punishment. We have seen that the Peaceable Schools Movement requires transforming the school organization, school climate, curriculum, and educational process, and replacing violence and symbolic violence, while operating at all levels of the organization with education for peace as opposed to education for war (Brock-Utne 1985; Caulfield 2000; Pepinsky 2000; Winslade and Williams, 2011). This approach encourages acts of kindness, forgiveness, trust building, responsibility, care, and love. Importantly, it requires a commitment from teachers and administrators themselves to model nonviolent approaches to conflict, and it also benefits them by relieving them of disciplinary burdens, allowing them to focus on their educational duties (Caulfield 2000). "It involves a mutual participatory sharing of thoughts ideas and experiences, rather than a hierarchical power relationship between teacher and learner. Educating for peace is ultimately about doing peace, not learning about it in mere abstraction" (Pepinsky 2000, p. 157).

In this concluding chapter we argue that the policies for addressing school violence need to be based not on emotion and fear, as in the punitive zero-tolerance model that emerged from the post-Columbine era, nor solely on its ideological counterpart of peacemaking, which imagines a society of structural equality that is not representative of the reality of late-modern society today. Rather, we argue that sound school antiviolence policy must be based on a rational, logical policy formation process that identifies, through a synchronized and integrated approach, the range of causes for school violence in its manifest forms and seeks to comprehensively address these as they occur at each level of a society's structure. Indeed, we have seen that recent developments in the school violence literature call for a recognition that school violence has multiple causes operating at different levels of society, and that an integrated, multicausal analysis of school violence demands "a comprehensive, policy response that takes account of the full range of constitutive elements" (Henry 2000, p. 16; see also Benbenishty and Astor 2005; Centers for Disease Control and Prevention [CDC] 2008; Espelage and Swearer 2004; Henry 2009; Henry and Bracy 2012; Hong et al. 2011; Muschert 2007b; Muschert and Peguero 2010).

Elsewhere we have argued that psychological, spatial, social, cultural, political, and structural causes reciprocally interact to generate occasions of escalating violence in schools over time, which can ultimately result in rampage shootings and mass homicide (Henry 2009; Henry and Bracy 2012). If our integrated multilevel analysis is correct, what policies offered by the variety of causal explanations can be brought together into a comprehensive integrative policy response to the complex social problem of school violence? This concluding chapter explores the insights on public policy designed to prevent school violence and the kind of interventions that an integrated, comprehensive public policy on school violence should contain in order to address its cocontributing multicausal factors. Importantly, we argue that such an integrated public policy would need to address the reciprocal and interactive nature of the problem of violence as it develops and changes over time. However, we also argue that such a comprehensive integrated policy is not simply a bundling together of the diverse range of policies that currently exist, regardless of their orientation, but that we need to draw specifically on policies that resonate with each other in addressing the identified causes to build a socially transformative, comprehensive approach.

An Interactive-Cumulative Approach to Understanding School Violence

In examining school violence as a subcategory of the more general phenomenon of violence, it has been noted that there are a complex set of influences, or multiple causes, that operate at the individual, community, and national levels and that these "incidents need to be understood as resulting from a constellation of contributing causes, none of which is sufficient in itself to explain a shooting" (Muschert 2007b, p. 68; see also CDC 2008; Garbarino 1999, p. 13; Henry 2000, p. 17; Henry 2009; Newman 2004, p. 229).

For example, Muschert (2007b, pp. 68–69) identifies thirteen categories of "cause" for school shootings, "ranging from the individual causes, community contexts, and social/cultural contexts in which the events occur" (Muschert 2007b, pp. 67–68). These include (1) "individual" causes such as mental illness, access to guns, peer relationships, and family neglect or abuse; (2) "community" contexts, such as youth and peer dynamics; (3) "institutional" contexts, such as school-based interaction that encompasses poor student-faculty relationships, ineffective school administration, inability of communities to respond to delinquency or excessively oppressive community responses to delinquency, and intolerant community climate; (4) the "social and cultural" level, such as the crisis in public school education, gender-based violence, conservative religious political climate, gun culture, and media violence (Muschert 2007b, p. 69).

Some school violence researchers have envisioned these levels not only as interacting, but as "nested" from the micro- to macro-structural levels (Benbenishty and Astor 2005; Henry 2000; Muschert

2007b; Welsh, Greene, and Jenkins 1999). For example, Benbenishty and Astor (2005, p. 113) state that school violence "is the product of many factors that are associated with multiple levels organized hierarchically (nested like a matryoshka doll): individual students within classes, classes within schools, schools within neighborhoods, and neighborhoods within societies and cultures."

Henry (2009) applied this integrated, multilevel analysis to school violence to show how different causal theories can be integrated to explain school violence. He argues that in order to examine such complex social problems, such as school violence, "we need to take a wide-angle interdisciplinary lens to the nature of what constitutes violence in schools and retain the connection between school violence and violence at various levels within the institution of the school and the wider society" (Henry 2009, p. 1248). While conventional analyses of school violence attempt to explain each subtype of school violence, without recognizing the cumulative interrelations and interaction between them, Henry argues that school violence is a broad phenomenon with multiple manifest forms that together compose a continuum of violence. Indeed, even within the structure of the school there are multiple levels of school violence that can be distinguished by the level of their perpetrators within the social structure of the school and in society more generally. In an earlier statement, Henry (2000) identifies five somewhat distinct levels. The levels embody power differentials between participants that shape the nature of the conflict, which manifests as violence with different targets or victims:

- Level 1 Violence: Student on student; student on teacher; student on school.
- Level 2 Violence: Teacher on student; administrator on student; administrator on teacher; teacher or administrator on parent; parent on teacher or administrator.
- Level 3 Violence: School board on school or parent; school district on school or parent; community on school or parent; local political decisions on school or parent.
- Level 4 Violence: State and national educational policy on school; state and national juvenile justice policy on student; media and popular culture on student and administrator; corporate exploitation on students; national and state policies on guns and drugs.
- Level 5 Violence: Harmful social processes and practices that pervade each of the previous four levels. Here social processes

are the patterns of interaction that, over time, take on the appearance of a natural order or social reality existing above the individuals whose actions constitute that structure (Henry 2000, pp. 25–26).

Policy analysis related to the problem of school violence tends to be restricted to Level 1 and some aspects of Level 4. Even within Level 1, some important distinctions can be made. For example, not all violence by students is similarly motivated or subject to the same causes. Kramer (2000) identified three types of school violence: (1) predatory economic crimes, which involve the pursuit of material goals by any means, including violence; (2) drug industry crimes, which involve violent gang turf wars; and (3) social relationship violence from powerless, angry youths who use acts of violence to resolve issues of humiliation from their alienation. These differently motivated forms of violence suggest different causal mechanisms at work and indicate that any policy designed to reduce school violence cannot operate effectively simply by gearing its intervention at the individual perpetrators, but must seek to address these more macro-level causes that produce the conditions conducive to violence. Indeed, not all school students respond in the same way to the conditions that generate violence, even within Level 1. How students act has much to do with the structural forces of class, race, and gender (Yogan and Henry 2000). Moreover, how the system targets some students rather than others for discipline and control and the severity of the punishment dispensed are subject to the same social forces (Welch and Payne in this volume).

In contrast to the excessive discussion of micro-level causes and targeted policies focused on harsh control, there has been virtually no analysis of the wider contextual cultural and structural causes and the appropriate policies to deal with them. Where this has occurred (see CDC 2008; Hong et al. in this volume; Kellner in this volume) there has not been an attempt to integrate these policies at different levels so that they are consistent with an overall societal objective or principle. Moreover, given the interrelations between these types, the manifestation of different causes, and the partial nature of the policy, this fragmented approach leaves much of the complexity unaddressed. Indeed, it is the culmination of these processes that can make the difference between a crescendo outcome in the form of extreme violence or less violent results. Existing policies designed to prevent and control school violence are largely based on assumptions found in criminal justice ideologies and crime control practices, without addressing the multiple root causes, interaction between causes, or the wider social and cultural contexts in which they are embedded. These policies can, therefore, be both contradictory and counterproductive.

As shown in this volume, Jun Sung Hong and Dorothy L. Espelage and colleagues (see Espelage and Swearer, 2003, 2004, 2011; Hong et al. 2011) advocate a multilevel social ecology approach to the analysis of school violence and bullying. In particular, they draw on Bronfenbrenner's (1979) ecological systems theory to demonstrate that cause and policy intervention need to address micro-, meso-, macro-levels of society, as well as the exo-system involving the interaction between various levels. They state, "It is imperative that school violence interventions need to consider the multilevel ecological environment in which youths and their schools are situated . . . rather than simply identifying factors that contribute to violence" (Hong et al. in this volume).

Thus, although there seems to be considerable agreement among our contributors that a multilevel ecological approach offers the best basis for the future development of school antiviolence policy, the integration of that policy falls short. The problem is that which policies we include at each level of analysis makes a critical difference to our ability to transform the problem. We argue, based on the analysis of the contributors to this volume, that not all policies and interventions are equal, and that simply because they can be developed, targeted, and implemented for different analytical *levels* does not mean that they are equally effective or desirable. The simple solution to this dilemma might seem to be to suggest that policies at different levels be subject to empirical evaluation to see which are effective and which are not. While such an evidence-based approach might seem helpful, it lacks a holistic framework. What might be effective at a micro-level might have negative or unintended consequences at a meso- or macro-level, and vice versa. We are reminded of Popisil's (1971, p. 125) insightful observations about the contradictions of the plurality of law and subsystems that impose different and oppositional normative imperatives on their members; so too with antiviolence policy. Rather, we believe that the policy approach to school violence needs to be multilevel, comprehensive, and synchronized between its various levels. Such an approach begs the question about the characteristics of the various policy elements operative at the different levels.

Synchronization of Policy
Toward a Comprehensive Integrated Approach

As we have seen, the term *Columbine Effect* (Cloud 1999; Muschert and Peguero 2010) has been used to characterize the popular discourse around school violence in America; specifically, that school rampage shootings, despite their rarity, strongly define how the public thinks about school violence, perpetrators of school violence, and their victims. The fear generated by school rampage shootings has played a significant role in shaping contemporary school security and discipline policies. We have seen that these policies operate at multiple levels and draw on different disciplinary-based theoretical assumptions (Henry 2009; Henry and Bracy 2012) in order to achieve a variety of policy outcomes (Hong et al. 2011; Hong et al. in this volume). Consequently, we argue that these policies are limited in their ability to comprehensively address the complex problem of school violence and, in some cases, exacerbate student misbehavior and make the school climate deteriorate.

Acknowledging the CDC's (2008) point that societal-level changes are difficult to achieve, this is not the whole reason for the imbalance toward the micro- and meso-levels of policy intervention, nor is it because macro-level changes have distal effects. Rather, this policy bias has to do with our society's ideological position that the problems of school violence stem mainly from individuals, specifically the students and their parents, rather than the system, the community, or the wider culture or social structure (see Muschert and Ragnedda 2010). As long as we continue to view school violence in this way, we will continue to fall short in our goals of creating safer schools.

Rather than taking policies in isolation or as alternatives, we argue that effective prevention policy requires the multiple, cumulative causes of school violence to be simultaneously addressed through a comprehensive web of synchronous policies. It is helpful in this analysis to expand the policy framework advocated by Morrison (2007; Morrison and Vaandering 2012) in her restorative justice approach to building relationships. Here she draws on the public health triangle to produce a whole school approach to safe schools as communities of relationships based on strengthening social and emotional skills. The paradigm shift that this whole school approach takes is justified on the basis that problems of discipline and violence are part of a wider set of relationships and cannot be treated in isolation.

Indeed, the model supports a holistic approach: "Social engagement with its emphasis on human beings as worthy, interconnected, and relational, creates a school context where students are respected within the institution's main practices of pedagogy and praxis" (Morrison and Vaandering 2012, p. 151). Instead of excluding and punishing, restorative justice sees violence as a form of conflict and acts proactively to find alternative ways to resolve conflict, such as peer mediation, or other forms of settlement-directed talking, such as restorative conferencing and peacemaking circles (Morrison and Vaandering 2012; Stinchcomb, Bazemore, and Riestenberg 2006; Stutzman-Amstutz and Mullet, 2005). Restorative justice can operate as these specific policy practices or as a whole school or universal approach:

> Primary restorative practices involve the entire school community and aim at establishing a values ethic, as well as skill base, for developing relational ecologies and resolving differences in respectful and caring ways. Secondary restorative practices address specific behaviors that disrupt the harmony and social relations of classrooms (e.g., problem-solving circles), hallways (e.g., corridor conferences) and playgrounds (e.g., peer mediations). Tertiary restorative practices are the most intensive, often responding to serious harm, and involve all those affected (including families, professionals, fellow students, and others affected) in a face-to-face restorative justice process. (Morrison and Vaandering 2012, p. 144)

At the whole school level, restorative justice practices create a relational ecology that operates from "classroom, playground, school, or neighborhood," and provides "a distinct institutional space" that responds to "all relationships occurring in schools, such as an administrator's interactions, policy decisions, a teacher's pedagogy and curriculum, as well as professional and institutional development" (Morrison and Vaandering 2012, p. 145). The change goes beyond the micro-level in that it represents "a shift away from being a rule-based institution to a relationship-based institution, or from being an institution whose purpose is social control to being an institution that nurtures social engagement" (Morrison and Vaandering 2012, p. 145).

If this is true for individual behavior within a school, it is surely true for individual behavior within neighborhoods and communities, for communities within societies, and for societies as a whole. We need a whole-society synchronous approach to building relationships between schools and institutions within communities, and between communities, such that each reinforces the same ethos and values that sees people as embedded in webs of networks of relationships that are interdependent and interrelated. As relationship networks in schools are replicated in the wider social contexts, these contexts of caring become more inclusive, less alienating, and less divisive. Policy at each level resonates with and reinforces policy at the other levels. However, we also need to implement societal-level policies that deconstruct the fragmentation and individualized punishment that are part of our wider structure and culture. Restorative justice in the classroom, or even in the school, requires restorative justice in the community and in the society at large, if we are to reverse the Columbine Effect.

As stated, societal macro-level policy that is synchronous with the relational work that can be implemented in the school context is difficult to reproduce. Societal-level change refers to policy changes that go beyond individual psychological and interactional causes (the micro-level), and also beyond the organizational and institutional causes (meso-level or mid-level), to address macro-level cultural and structural causes and their policy and practice implications. Approaches to school violence at the societal level recognize that schools are microcosms of larger society and that, in order to be effective, violence prevention must involve changes to the wider context of social organization:

> School violence . . . prevention should address all levels of school violence: individual, relationship, community and society. . . . Strategies to change the social and cultural climate to reduce youth violence are often difficult and infrequently used. Examples of strategies that may facilitate lasting change include addressing social norms via information campaigns, reducing media violence, reforming institutional educational systems at the institutional level. (CDC 2008, p. 4)

The media, for example, focus on the institution of the school as the theater of violence, but do not look for the macro-level scriptwriters. One set of scriptwriters is the media itself. Through sensationalized stories of extreme instances of school violence, students and parents are led by the media to distorted beliefs that schools are violent environments, beliefs reinforced by increased security measures in schools (Kupchik and Bracy 2009). In addition to the media's distortion of school violence, the media sensationalizes violence more broadly and exaggerates its incidence so that youth are swamped with violent messages involving images of injury and death. The effects of this are a brutalization of our youth. Research clearly documents that exposure to violence in the media has a consistent and substantial impact on youth aggressive behavior (see Bushman and Huesmann 2006, for example). The clear policy implication is that any comprehensive policy addressing school violence must address the wider media in ways that provide a replacement discourse focusing on community building, relationship building, and problem-solving restorative practices.

Parting Words

This volume has brought together experts in the fields of education, criminology, sociolegal studies, gender studies, psychology, and sociology to reflect on the ways in which schools are responding to school violence—both the actual violence that occurs in schools and the omnipresent threat of a "Columbine-style" mass homicide. As the authors and editors argue, what schools have largely neglected to notice is the manner in which they are reproducing violence and harm through their prevention policies. The project has involved an effort to connect three areas of academic work that rarely converge: (1) discursive studies of the social construction of the social problem of school violence in the media discourse and beyond; (2) policy studies that examine the philosophy, implementation, and effects of contemporary school antiviolence policies (including their oftentimes unintended negative consequences); and (3) studies that examine the complex etiology of school violence, with an eye toward prescribing policy responses that have been empirically demonstrated to be effective at reducing violence in schools while resolving conflict in the social ecology. An important point of these perspectives, which are often restorative and peacemaking in their approach, is that they typically consider the unintended negative consequences of more punitive approaches such as zero-tolerance policies, school exclusion, and increased surveillance.

By producing a volume connecting discursive studies of the social construction of the problem with analytical and proscriptive policy studies, it is our hope that we can push the discourse of school violence in a fruitful direction: toward understanding the complexity of the problem, and the extent to which violence is integrated into fundamental social institutions and relations. As one of our editorial team has written elsewhere, Columbine is a "keyword for a complex set of emotions surrounding youth, fear, risk, and delinquency in 21st

Century America" (Muschert 2007a, p. 365). Indeed, the Columbine Effect stems from equally complex rhetorical and practical positions, which have viewed incidents of school violence as a problem in need to control, rather than as symptoms of underlying social conflict and perhaps the dysfunction of our social ecologies on the meso- and macro-levels. In recent decades, the regime of social control in schools has tended toward the punitive, and as has been demonstrated here, the Columbine event and the discussion that ensued served as a catalyst for such development. However, as the pendulum eventually swings back, we observe that many stakeholders (academics, administrators, school security professionals, and policymakers) seem increasingly aware of the unintended negative consequences of punitive measures, and it is our hope that our volume will contribute in a modest way both to a reassessment of the current regime of control and to a movement to create more positive, constructive, and efficacious antiviolence policies for our children, our schools, our communities, and our societies.

Postscript

Shortly before this volume went to press, the United States experienced a horrific instance of school violence when twenty children and six adults were killed at Sandy Hook Elementary School in Newtown, Connecticut. This was the most deadly episode of school violence in the United States since the Virginia Tech shootings in 2007 and the most deadly involving elementary school children since the Bath, Michigan, School Massacre in 1927.

Not surprisingly, the media response to the Sandy Hook shootings was immediate and intense. In fact, many of the editors and authors of this volume, recognized as experts on the topic of school violence, were called on by various news media outlets across the country to provide context, explanation, and advice. Even for experts, these are difficult questions to answer. Despite the attention given by the media to this event and others that have preceded it, homicides in schools are rare events and mass homicides even rarer (Robers, Zhang, and Truman 2012). So while in the aftermath this tragedy it may offer little consolation, schools are still among the safest places for children and youth.

Multiple solutions have been publicly proposed in the days and weeks immediately following Sandy Hook, ranging from stricter gun control laws and increased police power to confiscate guns from potentially mentally ill gun owners to placing armed security guards in every school, each with its own laundry list of shortcomings and caveats. What occurred at Sandy Hook was a different type of school violence than is discussed throughout the chapters in this book. Unlike at Columbine or Virginia Tech, where students turned guns on their peers and teachers, the tragedy at Sandy Hook Elementary was committed by an outsider—someone with no apparent ties to the school, the staff, or the students. This particular act could not have been prevented via more harmonious school discipline policies or a more positive school climate, as authors in this volume argue are instrumental to school violence prevention. Indeed, as we argue in the conclusion of this book, what is needed is a synchronous, integrated policy that operates at multiple levels of society. The safest, most peaceful schools, which preempt conflict before it manifests into escalating violence and replace escalating violence with restorative justice practices, do nothing to engage the community. The result is that peaceable schools in fragmented communities are not sustainable. The community and the society each need to also develop integrated peacemaking approaches that would lead to early identification to pinpoint and help community outliers and potential threats.

The editors and authors of this volume share the nation's grief over the tragic loss of lives at Sandy Hook Elementary School and call for balanced, evidence-based responses that repair rather than replicate harm.

References

Addington, L. 2008. *Columbine ten years later: The effect of deadly school violence on school security and student civil liberties.* Paper presented at the Annual Meeting of the American Society of Criminology, Philadelphia.

Addington, L.A. 2009. Cops and cameras: Public school security as a policy response to Columbine. *American Behavioral Scientist, 52*, pp. 1426–1446.

Advancement Project. 2005. Education on lockdown: The schoolhouse to jailhouse track. Retrieved June 5, 2012 (http://www.advancementproject.org/sites/default/files/publications/FINALEOLrep.pdf).

Advancement Project and the Civil Rights Project. 2000. Opportunities suspended: The devastating consequences of zero tolerance and school discipline policies. Accessed from http://www.eric.ed.gov/ERICWebPortal/search/detailmini.jsp?_nfpb=trueand_andERICExtSearch_SearchValue_0=ED454314andERICExtSearch_SearchType_0=noandaccno=ED454314.

Aitken, S.C. 2001. Schoolyard shootings: Racism, sexism and moral panics over teen violence. *Antipode, 33*(4), pp. 594–600.

Akers, R. 1998. *Social learning and social structure: A general theory of crime and delinquency.* Boston: Northeastern University Press.

Akiba, M. 2010. What predicts fear of school violence among US adolescents? *Teachers College Record, 112*(1), pp. 68–102.

Alexander, J., and M.S. Robbins. 2010. Functional family therapy: A phase-based and multi-component approach to change. In R.C. Murrihy, A.D. Kidman, and T.H. Ollendick, eds., *Clinical handbook of assessing and treating conduct problems in youth* (pp. 245–271). New York: Springer.

Allison, P.D. 2002. *Missing data.* Thousand Oaks, CA: Sage.

Altheide, D.L. 2002. *Creating fear: News and the construction of crisis.* New York: Aldine de Gruyter.

American Academy of Pediatrics. 2000. Joint statement on the impact of entertainment violence on children. Accessed May 10, 2011, from http://www.aap.org/advocacy/releases/jstmtevc.htm.

American Bar Association. 2001. *Zero tolerance policy report.* Accessed January 20, 2011, from www.abanet.org/crimjust/juvjus/zerotolreport.html.

American Psychological Association. 1999. *Warning signs: A violence prevention guide for youth.* Accessed January 20, 2011, from http://helping.apa.org/warningsigns/index.html.

231

American Psychological Association. 2005. Resolution on violence in video games and interactive media. Accessed May 22, 2011, from http://www.apa.org/releases/resolutiononvideoviolence.pdf.

American Psychological Association Zero Tolerance Task Force. 2008. Are zero tolerance policies effective in the schools? An evidentiary review and recommendations. *American Psychologist, 63*(9), pp. 852–862.

American School Counselor Association. 2005. *The ASCA national model: A framework for school counseling programs.* 2nd ed. Alexandria, VA: Author. Accessed from http://www.schoolcounselor.org/files/appropriate.pdf.

Anderson, D.R., A.C. Huston, K.L. Schmitt, D.L. Linebarger, and J.C. Wright. 2001. Early childhood television viewing and adolescent behavior: The recontact study. *Monographs of the Society for Research in Child Development, 66*, pp. vii–147. DOI:10.1111/1540-5834.00120.

Andrade, J.T. Ed. 2009. *Handbook of violence risk assessment and treatment: New approaches for mental health professionals.* New York: Springer.

Andrade, J.T., K. O'Neill, and R.B. Diener. 2009. Violence risk assessment and risk management: A historical overview and clinical application. In J. Andrade, ed., *Handbook of violence risk assessment and treatment: New approaches for mental health professionals* (pp. 3–40). New York: Springer.

Angell, A.V. 1998. Practicing democracy at school: A qualitative analysis of an elementary class council. *Theory and Research in Social Education, 26*, pp. 149–172.

Apple, M.W. 2004. *Ideology and curriculum.* 3rd ed. New York: Routledge-Falmer.

Apple, M.W., and J.A. Beane. 1999. *Democratic schools: Lessons from the chalk face.* Buckingham, UK: Open University Press.

Ashford, R. 2000. Can zero tolerance keep our school safe? *Principal, 34*, pp. 28–30.

Ashworth, J., S. Van Bockern, J. Ailts, J. Donnelly, K. Erickson, and J. Woltermann. 2008. The restorative justice center: An alternative to school detention. *Reclaiming Children and Youth, 17*, pp. 22–27.

Astor, R.A., R. Benbenishty, A. Zeira, and A. Vinokur. 2002. School climate, observed risky behaviors, and victimization as predictors of high school students' fear and judgments of school violence as a problem. *Health, Education and Behavior, 29*(6), pp. 716–736.

Astor, R.A., R.O. Pitner, and B.B. Duncan. 1996. Ecological approaches to mental health consultation with teachers on issues related to youth and school violence. *Journal of Negro Education, 65*, pp. 336–355.

Atkinson, A.J., and R.J. Kipper. 2000. *Virginia School Resource Officer Program Guide.* Richmond, VA. Accessed from http://www.ncjrs.gov/App/Publications/abstract.aspx?ID=190036.

Austin, J., and J. Irwin. 2001. *It's about time: America's imprisonment binge.* Belmont, CA: Wadsworth.

Australian Government Attorney General's Department. 2010. *Literature review on the impact of playing violent video games on aggression.* Barton, Australia: Attorney General's Department.

Aviel, R. 2006, Summer. Compulsory education and substantive due process: Asserting student rights to a safe and healthy school facility. *Lewis and Clark Law Review, 10*, 201–235.

Ayers, W., R. Ayers, and B. Dohrn. 2001. *Zero tolerance: Resisting the drive for punishment in our schools.* New York: Free Press.

Ayyash-Abdo, H. 2002. Adolescent suicide: An ecological approach. *Psychology in the Schools, 39*, pp. 459–475.

Ball, S.J. 2001, December. Global policies and vernacular politics in education. *Currículo sem Fronteiras, 1*(2), pp. xxvii–xliii. Accessed from http://www.curriculosemfronteiras.org/vol1iss2articles/balleng.pdf.

Ball, S.J. 2003. The teacher's soul and the terrors of performativity. *Journal of Education Policy, 18*(2), pp. 215–228.

Band, S.R., and J.A. Harpold. 1999. School violence: Lessons learned. *FBI Law Enforcement Bulletin, 6*, pp. 9–16.

Barak, G. 2003. *Violence and nonviolence: Pathways to understanding.* Thousand Oaks, CA: Sage.

Barnes, L.M. 2008. Policing the schools: An evaluation of the North Carolina school resource officer program. Doctoral dissertation, Rutgers University, 2008. *Dissertation Abstracts International, 69*(08). UMI No. 3326961.

Bastian, L., and B. Taylor. 1991. School crime: A national crime victimization survey report. US Department of Justice, Justice Statistics Clearinghouse/NCJRS.

Battistich, V., and A. Hom. 1997. The relationship between students' sense of their school as a community and their involvement in problem behavior. *American Journal of Public Health, 87*, 1997–2001.

Battistich, V., and D. Solomon. 1997. Caring school communities. *Educational Psychologist, 32*, pp. 137–151.

Battistich, V., D. Solomon, D.I. Kim, M. Watson, and E. Schaps. 1995. Schools as communities, poverty levels of student populations, and students' attitudes, motives, and performance: A multilevel analysis. *American Educational Research Journal, 32*, pp. 627–658.

Bauer, N.S., P. Lozano, and F.P. Rivara. 2007. The effectiveness of the Olweus Bullying Prevention Program in public middle schools: A controlled trial. *Journal of Adolescent Health, 40*, pp. 266–274.

Baumer, E., S.F. Messner, and R. Rosenfeld. 2003. Explaining spatial variation in support for capital punishment: A multilevel analysis. *American Journal of Sociology, 108*, pp. 844–875.

Bazemore, G., L.A. Leip, and J. Stinchcomb. 2004. Boundary changes and the nexus between formal and informal social control: Truancy intervention as a case study in criminal justice expansion. *Notre Dame Journal of Law, Ethics and Public Policy, 18*, pp. 521–570.

Bazemore, G., and M. Schiff. 2010. *No time to talk: A cautiously optimistic tale of restorative justice and related approaches to school discipline.* Paper presented at the American Society of Criminology 2010 meetings, San Francisco, CA.

Beachum, F., A.M. Dentith, C.R. McCray, and T.M. Boyle. 2008. Havens of hope or the killing fields: The paradox of leadership, pedagogy, and relationships in an urban middle school. *Urban Education, 43*(2), pp. 189–215.

Beatty, B. 2007. Going through the emotions: Leadership that gets to the heart of school renewal. *Australian Journal of Education, 51*(3), pp. 328–340.

Beck, U. 1992. *The risk society: Towards a new modernity.* London: Sage.

Beck, U. 1999. *World risk society.* Malden, MA: Polity Press.

Beckham, J. E. 2009. *Zero tolerance discipline policies: Urban administrators' perspectives.* Doctoral dissertation, Miami University, Educational Leadership.

Beger, R.R. 2002. Expansion of police power in public schools and the vanishing rights of students. *Social Justice, 29*, 119–130.

Behrens, A., C. Uggen, and J. Manza. 2003. Ballot manipulation and the menace of Negro domination: Racial threat and felon disenfranchisement in the United States, 1850–2002. *American Journal of Sociology, 109,* pp. 559–605.

Bellesiles, M.A. 2000. *Arming America: The origins of a national gun culture.* New York: Alfred A. Knopf.

Benbenishty, R., and R.A. Astor. 2005. *School violence in context: Culture, neighborhood, family, school and gender.* New York: Oxford University Press.

Bentham, J. [1789] 1970. *An introduction to the principles of morals and legislation,* ed. J.H. Burns and H.L.A. Hart. Oxford, UK: Oxford University Press.

Bergin, C., and D.A. Bergin. 1999. Classroom discipline that promotes self-control. *Journal of Applied Developmental Psychology, 20*(2), pp. 189–206.

Best, S., and D. Kellner. 2001. *The postmodern adventure: Science, technology, and cultural studies at the third millennium.* New York: Guilford.

Biglan, T., M. Wang, and H. Walberg. 2003. *Preventing youth problems.* New York: Kluwer Academic/Plenum Publishers.

Bird, T., and J.W. Little. 1986. How schools organize the teaching occupation. *Elementary School Journal, 86,* pp. 493–511.

Blaber, C., and C. Bershad. 2011. *Realizing the promise of the whole-school approach to children's mental health: A practical guide for schools.* Washington, DC: American Institutes for Research: National Center for Mental Health Promotion and Youth Violence Prevention Education Development Center, Inc., Health and Human Development Division.

Black, D. 1976. *The behavior of law.* San Diego, CA: Academic Press.

Blalock, H. 1967. *Toward a theory of minority group relations.* New York: Capricorn Books.

Block, J., and B. Crain. 2007. Omissions and errors in "Media violence and the American public." *American Psychologist, 62,* pp. 252–253.

Blood, P., and M. Thorsborne. 2005. The challenge of culture change: Embedding restorative practice in schools. Paper presented at the Sixth International Conference on Conferencing, Circles and other Restorative Practices: "Building a Global Alliance for Restorative Practices and Family Empowerment." Sydney, Australia, March 3–5, 2005.

Blueprint for Violence Prevention 2002–2004. Blueprint model programs: Olweus Bullying Prevention Program (BPP). Accessed May 18, 2011, from http://www.colorado.edu/cspv/blueprints/model/programs/BPP.html.

Blum, R.W. 2005. A case for school connectedness. *Educational Leadership, 62,* pp. 6–20.

Blumenson, E., and E.S. Nilsen. 2002. How to construct an underclass, or how the war on drugs became a war on education. *University of Iowa Journal of Gender, Race, and Justice, 6,* p. 65.

Boland, J.B., A.W. Todd, R. Horner, and G. Sugai. 2006. Positive behavior supports surveys: Self assessment (Version 2.0). Eugene: Educational and Community Supports, University of Oregon. Accessed from www.pbssurveys.org.

Borum, R. 2000. Assessing violence risk among youth. *Journal of Clinical Psychology, 56,* pp. 1263–1288.

Borum, R., D. Cornell, W. Modzeleski, and S. Jimerson. 2010. What can be done about school shootings? A review of the evidence. *Educational Researcher, 39*(1), pp. 27–37.

Bough, A.G. 1999. Searches and seizures in schools: Should reasonable suspicion or probable cause apply to school resource/liaison officers? *University of Missouri–Kansas City Law Review, 67*, p. 3.

Bourdieu, P., and J.-C. Passeron. 1990. *Reproduction in education, society and culture.* 2nd ed. Thousand Oaks, CA: Sage.

Bowles, S., and H. Gintis. 1977. *Schooling in capitalist America: Educational reform and the contradictions of economic life.* New York: Basic Books.

Boyes-Watson, C. 2005. Community is not a place but a relationship: Lessons for organizational development. *Public Organization Review: A Global Journal, 5*, pp. 359–374.

Bracy, N.L. 2010. Circumventing the law: Students' rights in schools with police. *Journal of Contemporary Criminal Justice, 26*, pp. 294–315.

Bracy, N.L, and A. Kupchik. 2009. The news media on school crime and violence: Constructing dangerousness and fueling fear. *Youth Violence and Juvenile Justice, 7*, pp. 136–155.

Bradshaw, C.P., M.M. Mitchell, and P.J. Leaf. 2010. Examining the effects of schoolwide positive behavioral interventions and supports on student outcomes. *Journal of Positive Behavior Interventions, 12*(3), pp. 133–148. DOI: 10.1177/1098300709334798.

Brady, H.E., S. Verba, and K.L. Schlozman. 1995. Beyond SES: A resource model of political participation. *American Political Science Review, 89*, pp. 271–297.

Brady, K.P. 2002. Weapons of choice: Zero tolerance school discipline policies and the limitations of student procedural due process. *Children's Legal Rights Journal, 22*, pp. 2–10.

Brady, K.P., S. Balmer, and D. Phenix. 2007. School-police partnership effectiveness in urban schools: An analysis of New York City's impact schools initiative. *Education and Urban Society, 39*, pp. 455–478.

Braithwaite, V., E. Ahmed, B. Morrison, and M. Reinhart. 2001. Researching prospects for restorative justice practice in schools: The Life at School survey 1996–1999. Restorative Justice Conference, Leuven, September 2001. Research School of Social Sciences, Australian National University.

Breunlin, D.C., R.A. Cimmarusti, T.L. Bryant-Edwards, and J.S. Hetherington. 2002. Conflict resolution training as an alternative to suspension for violent behavior. *The Journal of Educational Research, 95*, pp. 349–357.

Brock-Utne, B. 1985. *Educating for peace: A feminist perspective.* New York: Pergamon.

Bronfenbrenner, U. 1976. The experimental ecology of education. *Educational Researcher, 5*, pp. 5–15.

Bronfenbrenner, U. 1979. *The ecology of human development.* Cambridge, MA: Harvard University Press.

Brookmeyer, K.A., K.A. Fanti, and C.C. Henrich. 2006. Schools, parents, and youth violence: A multilevel, ecological analysis. *Journal of Clinical Child and Adolescent Psychology, 35*, pp. 504–514.

Brooks, K., V. Schiraldi, and J. Ziedenberg. 2000. School house hype: Two years later. Policy Report. Washington, DC: Justice Policy Institute. ERIC database (ED446164). Accessed from http://www.justicepolicy.org/images/upload/00-04_REP_SchoolHouseHype2_JJ.pdf.

Brown, B. 2006. Understanding and assessing school police officers: A conceptual and methodological comment. *Journal of Criminal Justice, 34*, pp. 591–604.

Brown, B., and R. Merritt. 2002. *No easy answers: The truth behind death at Columbine*. New York: Lantern Books.

Brown, L.D., and L.R. Jacobs. 2008. *The private abuse of the public interest: Market myths and policy muddles*. Chicago: University of Chicago Press.

Bryk, A.S., and M.E. Driscoll. 1988. *The high school as community: Contextual influences and consequences for students and teachers*. Madison: University of Wisconsin, National Center on Effective Secondary Schools.

Bryk, A.S., and M.E. Driscoll. 1989. *The school as community: Shaping forces and consequences for students and teachers*. Madison: University of Wisconsin, National Center on Effective Secondary Schools.

Bryn, S. 2011. Stop bullying now! A federal campaign for bullying prevention and intervention. *Journal of School Violence, 10*, pp. 213–219.

Burns, R., and C. Crawford. 1999. School shootings, the media, and public fear: Ingredients for a moral panic. *Crime, Law & Social Change, 32*(2), pp. 147–168.

Bushman, B.J., and L.R. Huesmann. 2006. Short-term and long-term effects of violent media on aggression in children and adults. *Archives of Pediatrics and Adolescent Medicine, 160*, pp. 348–352.

Butts, J. 2000. *Youth crime drop: Crime and policy report*. Washington, DC: The Urban Institute Justice Policy Center.

Calefati, J. 2009. School safety, 10 years after Columbine. *US News and World Report*. Accessed May 11, 2011, from http://www.usnews.com/education/articles/2009/04/17/school-safety-10-years-after-columbine.

Calhoun, A., and G. Daniels. 2008. Accountability in school responses to harmful incidents. *Journal of School Violence, 7*, pp. 21–47.

Cameron, L., and M. Thorsborne. 1999. Restorative justice and school discipline: Mutually exclusive? A practitioner's view of the impact of community conferencing in Queensland Schools. Accessed from http://www.realjustice.org/Pages/schooldisc.html.

Cameron, M. 2006. Managing school discipline and implications for social workers: A review of the literature. *Children and Schools, 28*(4), pp. 219–227.

Cameron, M., and S.M. Sheppard. 2006. School discipline and social work practice: Application of research and theory to intervention. *Children and Schools, 28*(1), pp. 15–22.

Campbell, C.Z. 2003. The effective use of school resource officers: The constitutionality of school searches and interrogations. *School Law Bulletin, 34*, p. 1.

Campbell, D.E. 2006. *Why we vote: How schools and communities shape our civic life*. Princeton, NJ: Princeton University Press.

Canadian Broadcasting Corporation (CBC). 2000a. Alberta town reeling after school shooting. CBCnews.com. Accessed from http://www.cbc.ca/news/canada/story/1999/04/29/tabor_shoot990429.html.

Canadian Broadcasting Corporation (CBC). 2000b. Boy charged in Taber shooting gets three years. CBCnews.com. Accessed from http://www.cbc.ca/news/story/2000/11/17/taber_shooting001117.html.

Canter, D., and D. Youngs. 2009. *Investigative psychology: Offender profiling and the analysis of criminal action*. New York: Wiley.

Caplan, A.H. 2003. Public school discipline for creating uncensored anonymous internet forums. *Willamette Law Review, 39*, pp. 93–193.

Carr, B. 2007. *Universe or multiverse?* Cambridge: Cambridge University Press.

Casella, R. 2001. *Being down: Challenging violence in urban schools*. New York: Teachers College Press.

Casella, R. 2003a. The false allure of security technologies. *Social Justice, 30*(3), pp. 82–93.

Casella, R. 2003b. Zero tolerance policies in schools: Rationale, consequences, and alternatives. *Teachers College Record, 105*, pp. 872–892.

Casella, R. 2006. *Selling us the fortress: The promotion of techno-security equipment for schools.* New York: Routledge.

Catalano, R. F., K.P. Haggerty, S. Oesterle, C.B. Fleming, and J.D. Hawkins. 2004. The importance of bonding to school for healthy development: Findings from the Social Development Research Group. *Journal of School Health, 74*, pp. 252–261.

Catlaw, T.J. 2007. *Fabricating the people: Politics and administration in the biopolitical state.* Tuscaloosa: University of Alabama Press.

Caulfield, S. 2000. Creating peaceable schools. *The Annals of the American Academy of Political and Social Science, 567*, pp. 170–185.

Center for Problem-Oriented Policing. 2002. Nomination for the 2002 Herman Goldstein Award for Excellence in Problem-Oriented Policing. Accessed from http://www.popcenter.org/library/awards/goldstein/2002/02-17.pdf.

Center for the Prevention of School Violence. 2009. *School resource officer.* Raleigh, NC: North Carolina Department of Juvenile Justice and Delinquency Prevention. Accessed from http://www.ncdjjdp.org/cpsv/school _resource_officer.html.

Centers for Disease Control and Prevention (CDC). 2008. Understanding school violence: Fact sheet. Accessed January 3, 2009, from http://www.cdc.gov/ violenceprevention/pdf/SchoolViolence_FactSheet-a.pdf.

Cernkovich, S., and P. Giordano. 1987. Family relationships and delinquency. *Criminology, 25*, pp. 295–321.

Cernkovich, S. and P. Giordano. 1992. School bonding, race and delinquency. *Criminology, 30*, pp. 261–291.

Cerulo, K. 1998. *Deciphering violence: The cognitive structure of right and wrong.* New York: Routledge.

Chamlin, M.B. 1989. A macro social analysis of change in police force size 1972–1982: Controlling for static and dynamic influences. *Sociological Quarterly, 30*, pp. 615–624.

Chesler, M., J. Crowfoot, and B.I. Bryant. 1979. Organizational context of school discipline: Analytic models and policy options. *Education and Urban Society, 11*(4), pp. 496–510.

Chesney-Lind, M., and K. Irwin. 2008. *Beyond bad girls: Gender, violence, and media hype.* New York: Routledge.

Chmelynski, C. 2005. Restorative justice for discipline with respect. *The Education Digest, 71*, pp. 17–20.

Christenson, S.L. 2004. The family-school partnership: An opportunity to promote the learning competence of all students. *School Psychology Review, 33*, pp. 83–104.

civicyouth.org. n.d. CIRCLE (The Center for Information and Research on Civic Learning and Engagement). Accessed May 6, 2013, at http://www.civicyouth.org/.

Clarke, A.E., and C. Friese. 2007. Grounded theory using situational analysis. In A. Bryant and K. Charmaz, eds., *The Sage handbook of grounded theory* (pp. 365–397). London: Sage.

Cloud, J. 1999. The Columbine effect. *Time, 154*(23), pp. 51–53.

Cobb, C., and B. Avery. 1977. *The rape of a normal mind.* Markham, Ontario: PaperJacks.

Cohen, S. 1972. *Folk devils and moral panics: The creation of the mods and rockers.* London: MacGibbon and Kee.

Colomy, P., and L.R. Greiner. 2000. Making youth violence visible: The news media and the summer of violence. *Denver University Law Review, 77,* pp. 661–688.

Committee for Children. n.d. Second step: Skills for economic and social success. Online document, accessed May 14, 2013, at http://www.cfchildren .org/second-step.aspx.

Conrad, P.J. 1980. *Deviance and medicalization: From badness to sickness.* Philadelphia, PA: Temple University Press.

Corbin, J., and A. Strauss. 2008. *Basics of qualitative research.* 3rd ed. Los Angeles, CA: Sage.

Cornell, D.G. 2003. Guidelines for responding to student threats of violence. *Journal of Educational Administration, 41,* pp. 705–719.

Cornell, D.G. 2006. *School violence: Fear versus facts.* Mahwah, NJ: Lawrence Erlbaum.

Cornell, D.G., and P.L. Sheras. 2006. *Guidelines for responding to student threats of violence.* Longmont, CO: Sopris West.

Cornell, D.G., P.L. Sheras, S. Kaplan, D. McConville, J. Douglass, A. Elkon, L. McKnight, C. Branson, and J. Cole. 2004. Guidelines for student threat assessment: Field-test findings. *School Psychology Review, 33*(4), pp. 527–546.

Cramer, C.E. 2006. *Armed America. The story of how and why guns became as American as apple pie.* Nashville, TN: Nelson Current.

Crawford, C., T. Chiricos, and G. Kleck. 1998. Race, racial threat, and sentencing of habitual offenders. *Criminology, 36,* pp. 481–511.

Cremin, H. 2010. Talking back to Bazemore and Schiff: A discussion of restorative justice interventions in schools. American Society of Criminology 2010 meetings, San Francisco, CA.

Crews, G.A., and M.R. Counts. 1997. *The evolution of school disturbance in America: Colonial times to modern day.* Westport, CT: Praeger.

Cullen, D. 2009. *Columbine.* New York: Twelve.

Currie, E. 1998. *Crime and punishment in America.* New York: Henry Holt.

Daly, A.J. 2009. Rigid response in an age of accountability: The potential of leadership and trust. *Educational Administration Quarterly, 45*(2), pp. 168–216.

Danitz, T., and J. Nagy. 2000, April. States cool on unfettered gun rights. *USA Today.* Accessed May 22, 2011, from http://www.usatoday.com/news/ columbine/stline01.htm.

Davis, A., with E. Mendietta. 2005. *Abolition democracy: Beyond empire, prisons, and torture.* New York: Seven Stories Press.

Day, D.M., C.A. Golench, J. MacDougall, et al. 1995. *School-based violence prevention in Canada: Results of a national survey of policies and programs.* Toronto: Solicitor General of Canada.

Dayan, D. and E. Katz. 1992. *Media events: The live broadcasting of history.* Cambridge, MA: Harvard University Press.

Dean, M. 2010. *Governmentality: Power and rule in modern society.* 2nd ed. Thousand Oaks, CA: Sage.

Debord, G. 1970 [1967]. *The sociology of the spectacle.* Detroit, MI: Black and Red.

Deisinger, G., M. Randazzo, D. O'Neill, and J. Savage. 2008. *The handbook for campus threat assessment and management teams.* Stoneham, MA: Applied Risk Management, LLC.

Demuth, S., and D. Steffensmeier. 2004. Ethnicity effects on sentence outcomes in large urban courts: Comparisons among white, Black, and Hispanic defendants. *Social Science Quarterly, 85,* pp. 994–1011.

Derber, C. 1996. *The wilding of America.* New York: St. Martin's Press.

Detrich, R., R. Keyworth, and J. States. 2008. *Advances in evidence-based education: A roadmap to evidence-based education.* Oakland, CA: Wing Institute.

Devine, J. 1996. *Maximum security: The culture of violence in inner-city schools.* Chicago: University of Chicago Press.

DeVoe, J.F., K. Peter, M. Noonan, T.D. Snyder, and K. Baum. 2005. *Indicators of school crime and safety: 2005.* NCES 2006–001/NCJ 210697. US Departments of Education and Justice. Washington, DC: US Government Printing Office.

Dewey, J. [1909] 1959. *Moral principles in education.* New York: Philosophical Library.

Dewey, J. [1916] 1997. *Democracy and education.* New York: Simon and Schuster.

Dewey, J. 1964. *John Dewey on education: Selected writings.* R.D. Archambault, ed. New York: Modern Library.

Dewey, J. 1989. *Freedom and culture.* Amherst, MA: Prometheus Books.

Dilulio, J.J., Jr. 1995. The coming of the superpredators. *Weekly Standard,* 23.

Dimitriadis, G., and C. McCarthy. 2003. Creating a new panopticon: Columbine, cultural studies, and the uses of Foucault. In J.Z. Bratich, J. Packer, and C. McCarthy, eds., *Foucault, cultural studies, and govermentality* (pp. 273–294). Albany: State University of New York Press.

Dinkes, R., E.F. Cataldi, G. Kena, and K. Baum. 2006. *Indicators of school crime and safety: 2006.* NCES2007–003/NCJ 214262. US Departments of Education and Justice. Washington, DC: US Government Printing Office.

Dinkes, R., E.F. Cataldi, and W. Lin-Kelly. 2007. *Indicators of School Crime and Safety: 2007.* NCES 2008-021/NCJ 219553. US Departments of Education and Justice. Washington, DC: US Government Printing Office.

Dinkes, R., J. Kemp, and K. Baum. 2009. *Indicators of school crime and safety: 2009.* NCES 2010–012/NCJ 228478. Washington, DC: National Center for Education Statistics, Institute of Education Sciences, US Department of Education, and Bureau of Justice Statistics, Office of Justice Programs, US Department of Justice.

Dobozy, E. 2007. Effective learning of civic skills: Democratic schools succeed in nurturing capacities of students. *Education Studies, 33,* pp. 115–128.

Donohue, E., V. Schiraldi, and J. Ziedenberg. 1998. *School house hype: School shootings and the real risks kids face in America.* Washington, DC/Covington, KY: Justice Policy Institute/Children's Law Center.

Douglas, J.E., R.K. Ressler, A.W. Burgess, and C.R. Hartman. 1986. Criminal profiling from crime scene analysis. *Behavioral Sciences and the Law, 4,* pp. 401–21.

Drewery, W. 2004. Conferencing in schools: Punishment, restorative justice, and the productive importance of the process of conversation. *Journal of Community and Applied Social Psychology, 14,* pp. 332–344.

Duke, D.L. 1989. School organization, leadership, and student behavior. In O.C. Moles, ed., *Strategies to reduce student behavior.* Washington, DC: US Department of Education.

Dunbar, C., and F.A. Villarruel. 2004. What a difference the community makes: Zero tolerance policy interpretation and implementation. *Equity and Excellence in Education, 37*(4), pp. 351–359.

Duncan, A. 2011, March 10. *Enough is enough: Secretary Duncan's remarks at the White House conference on bullying prevention.* Washington, DC: US Department of Education. Accessed from http://www.ed.gov/news/speeches/ enough-enough-secretary-duncans-remarks-white-house-conference-bullying -prevention.

Durkheim, E. [1903] 1961. *Moral education: A study in the theory and application of the sociology of education.* H. Schnurer and E.K. Wilson, trans. Glenco, IL: Free Press.

Dwyer, K., D. Osher, and C. Warger. 1998. *Early warning, timely response: A guide to safe schools.* Washington, DC: US Department of Education.

Eber, L., K. Hyde, J. Rose, K. Breen, D. McDonald, and H. Lewandowski. 2009. Completing the continuum of schoolwide positive behavior support: Wrap-around as a tertiary-level intervention. In W. Sailor, G. Dunlap, G. Sugai, and R. Horner, eds., *Handbook of Positive Behavior Support* (pp. 671–709). New York: Springer.

Eck, J.E. 1994. Drug markets and drug places: A case-control study of the spatial structure of illicit drug dealing. Doctoral dissertation. University of Maryland, College Park.

Ehman, L.H. 1980. The American school in the political socialization process. *Review of Educational Research, 50,* pp. 99–119.

Epstein, J.L., and S. Lee. 1995. National patterns of school and family connections in the middle grades. In B.A. Ryan, G. Adams, T.P. Gullotta, R.P. Weissberg, and R.L. Hampton, eds., *The family-school connection, Vol. 2. Theory, research and practice* (pp. 108–154). Thousand Oaks, CA: Sage.

Erikson, W.H. 2001. *The Report of Governor Bill Owens' Columbine Review Commission.* Accessed March 13, 2011, from http://www.state.co.us/ columbine/Columbine_20Report_WEB.pdf.

Espelage, D.L., and S.M. Swearer. 2003. Research on school bullying and victimization: What have we learned and where do we go from here? *School Psychology Review, 32,* pp. 365–383.

Espelage, D.L., and S.M. Swearer. Eds. 2004. *Bullying in American schools: A social-ecological perspective on prevention and intervention.* Mahwah, NJ: Lawrence Erlbaum.

Espelage, D.L., and S.M. Swearer. Eds. 2011. *Bullying in North American schools.* New York: Routledge.

Fantz, A. 2008. Children forced into cell-like school seclusion rooms. CNN.com. Accessed December 17, 2008, from http://www.cnn.com/2008/US/12/17/ seclusion.rooms/index.html.

Farrell, A.D., A.L. Meyer, E.M. Kung, and T.N. Sullivan. 2001. Development and evaluation of school-based violence prevention programs. *Journal of Clinical Child & Adolescent Psychology, 30,* pp. 207–220.

Fast, J.D. 2008. *Ceremonial violence: A psychological explanation of school shootings.* Woodstock, NY, and New York: Overlook Press.

Feeley, M., and J. Simon. 1994. Actuarial justice: The emerging new criminal law. In D. Nelken, ed., *The futures of criminology* (pp. 173–201). London: Sage.

Fein, R.A., B. Vossekuil, and G. Holden. 1995. Threat assessment: An approach to prevent targeted violence. In *Research in action* (pp. 1–7). Washington, DC: US Department of Justice, Office of Justice Programs, National Institute of Justice.

Fein, R.A., B. Vossekuil, W. Pollack, R. Borum, W. Modzeleski, and M. Reddy. 2002. *Threat assessment in schools: A guide to managing threatening situations and to creating safe school climates.* Washington, DC: US Department of Education, Office of Elementary and Secondary Education, Safe and Drug-Free Schools Program and US Secret Service, National Threat Assessment Center.

Feld, B.C. 1998. Juvenile and criminal justice systems' responses to youth violence. *Crime and Justice, 24,* pp. 189–261.

Feldman, L., J. Pasek, D. Romer, and K.H. Jamieson. 2007. Identifying best practices in civic education: Lessons from the Student Voices program. *American Journal of Education, 114,* pp. 75–100.

Felitti, V.J., R.F. Anda, and D. Nordenberg. 1998, May. Relationship of childhood abuse and household dysfunction to many of the leading causes of death in adults. The Adverse Childhood Experiences (ACE) Study. *American Journal of Preventive Medicine, 14*(4), pp. 245–258.

Felson, M. 1993. Social indicators for criminology. *The Journal of Research in Crime and Delinquency, 30,* pp. 400–411.

Ferguson, A.A. 2000. *Bad boys: Public schools in the making of Black masculinity.* Ann Arbor: University of Michigan Press.

Ferguson, C.J. 2009. Media violence effects: Confirmed truth, or just another X-File? *Journal of Forensic Psychology Practice, 9*(2), pp. 103–126.

Ferguson, C.J. 2011. Video games and youth violence: A prospective analysis in adolescents. *Journal of Youth and Adolescence, 40*(4), pp. 377–391.

Ferguson, C.J., and K.M. Beaver. 2009. Natural born killers: The genetic origins of extreme violence. *Aggression and Violent Behavior, 14*(5), pp. 286–294.

Ferguson, C J., and A. Garza. 2011. Call of (civic) duty: Action games and civic behavior in a large sample of youth. *Computers in Human Behavior, 27,* pp. 770–775.

Fields, B.A. 2003. Restitution and restorative justice. *Youth Studies Australia, 22,* pp. 44–51.

Fine, M., A. Burns, Y.A. Payne, and M.E. Torre. 2004. Civics lessons: The color and class of betrayal. *Teachers College Record, 106,* pp. 2193–2223.

Finn, P., J. McDevitt, W. Lassiter, M. Shively, and T. Rich. 2005. *Case studies of 19 school resource officer (SRO) programs.* Report by the National Institute of Justice. US Department of Justice. Document Number 209271.

Fixsen, D.L., S.F. Naoom, K.A. Blase, R.M. Friedman, and F. Wallace. 2005. *Implementation research: A synthesis of the literature.* Tampa, FL: University of South Florida, Louis de la Parte Florida Mental Health Institute, The National Implementation Research Network. FMHI Publication 231.

Fixsen, D.L., S.F. Naoom, K.A. Blase, and F. Wallace. 2007. Implementation: The missing link between research and practice. *APSAC Advisor, 19,* pp. 4–11.

Flannery, D.J., A.T. Vazsonyi, A.K. Liau, S.G. Guo, K.E. Powell, H. Atha, et al. 2003. Initial behavior outcomes for the PeaceBuilders universal school violence prevention program. *Developmental Psychology, 39,* pp. 292–308.

Foney, D.M., and M. Cunningham. 2002. Why do good kids do bad things? Considering multiple contexts in the study of antisocial fighting behaviors in African American urban youth. *The Journal of Negro Education, 71,* pp. 143–157.

Foucault, M. 1979. *Discipline and punish: The birth of the prison.* New York: Knopf Doubleday.

Foucault, M. [2004] 2008. *The birth of biopolitics: Lectures at the college de France, 1978–1979.* G. Burchell, trans. New York: Palgrave MacMillan.

Fox, J.A. 1996. The calm before the crime wave storm. *Los Angeles Times,* B9.

Fox, J.A., and H. Burstein. 2010. *Violence and security on campus: From preschool through college.* Santa Barbara, CA: Praeger.

Fox, J.A., J. Levin, and K. Quinet. 2008. *The will to kill: Making sense of senseless murder,* 3rd ed. Boston: Allyn and Bacon.

Freedman, J. 2002. *Media violence and its effect on aggression: Assessing the scientific evidence.* Toronto: University of Toronto Press.

Freiberg, H.J., and J.M. Lapointe. 2006. Research-based programs for preventing and solving discipline problems. In C.M. Evertson and C.S. Weinstein, eds., *Handbook of classroom management* (pp. 735–786). Mahwah, NJ: Lawrence Erlbaum.

Freire, P. 1972. *Pedagogy of the oppressed.* New York: Herder and Herder.

Freire, P. 1998. *A Paulo Freire reader.* New York: Herder and Herder.

Frey, K.S., M.K. Hirschstein, and B.A. Guzzo. 2000. Second step. Preventing aggression by promoting social competence. In M.H. Epstein and H. Walker, eds., *Making schools safer and violence free: Critical issues, solutions, and recommended practices.* Austin, TX: Pro-Ed.

Fries, K., and T.A. DeMitchell. 2007. Zero tolerance and the paradox of fairness: Viewpoints from the classroom. *Journal of Law and Education, 36*(2), pp. 211–229.

Fullan, M.G., and A. Hargreaves. 1996. *What's worth fighting for in your school?* New York: Teachers College Press.

Gabor, T. 1995. *School violence and the zero tolerance alternative.* Ottawa, ON: Solicitor General Canada.

Gagnon, J.C., and P.E. Leone. 2001. Alternative strategies for school violence prevention. *New Directions for Youth Development, 92,* pp. 101–125.

Gallup, G., Jr. 1999. Many teens report copycat-related problems at school in wake of Littleton shooting: Nearly half say their school has violent or violence-prone groups. Accessed February 12, 2011, from http://www.gallup .com/poll/3838/Many-Teens-Report-CopycatRelated-Problems-School-Wake-Little.aspx.

Garbarino, J. 1999. *Lost boys: Why our sons turn violent and how we can save them.* New York: Free Press.

Garbarino, J. 2004. Foreword. In D.L. Espelage and S.M. Swearer, eds., *Bullying in American schools: A social-ecological perspective on prevention and intervention* (pp. xi–xiii). Mahwah, NJ: Lawrence Erlbaum.

Garbarino, J., C.P. Bradshaw, and J.A. Vorrasi. 2002. Mitigating the effects of gun violence on children and youth. *Future of Children, 12,* pp. 73–85.

Garbarino, J., and U. Bronfenbrenner. 1976. The socialization of moral judgment and behavior in cross-cultural perspective. In T. Lickona, ed., *Moral development and behavior: Theory, research and social issues* (pp. 70–83). New York: Holt, Rinehart and Winston.

Garcia, C.A. 2003. School safety technology in America: Current use and perceived effectiveness. *Criminal Justice Policy Review, 14,* pp. 30–54.

Garland, D. 2001. *The culture of control: Crime and social order in contemporary society.* Chicago: University of Chicago Press.

Gauntlett, D. 1995. *Moving experiences: Understanding television's influences and effects.* Luton, UK: John Libbey.

Gaustad, J. 1999. *The fundamentals of school security.* ERIC Digest No. 132. Eugene, OR: ERIC Clearinghouse on Educational Management, University of Oregon.

Giddens, A. 1991. *Consequences of modernity.* Stanford, CA: Stanford University Press.

Giddens, A. 1999. Risk and responsibility. *Modern Law Review, 62*(1), pp. 1–10.

Gilligan, C. 1982. *In a different voice.* Cambridge, MA: Harvard University Press.

Girouard, C. 2001. School resource officer training program. OJJDP Fact Sheet. Washington, DC: Office of Juvenile Justice and Delinquency Prevention.

Giroux, H.A. 2003. Racial injustice and disposable youth in the age of zero tolerance. *Qualitative Studies in Education, 16*(4), pp. 553–565.

Giroux, H.A., and D. Purpel. Eds. 1983. *The hidden curriculum and moral education.* Berkeley, CA: McCutchan Publishing.

Goodman, J.F. 2008. Responding to children's needs: Amplifying the caring ethic. *Journal of Philosophy of Education, 42*(2), pp. 233–248.

Gorman, K., and P. Pauken. 2003. The ethics of zero tolerance. *Journal of Educational Administration, 41*, pp. 24–36.

Gottfredson, D.C. 1987. An evaluation of an organization development approach to reducing school disorder. *Evaluation Research, 11*, pp. 739–763.

Gottfredson, D.C. 2001. *Schools and delinquency.* Cambridge: Cambridge University Press.

Gottfredson, D.C., C.M. Fink, S. Skroban, and G. Gottfredson. 1997. Making prevention work. In R.P. Weissberg, T.P. Gullotta, R.L. Hampton, and G.R. Adams, eds., *Healthy children 2010: Establishing preventative services.* Thousand Oaks, CA: Sage.

Gottfredson, D.C., and G.D. Gottfredson. 2002. Quality of school-based prevention programs: Results from a national survey. *Journal of Research in Crime and Delinquency, 39*(1), pp. 3–35.

Gottfredson, D.C., D.B. Wilson, and S.S. Najaka. 2002. School-based prevention of problem behaviors. In L. Sherman, D. Farrington, B. Welsh, and D. MacKenzie, eds., *Evidence-based crime prevention.* London, UK: Routledge.

Gottfredson, G.D., and D.C. Gottfredson. 1985. *Victimization in schools.* New York: Plenum.

Gottfredson, G.D., and D.C. Gottfredson. 2001. What schools do to prevent problem behavior and promote safe environments. *Journal of Educational and Psychological Consultation, 12*, pp. 313–344.

Gottfredson, G.D., D. Gottfredson, and E. Czeh. 2000. *National study of delinquency prevention in schools.* Ellicott City, MD: Gottfredson Associates, Inc.

Gottfredson, G.D., D.C. Gottfredson, A.A. Payne, and N.D. Gottfredson. 2005. School climate predictors of school disorder: Results from the national study of delinquency prevention in schools. *Journal of Research in Crime and Delinquency, 42*, pp. 412–444.

Gowri, A. 2003. Community policing is an epicycle. *Policing: An International Journal of Police Strategies and Management, 26*, pp. 591–611.

Grant, J., and F. Capell. 1983. *Reducing school crime: A report on the school team approach.* San Rafael, CA: Social Action Research Center.

Green, M. 1999. *The appropriate and effective use of security technologies in US schools. A guide for schools and law enforcement agencies.* Washington, DC: US Department of Justice.

Greene, M.B. 2005. Reducing violence and aggression in schools. *Trauma, Violence and Abuse, 6*, pp. 236–253.

Gregory, A., and D. Cornell. 2009. "Tolerating" adolescent needs: Moving beyond zero tolerance policies in high school. *Theory into Practice, 48*, pp. 106–113.

Gregory, A., R.J. Skiba, and P.A. Noguera. 2010. The achievement gap and the discipline gap: Two sides of the same coin? *Educational Researcher, 39*(1), pp. 59–68.

Grisso, T. 2009. Foreword. In J.T. Andrade, ed., *Handbook of violence risk assessment and treatment: New approaches for mental health professionals* (pp. xv–xvii). New York: Springer.

Grubin, D., and S. Wingate. 1996. Sexual offence recidivism: Prediction versus understanding. *Criminal Behaviour and Mental Health, 6,* pp. 349–359.

Gutmann, A. [1987] 1999. *Democratic education.* Princeton, NJ: Princeton University Press.

Halbig, W.W. 2000. Breaking the code of silence. *American School Board Journal, 187*(3), pp. 34–36.

Hallett, M., et al. 2004. Children, not offenders. Center for Race and Juvenile Justice Studies. University of North Florida. March 24. http://www.unf.edu/coas/crjjp/Children%20Not%20Offenders.pdf.

Hammer, R., and D. Kellner. Eds. 2009. *Media/cultural studies: Critical approaches.* New York: Peter Lang Publishing.

Harding, D., C. Fox, and J.D. Mehta. 2002. Studying rare events through qualitative case studies: Lessons from a study of rampage school shootings. *Sociological Methods and Research, 31*(2), pp. 174–217.

Harris, M.K. 1991. Moving into the new millennium: Toward a feminist vision of justice. In H.E. Pepinsky and R. Quinney, eds., *Criminology as peacemaking* (pp. 83–97). Bloomington: Indiana University Press.

Harvey, D. 2005. *A brief history of neoliberalism.* Oxford: Oxford University Press.

Hawkins, D., R. Catalano, R. Kosterman, R. Abbott, and K. Hill. 1999. Preventing adolescent health-risk behaviors by strengthening protection during childhood. *Archives of Pediatrics and Adolescent Medicine, 153,* pp. 226–234.

Heeringa, S.G., B.T. West, and P.A. Berglund. 2010. *Applied survey data analysis.* Boca Raton, FL: Chapman and Hall/CRC.

Held, D. 1996. From post-war stability to political crisis: The polarization of political ideals. In *Models of democracy* (pp. 233–273). Stanford, CA: Stanford University Press.

Henry, S. 2000. What is school violence: An integrated definition. *Annals of the American Academy of Political and Social Science, 567,* pp. 16–29.

Henry, S. 2009. School violence beyond Columbine: A complex problem in need of an interdisciplinary analysis. *American Behavioral Scientist, 52*(9), pp. 1246–1265.

Henry, S., and N.L. Bracy. 2012. Integrative theory in criminology applied to the complex social problem of school violence. In A.F. Repko, W. H. Newell, and R. Szostak, eds., *Case Studies in Interdisciplinary Research* (pp. 259–282). Thousand Oaks, CA: Sage.

Herda-Rapp, A. 2003. The social construction of local school violence threats by the news media and professional organizations. *Sociological Inquiry, 73*(4), pp. 545–574.

Heydenberk, R.A., and W.R. Heydenberk. 2007. The conflict resolution connection: Increasing school attachment in cooperative classroom communities. *Reclaiming Children and Youth: The Journal of Strength-based Interventions, 16,* pp. 18–22.

Heydenberk, R.A., W.R. Heydenberk, and V. Tzenova. 2006. Conflict resolution and bully prevention: Skills for school success. *Conflict Resolution Quarterly, 24,* pp. 55–69.

Hickman, M.J., and B.A. Reaves. 2001. *Local police departments, 1999*. Washington, DC: Bureau of Justice Statistics; Law Enforcement Management and Administrative Statistics.

Hickman, M.J., and B.A. Reaves. 2003. *Local police departments, 2000*. Washington, DC: Bureau of Justice Statistics; Law Enforcement Management and Administrative Statistics.

Hickman, M.J., and B.A. Reaves. 2006. *Local police departments, 2003*. Washington, DC: Bureau of Justice Statistics.

Hillyard, D. 2007. The criminalization of deviance. In George Ritzer, ed., *The Blackwell Encyclopedia of Sociology*. Oxford: Blackwell Publishing.

Hinduja, S., and J. Patchin. 2011. State cyberbullying laws: A brief review of state cyberbullying laws and policies. Cyberbullying Research Center. Accessed from http://www.cyberbullying.us/Bullying_and_Cyberbullying _Laws.pdf.

Hirschfield, P.J., 2008. Preparing for prison? The criminalization of school discipline in the USA. *Theoretical Criminology, 12*(1), pp. 79–101.

Hirschfield, P.J. 2010. School surveillance in America: Disparate and unequal. In T. Monahan and R.D. Torres, eds., *Schools under surveillance: Cultures of control in public education* (pp. 38–54). New Brunswick, NJ: Rutgers University Press.

Hirschfield, P.J., and K. Celinska. 2011. Beyond fear: Sociological perspectives on the criminalization of school discipline. *Sociology Compass, 5*(1), pp. 1–12.

Hirschi, T. 1969. *Causes of delinquency*. Berkeley: University of California Press.

Holmes, M.D. 2000. Minority threat and police brutality: Determinants of civil rights criminal complaints in US municipalities. *Criminology, 38*, pp. 343–367.

Homant, R., and D. Kennedy. 1998. Psychological aspects of crime scene profiling: Validity research. *Criminal Justice and Behavior, 25*, pp. 319–343.

Hong, J.S. 2009. Feasibility of the Olweus bullying prevention program in low-income schools. *Journal of School Violence, 8*, pp. 81–97.

Hong, J.S., H. Cho, P. Allen-Meares, and D.L. Espelage. 2011. The social ecology of the Columbine High School shootings. *Children and Youth Services Review, 33*, pp. 861–868.

Hong, J.S., and M.K. Eamon. 2012. Students' perceptions of unsafe schools: An ecological systems analysis. *Journal of Child and Family Studies.*

Hong, J.S., and D.L. Espelage. 2012. A review of research on bullying and peer victimization in school: An ecological systems analysis. *Aggression and Violent Behavior.*

Honora, D., and A. Rolle. 2002. A discussion of the incongruence between optimism and academic performance and its influence on school violence. *Journal of School Violence, 1*(1), pp. 67–81.

Hope, A. 2010. Seductions of risk, social control, and resistance to school surveillance. In T. Monahan and R.D. Torres, eds., *Schools under surveillance: Cultures of control in public education* (pp. 230–246). New Brunswick, NJ: Rutgers University Press.

Hopkins, B. 2002. Restorative justice in schools. *Support for Learning, 17*, pp. 144–149.

Horner, R.H., G. Sugai, and C.M. Anderson. 2010. Examining the evidence base for School-Wide Positive Behavior Support. *Focus on Exceptional Children, 42*(8), pp. 1–15.

Horner, R.H., G. Sugai, K. Smolkowski, A. Todd, J. Nakasato, and J. Esperanza. 2009. A randomized control trial of school-wide positive behavior support in elementary schools. *Journal of Positive Behavioral Interventions, 11*, pp. 133–144.

Howell, S. 2009. Schools, youth crime and violence: Moral crisis or moral panic? Paper presented at the Annual Meeting of the American Society of Criminology, Philadelphia.

Hoy, W.K. 1971. *An investigation of the relationships between characteristics of secondary schools and student alienation.* Final Report—RMQ 66004. Washington, DC: Department of Health Education and Welfare, Bureau of Research, Office of Education.

Hudson, P.E., R.C. Windham, and L.M. Hooper. 2005. Characteristics of school violence and the value of family-school therapeutic alliances. *Journal of School Violence, 4*, pp. 133–146.

Huey, S.J., Jr., S.W. Henggeler, J. Brondino, and S.G. Pickrel. 2000. Mechanisms of change in multisystemic therapy: Reducing delinquent behavior through therapist adherence and improved family and peer functioning. *Journal of Consulting and Clinical Psychology, 63*, pp. 451–467.

Humes, K.R., N.A. Jones, and R.R. Ramirez. 2011. Overview of race and Hispanic origin: 2010. *U.S. Census Brief.* Accessed from http://www.census.gov/prod/cen2010/.

Husak, D. 2008. *Overcriminalization: The limits of the criminal law.* New York: Oxford University Press.

Illich, I. 1970. *Deschooling society.* New York: Marion Boyers Press.

Illich, I. 1971. *Celebration of awareness.* London: Marion Boyars Press.

Illich, I. 1973. *Tools for conviviality.* New York: Harper and Row.

Insley, A.C. 2001. Suspending and expelling children from educational opportunity: Time to reevaluate zero tolerance policies. *American University Law Review, 50*, p. 1039.

International Association of Chiefs of Police. 1999. *Guidelines for preventing and responding to school violence.* Alexandria, VA: Author.

Irvin, L.K., R.H. Horner, L.K. Ingram, A.W. Todd, G. Sugai, N. Sampson, and J. Boland. 2006. Using office discipline referral data for decision-making about student behavior in elementary and middle schools: An emperial investigation of validity. *Journal of Positive Behavior Interventions, 8*(1), pp. 10–23.

Irvin, L.K., T. Tobin, J. Sprague, G. Sugai, and C. Vincent. 2004. Validity of office discipline referral measures as indices of school-wide behavioral status and effects of school-wide behavioral interventions. *Journal of Positive Behavioral Interventions, 6*, pp. 131–147.

Jackson, A. 2002. Police-school resource officers' and students' perception of the police and offending. *Policing: An International Journal of Police Strategies and Management, 25*, pp. 631–650.

Jacobs, D., and R. Helms. 1999. Collective outbursts, politics, and punitive resources: Toward a political sociology of spending on social control. *Social Forces, 77*, pp. 1497–1524.

Jacobs, D., and R. Kleban. 2003. Political institutions, minorities, and punishment: A pooled cross-national analysis of imprisonment rates. *Social Forces, 80*, pp. 725–755.

James, S.D. 2009. Columbine shootings 10 years later: Students, teacher still haunted by post-traumatic stress. ABC News. Accessed September 20, 2010, from http://abcnews.go.com/Health/story?id=7300782andpage=1.

Jenkins, P.H. 1997. School delinquency and the school social bond. *Journal of Research in Crime and Delinquency, 34,* pp. 337–368.

Jennings, W.G., D.N. Khey, J. Maskaly, and C.M. Donner. 2011. Evaluating the relationship between law enforcement and school security measures and violent crimes in school. *Journal of Police Crisis Negotiations, 11,* pp. 109–124.

Jimerson, S.R., S.E. Brock, and K. Cowan. 2005. Threat assessment: An essential component of a comprehensive safe school program. *Principal Leadership, 6*(2), pp. 11–15.

Johnson, I.M. 1999. School violence: The effectiveness of a school resource officer program in a southern city. *Journal of Criminal Justice, 27,* pp. 173–192.

Jones, S. 2002. *The Internet goes to college: How students are living in the future with today's technology.* Washington, DC: Pew Internet and American Life Project. Accessed April 17, 2012, from http://www.eric.ed.gov/ERIC WebPortal/search/detailmini.jsp?_nfpb=trueand_andERICExtSearch_Search Value_0=ED472669andERICExtSearch_SearchType_0=noandaccno=ED47 2669.

Juvonen, J. 2001. School violence: Prevalence, fears, and prevention. Rand Issue Paper. Accessed July 15, 2008, from http://www.rand.org/pubs /issue_papers/2006/IP219.pdf.

Kadish, S. 1967. The crisis of overcriminalization. *Annals of the American Academy of Political and Social Science, 374*(1), pp. 157–170.

Kahn, R., and D. Kellner. 2003. Internet subcultures and oppositional politics. In D. Muggleton, ed., *The Post-Subcultures Reader* (pp. 299–314). Oxford and New York: Berg.

Kahn, R., and D. Kellner. 2005. Oppositional politics and the Internet: A critical/reconstructive approach. *Cultural Politics, 1*(1), pp. 75–100.

Kahn, R., and D. Kellner. 2006. Reconstructing technoliteracy: A multiple literacies approach. In J.R. Dakers, ed., *Defining Technological Literacy* (pp. 253–274). New York and Houndmills, UK: Palgrave Macmillan.

Kappeler, V.E., and G.W. Potter. 2005. *The mythology of crime and criminal justice.* 4th ed. Long Grove, IL: Waveland Press.

Karp, D.R., and B. Breslin. 2001. Restorative justice in school communities. *Youth and Society, 33,* pp. 249–272.

Kass, J. 2010. Media coverage of the Columbine shootings. *The Denver Post.* Accessed May 11, 2011, from http://www.denverpost.com/headlines/ci _14891787.

Kathi, P.C., and T.L. Cooper. 2005. Democratizing the administrative state: Connecting neighborhood councils and city agencies. *Public Administration Review, 65,* pp. 559–567.

Katz, E., and D. Dayan. 1992. *Media events: The live broadcasting of history.* Cambridge, MA: Harvard University Press.

Katz, J. 2006. *The macho paradox.* Naperville, IL: Sourcebook.

Kauffman, J.M. 1999. How we prevent the prevention of emotional and behavioral disorders. *Exceptional Children, 65,* pp. 448–469.

Keen, B., and D. Jacobs. 2009. Racial threat, partisan politics, and racial disparities in prison admissions: A panel analysis. *Criminology, 47,* pp. 209–238.

Kelling, G.L., and C. Coles. 1996. *Fixing broken windows.* New York: Simon and Schuster.

Kellner, D.K. 1995. *Media culture.* London and New York: Routledge.

Kellner, D.K. 1998. Multiple literacies and critical pedagogy in a multicultural society. *Educational Theory, 48,* pp. 103–122.

Kellner, D.K. 2003a. *From September 11 to terror war: The dangers of the Bush legacy.* Lanham, MD: Rowman and Littlefield.

Kellner, D.K. 2003b. *Media spectacle.* London and New York: Routledge.

Kellner, D.K. 2004. Technological transformation, multiple literacies, and the revisioning of education. *E-Learning, 1*(1), pp. 9–37.

Kellner, D.K. 2005. *Media spectacle and the crisis of democracy.* Boulder, CO: Paradigm Press.

Kellner, D.K. 2006. Toward a critical theory of education. In Gur-Ze'ev, ed., *Critical Theory and Critical Pedagogy Today: Toward a New Critical Language in Education* (pp. 49–69). University of Haifa, Israel: Studies in Education.

Kellner, D.K. 2008. *Guys and guns amok: Domestic terrorism and school shootings from the Oklahoma city bombings to the Virginia Tech massacre.* Boulder, CO: Paradigm Press.

Kellner, D.K. 2012. *Media spectacle and insurrection, 2011: From the Arab uprisings to occupy everywhere!* London and New York: Continuum/Bloomsbury.

Kellner, D.K., T. Cho, E. Lewis, and C. Pierce. Eds. 2009. *Marcuse's challenge to education.* Lanham, MD: Rowman and Littlefield.

Kellner, D.K., and M.G. Durham. Eds. 2012. *Media and cultural studies: KeyWorks.* 2nd ed. Malden, MA, and Oxford: Blackwell.

Kellner, D.K., and J. Share. 2007. Critical media literacy, democracy, and the reconstruction of education. In D. Macedo and S.R. Steinberg, eds., *Media literacy. A Reader* (pp. 3–23). New York: Peter Lang.

Keppel, R.D. 2006. *Offender profiling.* Mason, OH: Thomson Custom Publishing.

Kerns, S.E.U., and R.J. Prinz. 2002. Critical issues in the prevention of violence-related behavior in youth. *Clinical Child and Family Psychology Review, 5,* pp. 133–160.

Kiefer, H.M. 2005. Public: Society powerless to stop school shootings: Three-fourths say school shootings likely to happen in their communities. Accessed March 15, 2011, from http://www.gallup.com/poll/15511/Public-Society-Powerless-Stop-School-Shootings.aspx.

Killingbeck, D. 2001. The role of television news in the construction of school violence as a "moral panic." *Journal of Criminal Justice and Popular Culture, 8*(3), pp. 186–202.

Kim, C., D.L. Losen, and D.T. Hewitt. 2010. *The school-to-prison pipeline: Structuring legal reform.* New York: New York University Press.

Kimmel, M.S., and M. Mahler. 2003. Adolescent masculinity, homophobia, and violence. *American Behavioral Scientist, 46,* pp. 1439–1458.

King, K. A., R.A. Vidourek, B. Davis and W. McClellan. 2002. Increasing self-esteem and school connectedness through a multidimensional mentoring program. *Journal of School Health, 72,* pp. 294–299.

Kinney, P. 2009. Safety relies on climate. *Principal Leadership: High School Edition, 9*(5), p. 54.

Kjaer, A.-M. 2004. *Governance.* London: Polity Press.

Klem, A.M., and J.P. Connell. 2004. Relationships matter: Linking teacher support to student engagement. *Journal of School Health, 74,* pp. 262–273.

Kocsis, R.N. 2007. *Criminal profiling: International theory, research, and practice.* Totowa, NJ: Humana Press.

Kocsis, R.N., H.J. Irwin, A.F. Hayes, and R. Nunn. 2000. Expertise in psychological profiling: A comparative assessment. *Journal of Interpersonal Violence, 15*(3), pp. 311–331.

Kramer, R.C. 2000. Poverty, inequality and youth violence. *Annals of the American Academy of Political and Social Science, 567,* pp. 123–139.

Krohn, M., and J.L Massey. 1980. Social control and delinquent behavior: An examination of the elements of the social bond. *The Sociological Quarterly, 21,* pp. 529–544.

Kupchik, A. 2010. *Homeroom security: School discipline in an age of fear.* New York: New York University Press.

Kupchik, A., and N.L. Bracy. 2009. The news media on school crime and violence: Constructing dangerousness and fueling fear. *Youth Violence and Juvenile Justice, 7*(2), pp. 136–155.

Kupchik, A., and N.L. Bracy. 2010. To protect, serve, and mentor: Police officers in public schools. In T. Monahan and R.D. Torres, eds., *Schools under surveillance: Cultures of control in public education* (pp. 21–37). New Brunswick, NJ: Rutgers University Press.

Kupchik, A., and N.D. Ellis. 2008. School discipline and security: Fair for all students? *Youth and Society, 39,* pp. 549–574.

Kupchik, A., and T. Monahan. 2006. The new American school: Preparation for post-industrial discipline. *British Journal of Sociology of Education, 5,* pp. 617–631.

Kutash, K., A. Duchnowski, and N. Lynn. 2006. *School-based mental health: An empirical guide for decision-makers.* The Research and Training Center for Children's Mental Health, Florida Mental Institute, University of South Florida.

Lakoff, G. 2002. *Moral politics: How conservatives and liberals think.* 2nd ed. Chicago: University of Chicago Press.

Langman, P. 2009. *Why kids kill: Inside the minds of school shooters.* Houndmills, UK: Palgrave Macmillan.

Lareau, A. 2003. *Unequal childhoods: Class, race and family life.* Berkeley: University of California Press.

Larkin, R.W. 2007. *Comprehending Columbine.* Philadelphia: Temple University Press.

Lawrence, R.G. 2001. Defining events: Problem definition in the media arena. In R.P. Hart and B.H. Sparrow, eds., *Politics, discourse, and American society: New agendas* (pp. 91–110). Lanham, MD: Rowman and Littlefield.

Lawrence, R.G. 2007. *School crime and juvenile justice.* 2nd ed. New York: Oxford University Press.

Leary, M.R., R.M. Kowalski, L. Smith, and S. Phillips. 2003. Teasing, rejection, and violence: Case studies of the school shootings. *Aggressive Behavior, 29,* pp. 202–214.

Lee, V.E., A.S. Bryk, and J.B. Smith. 1992. The organization of effective secondary schools. *Review of Research in Education, 19,* pp. 171–267.

Levin, B. 1998. An epidemic of education policy: What can we learn from each other? *Comparative Education, 34*(2), pp. 131–142.

Levin, J., and E. Madfis. 2009. Mass murder at school and cumulative strain: A sequential model. *American Behavioral Scientist, 52*(9), pp. 1227–1245.

Lezotte, L.W., and J. Passalacqua. 1978. Individual school buildings: Accounting for differences in measured pupil performance. *Urban Education, 13*(3), pp. 283–293.

Lieberman, J. 2006. *The shooting game: The making of school shooters.* Santa Ana, CA: Seven Locks Press.

Limber, S.P., M.N. Nation, A.J. Tracy, G.B. Melton, and V. Flerx. 2004. Implementation of the Olweus Bullying Prevention programme in Southeastern

United States. In P. K. Smith, D. Pepler, and K. Rigby, eds., *Bullying in schools: How successful can interventions be?* (pp. 55–80). Cambridge: Cambridge University Press.

Limber, S.P., and M.A. Small. 2003. Laws and policies to address bullying in U.S. schools. *School Psychology Review, 32*, pp. 445–455.

Lindle, J.C. 2008. School safety: Real or imagined fear? *Educational Policy, 22*(1), pp. 28–44.

Liska, A.E. 1992. *Social threat and social control.* Albany: State University of New York Press.

Liska, A.E., and M. Reed. 1985. Ties to conventional institutions and delinquency: estimating reciprocal effects. *American Sociological Review, 50,* pp. 547–560.

Little, J.W. 1985. Contested ground: The basis of teacher leadership in two restructuring high schools. *The Elementary School Journal, 96*(1), pp. 47–63.

Lodge, J., and E. Frydenberg. 2005. The role of peer bystanders in school bullying: Positive steps toward promoting peaceful schools. *Theory into Practice, 44*(4), pp. 329–336.

Lorenz, A. 2010. The windows remain broken. How zero tolerance destroyed due process. *Public Integrity, 12,* pp. 247–259.

Loukas, A., R. Suzuki, and K.D. Horton. 2006. Examining school connectedness as a mediator of school climate effects. *Journal of Research on Adolescence, 16,* pp. 491–502.

Luhman, N. 1991. *Risk: A sociological theory.* New York: Aldine de Gruyter.

Luke, A., and C. Luke. 2002. Adolescence lost/childhood regained: On early intervention and the emergence of the techno-subject. *Journal of Early Childhood Literacy, 1*(1), pp. 91–120.

Lumby, J. 2009. Performativity and identity: Mechanisms of exclusion. *Journal of Education Policy, 24*(3), pp. 353–369.

Lyons, W., and J. Drew. 2006. *Punishing schools, fear and citizenship in American public education.* Ann Arbor: University of Michigan Press.

Lyotard, J. 1984. *The postmodern condition: A report on knowledge.* Manchester, UK: Manchester University Press.

Macallair, D. 2002. *School house hype: Two years later.* Executive summary. San Francisco: Center on Juvenile and Criminal Justice. Accessed from http://www.cjcj.org/files/schoolhouse.pdf.

MacGregor, K. 1995. Tighten custody, gun laws to curb family violence, say critics; West end slaying of two children angers activists. *Ottawa Citizen,* B4.

MacNeil, A.J., and D. Prater. 2010. Teachers and principals differ on the seriousness of school discipline: A national perspective. *National Forum of Applied Educational Research Journal, 23*(3), pp. 1–7.

Macready, T. 2009. Learning social responsibility in schools: A restorative practice. *Educational Psychology in Practice, 25,* pp. 211–220.

Madfis, E. 2012. Averting the unlikely: Fearing, assessing, and preventing threats of rampage violence in American public schools. Unpublished Doctoral Dissertation, Northeastern University.

Marcuse, H. 1970. *Five lectures.* Boston: Beacon Press.

Marcuse, H. 2001. *Toward a critical theory of society.* Vol. 2 in Douglas Kellner, ed., *Collected papers of Herbert Marcuse.* London and New York: Routledge.

Marcuse, H. 2004. *Herbert Marcuse. The new left and the 1960s.* Vol. 3. in Douglas Kellner, ed., *Collected Papers of Herbert Marcuse.* London and New York: Routledge.

Marcuse, H. 2006. *Art and liberation.* Vol. 4 in Douglas Kellner, ed., *Collected Papers of Herbert Marcuse.* London and New York: Routledge.

Marx, G.T., and V. Steeves. 2010. From the beginning: Children as subjects and agents of surveillance. *Surveillance and Society, 7,* pp. 192–230.

Marzano, R.J. 2003. *What works in schools: Translating research into action.* Alexandria, VA: Association for Supervision and Curriculum Development (ASCD).

Matthew, R.A. 2010. Reading, writing and readiness. In T. Monahan and R.D. Torres, eds., *Schools under surveillance: Cultures of control in public education* (pp. 123–139). New Brunswick, NJ: Routledge.

Mawson, A.R., P.M. Lapsley, A.M. Hoffman, and J.C. Guignard. 2002. Preventing lethal violence in schools: The case for entry-based weapons screening. *Journal of Health Politics, Policy and Law, 27,* pp. 243–260.

May, S., W.I. Ard, A.W. Todd, R.H. Horner, A. Glasgow, G. Sugai, and J.R. Sprague. 2000. School-wide information system. Accessed from www.swis.org.

Mayer, G.R., and B. Sulzer-Azaroff. 1991. Interventions for vandalism. In G. Stoner, M.R. Shinn, and H.M. Walker, eds., *Interventions for achievements and behavior problems* (pp. 559–580). Silver Spring, MD: National Association of School Psychologists.

McCluskey, G., G. Lloyd, J. Kane, S. Riddell, J. Stead, and F. Weedon. 2008. Can restorative practices in schools make a difference? *Educational Review, 60,* pp. 405–417.

McDermott, M.J. 1994. Criminology as peacemaking, feminist ethics, and the victimization of women. *Women and Criminal Justice, 5*(20), pp. 21–44.

McDevitt, J., and P. Finn. 2005. *National assessment of school resource officer programs final project report.* Washington, DC: National Institute of Justice, US Department of Justice. Document No. 209273.

McDevitt, J., and J. Panniello. 2005. *National assessment of the School Resource Officer Programs: Survey of students in three large new SRO programs.* NIJ Final Report. Accessed July 23, 2008, from http://www.cj.neu.edu/pdf/BOOK_NEU_Survey_D10.pdf.

McFarland, D.A., and R.J. Thomas. 2006. Bowling young: How youth voluntary associations influence adult political participation. *American Journal of Sociology, 71,* pp. 401–425.

McGee, J.P., and C.R. DeBernardo. 1999. The classroom avenger: A behavioral profile of school based shootings. *The Forensic Examiner, 8,* pp. 16–18.

McLaren, P. 2007. *Life in schools: An introduction to critical pedagogy in the foundations of education.* 5th ed. Boston: Pearson Allyn and Bacon.

McLaughlin, M.W. 1990. The Rand change agent study revisited: Macro perspectives and micro realities. *Educational Researcher, 19,* pp. 11–16.

McLuhan, M. 1964. *Understanding media: The extensions of man.* New York: Signet Books.

McNeely, C.A., J.M. Nonnemaker, and R.W. Blum. 2002. Promoting school connectedness: Evidence from the National Longitudinal Study of Adolescent Health. *Journal of School Health, 72,* pp. 138–146.

Merida, K. 1999. Fearful kids maintain code of silence. *Washington Post.* Accessed May 3, 2011, from http://www.washingtonpost.com/wp-srv/national/daily/april99/snitch042799.htm.

Messerschmidt, J.W. 1993. *Masculinities and crime.* Lanham, MD: Rowman and Littlefield.

Messerschmidt, J.W., and R.W. Connell. 2005. Hegemonic masculinity: Rethinking the concept. *Gender & Society, 19,* pp. 829–859.

Michigan American Civil Liberties Union (ACLU). 2009. *Reclaiming Michigan's throwaway kids: Students trapped in the school-to-prison pipeline.* Detroit, MI: Author.

Mill, J.S. [1859] 1869. *On liberty.* London: Longman, Roberts and Green. Accessed July 24, 2011, from www.bartleby.com/130/.

Miller, J. 2008. *Getting played: African American girls, urban inequality, and gendered violence.* New York: New York University Press.

Mohr, D., P. Cuijpers, and K. Lehman. 2011. Supportive accountability: A model for providing human support to enhance adherence to eHealth interventions. *Journal of Medical Internet Research, 13*(1):e30(1), pp. 1–11. DOI:10.2196/jmir.1602.

Monahan, T. 2006. The surveillance curriculum: Risk management and social control in the neoliberal school. In T. Monahan, ed., *Surveillance and security: Technological politics and power in everyday life* (pp. 109–124). New York: Routledge.

Monahan, T., and R.D. Torres. Eds. 2010. *Schools under surveillance: Cultures of control in public education.* New Brunswick, NJ: Rutgers University Press.

Morbidity and Mortality Weekly Report (MMWR). 2007. The effectiveness of universal school-based programs for the prevention of violent and aggressive behavior: A report on recommendations of the task force on community preventive services. *MMWR, 56*(RR-7), pp. 1–8.

Morozov, E. 2011. *The net delusion: The dark side of Internet freedom.* New York: PublicAffairs.

Morrill, C., K. Tyson, L.B. Edelman, and R. Arum. 2010. Legal mobilization in schools: The paradox of rights and race among youth. *Law and Society Review, 44*, pp. 651–694.

Morris, E.W. 2005. "Tuck in that shirt!" Race, class, gender and discipline in an urban school. *Sociological Perspectives, 48*(1), pp. 25–48.

Morris, N., and G. Hawkings. 1970. *The honest politician's guide to criminal control.* Chicago: University of Chicago Press.

Morrison, B.E. 2002. Bullying and victimisation in schools: A restorative justice approach. *Trends and Issues in Crime and Criminal Justice, 219.* Canberra, Australia: Australian Institute of Criminology. Accessed from http://www.aic.gov.au/publications/tandi/ti219.pdf.

Morrison, B.E. 2003. Regulating safe school communities: Being responsive and restorative. *Journal of Educational Administration, 41*, pp. 689–704.

Morrison, B.E. 2005. Restorative justice in schools. In E. Elliott and R.M. Gordon, eds., *New directions in restorative justice: Issues, practice, evaluation.* Gordon, UK: Willan Publishing.

Morrison, B.E. 2007. *Restoring safe school communities.* Sydney, Australia: Federation.

Morrison, B.E. 2010. From social control to social engagement: Enabling the "time and space" to talk through restorative justice and responsive regulation. Paper presented at the American Society of Criminology 2010 meetings, San Francisco, CA.

Morrison, B.E., P. Blood, and M. Thorsborne. 2005. Practicing restorative justice in school communities: The challenge of culture change. *Public Organization Review: A Global Journal, 5*, pp. 335–357.

Morrison B.E., and D. Vaanderling. 2012. Restorative justice: Pedagogy, praxis, and discipline. *Journal of School Violence, 11*, pp. 138–155.

Morrison, K.C. 2003. *School crime and school resource officers: A desk reference for prosecutors.* Special Topic Series, Alexandria, VA: American Prosecutors Research Institute, Office of Juvenile Justice and Delinquency Prevention.

Mosher, C. 2001. Predicting drug arrest rates: Conflict and social disorganization perspectives. *Crime and Delinquency, 47,* pp. 84–104.

Mossman, D. 1994. Assessing predictions of violence: Being accurate about accuracy. *Journal of Consulting and Clinical Psychology, 62,* pp. 783–792.

Mulvey, E.P., and E. Cauffman. 2001. The inherent limits of predicting school violence. *American Psychologist, 56,* pp. 797–802.

Muschert, G.W. 2007a. The Columbine victims and the myth of the juvenile superpredator. *Youth Violence and Juvenile Justice, 5*(4), pp. 351–366.

Muschert, G.W. 2007b. Research in school shootings. *Sociology Compass, 1*(1), pp. 60–80.

Muschert, G.W. 2009. Frame-changing in the media coverage of a school shooting: The rise of Columbine as a national concern. *Social Science Journal, 46*(1), pp. 164–170.

Muschert, G.W. 2012. School shootings as mediatized violence. In N. Böckler, T. Seeger, P. Sitzer, and W. Heitmeyer, eds., *School shootings: International research, case studies, and concepts for prevention.* New York: Springer.

Muschert, G.W., and D.C. Carr. 2006. Media salience and frame changing across events: Coverage of nine school shootings, 1997-2001. *Journalism & Mass Communication Quarterly, 83*(4), pp. 747-766.

Muschert, G.W., and A.A. Peguero. 2010. The Columbine effect and school anti-violence policy. *Research in Social Problems and Public Policy, 17,* pp. 117–148.

Muschert, G.W., and M. Ragnedda. 2010. Media and violence control: The framing of school shootings. In W. Heitmeyer, H.G. Haupt, S. Malthaner, and A. Kirschner, eds., *The control of violence in modern society: Multidisciplinary perspectives, from school shootings to ethnic violence* (pp. 345–361). New York: Springer.

Muschert, G.W., and J.W. Spencer. eds. 2009a. Lessons of Columbine, Part I. *American Behavioral Scientist, 52,* p. 9.

Muschert, G.W., and J.W. Spencer. eds. 2009b. Lessons of Columbine, Part II. *American Behavioral Scientist, 52,* p. 10.

Nalbandian, J. 2005. Professionals and conflicting forces of administrative modernization and civic engagement. *American Review of Public Administration, 35,* pp. 311–326.

National Association of School Resource Officers (NASRO). 2010. *Bylaws of the National Association of School Resources Officers, Inc.* Accessed from http://www.nasro.org/mc/page.do?sitePageId=114179andorgId=naasro.

National Association of School Resource Officers (NASRO). 2011. National Association of School Resource Officers. Accessed September 18, 2011, from http://www.nasro.org/mc/page.do?sitePageId=115971andorgId=naasro.

Neiman, S., and J.F. DeVoe. 2009. *Crime, violence, discipline, and safety in US public schools: Findings from the School Survey on Crime and Safety.* Washington, DC: US Department of Education.

Nettles, S., W. Mucheran, and D. Jones. 2000. Understanding resilience: The role of social resources. *Journal of Education for Students Placed at Risk, 5,* pp. 47–60.

Newman, K. 2004. *Rampage: The social roots of school shootings.* New York: Basic Books.

Newmann, F.M., R.A. Rutter, and M.S. Smith. 1989. Organizational factors affecting school sense of efficacy, community, and expectations. *Sociology of Education, 62,* pp. 221–238.

Newport, F. 2006. Before recent shootings, most parents not worried about school safety: Rise in concern after Columbine in 1999 has dissipated. Accessed May 4, 2011, from http://www.gallup.com/poll/24844/Before -Recent-Shootings-Most-Parents-Worried-About-School-Safety.aspx.

Newton, J.S., R. Horner, B. Algozzine, A. Todd, and K.M. Algozzine. 2009. Using a problem-solving model for data-based decision making in schools. In W. Sailor, G. Dunlap, G. Sugai, and R.H. Horner, eds., *Handbook of positive behavior support* (pp. 551–580). New York: Springer.

Nichols, J.D. 2004. An exploration of discipline and suspension data. *The Journal of Negro Education, 73,* pp. 408–423.

Nickerson, A.B., and S.E. Brock. 2011. Measurement and evaluation of school crisis prevention and intervention: Introduction to special issue. *Journal of School Violence, 10,* pp. 1–15.

Nickerson, A.B., and W.H. Spears. 2007. Influences on authoritarian and educational/therapeutic approaches to school violence. *Journal of School Violence, 6,* pp. 3–31.

Nicoletti, J., S. Spencer-Thomas, and C. Bollinger. 2001. *Violence goes to college: The authoritative guide to prevention and intervention.* Google e-book. Accessed April 13, 2012, at http://books.google.com/books/about/ Violence_Goes_to_College.html?id=T_ClourcxRwC.

Nimmo, B., and D. Scott. 2000. *Rachel's tears: The spiritual journey of Columbine martyr Rachel Scott.* Nashville, TN: Thomas Nelson Publishers.

Noddings, N. 1984. *Caring: A feminine approach to ethics and moral education.* Berkeley: University of California Press.

Noddings, N. 2002. *Starting at home: Caring and social policy.* Berkeley: University of California Press.

Noddings, N. 2006. *Critical lessons: What our schools should teach.* Cambridge: Cambridge University Press.

Noguera, P.A. 1995. Preventing and producing violence: A critical analysis of responses to school violence. *Harvard Educational Review, 65*(2), pp. 189– 213.

Noguera, P.A. 2003. Schools, prisons, and social implications of punishment: Rethinking disciplinary practices. *Theory into Practice, 42,* pp. 341–350.

Noguera, P.A. 2008. *The trouble with Black boys . . . and other reflections on race, equity, and the future of public education.* San Francisco, CA: Jossey-Bass.

Nye, J.S., P.D. Zelikow, and D.C. King. eds. 1997. *Why people don't trust government.* Cambridge, MA: Harvard University Press.

O'Dea, J., and C. Loewen. 1999. Life in the hallway: Students' perceptions of violent and disruptive behavior in their schools. In G. Malicky, B. Shapiro, and K. Mazurek, eds., *Building foundations for safe and caring schools: Research on disruptive behavior and violence.* Edmonton, Canada: Duval House Publishing.

O'Donovan, E. 2006. How to stay out of court. *District Administration, 42*(10), pp. 76–77.

Office of Community Oriented Policing Service, 2005. *COPS in schools fact sheet.* Washington, DC: U.S. Department of Justice. Available at http:// ric-zai-inc.com/Publications/cops-w0028-pub.pdf.

Office of Community Oriented Policing Services, 2008. *COPS evaluation brief no. 2: Evaluation of a pilot community policing program.* Washington, DC: U.S. Department of Justice. Available at http://ric-zai-inc.com/Publications/cops-p147-pub.pdf

O'Neill, R.E., R.H. Horner, R.W. Albin, J.R. Sprague, S. Newton, and K. Storey. 1997. *Functional assessment and program development for problem behavior: A practical handbook.* 2nd ed. Pacific Grove, CA: Brookes/Cole.

Ontario Ministry of Education. 2012. The provincial code of conduct and school board codes of conduct. Policy/program memorandum no. 128. Ontario, Canada.

Orr, M.T., B. Berg, R. Shore, and E. Meier. 2008. Putting the pieces together: Leadership for change in low-performing urban schools. *Education and Urban Society, 40*(6), pp. 670–693.

Osher, D., G.G. Bear, J.R. Sprague, and W. Doyle. 2010. How can we improve school discipline? *Educational Researcher, 39*(1), pp. 48–58.

Osher, D., K. Dwyer, and S.R. Jimerson. 2006. Safe, supportive, and effective schools: Promoting school success to reduce school violence. In S.R. Jimerson and M.J. Furlong, eds., *Handbook of school violence and school safety: From research to practice* (pp. 51–71). Mahwah, NJ: Lawrence Erlbaum.

Ostroff, C. 1992. The relationship between satisfaction, attitudes, and performance: An organizational level analysis. *Journal of Applied Psychology, 77,* pp. 963–974.

O'Toole, M.E. 2000. *The school shooter: A threat assessment perspective.* Washington, DC: Federal Bureau of Investigation. Accessed September 30, 2010, from http://www.fbi.gov/publications/school/school2.pdf.

Ottawa-Carleton District School Board. 2011. Letter to parents. Ottawa, Canada.

Ottawa Police Service. 2010a. *2008–2009 Crime trends for Ward 8—College.* Accessed from http://ottawapolice.ca/en/resources/crime_analysis_statistics/pdf/2008%20-%202009%20Crime%20Trends%20for%20Ward%208%20-%20College.pdf.

Ottawa Police Service. 2010b. *2008–2009 Crime trends for Ward 9—Knoxdale-Merivale.* Accessed from http://ottawapolice.ca/en/resources/crime_analysis_statistics/pdf/2008%20-%202009%20Crime%20Trends%20for%20Ward%209%20-%20Knoxdale-Merivale.pdf.

Otto, R.K. 2000. Assessing and managing violence risk in outpatient settings. *Journal of Clinical Psychology, 56,* pp. 1239–1262.

Ou, D. 2010. To leave or not to leave? A regression discontinuity analysis of the impact of failing the high school exit exam. *Economics of Education Review, 29*(2), pp. 171–186.

Packard, J.S. 1988. The Pupil Control studies. In N. Boyan, ed., *Handbook of research on educational administration: A project of the American Educational Research Association* (pp. 185–207). New York: Longman.

Packer, H. 1968. *The limits of the criminal sanction.* Stanford, CA: Stanford University Press.

Pagliocca, P.M., and A.B. Nickerson. 2001. Legislating school crisis response: Good policy or just good politics? *Law and Policy, 23,* pp. 373–407.

Paine, C.K., and J.R. Sprague. 2002. Dealing with a school shooting disaster: Lessons learned from Springfield, Oregon. *Emotional and Behavioral Disorders in Youth, 2*(2), pp. 35–40.

Palermo, G.B., and R.N. Kocsis. 2005. *Offender profiling: An introduction to the sociopsychological analysis of violent crime.* Springfield, IL: Charles C. Thomas Publisher.

Paquette, D., and J. Ryan. 2001. *Bronfenbrenner's ecological systems theory.* Accessed October 18, 2011, from http://pt3.nl.edu/paquetteryanwebquest .pdf#search=%22ecological%20theory%22.

Parenti, C. 2000. *Lockdown America: Police and prisons in the age of crisis.* New York: Verso.

Pasek, J., L. Feldman, D. Romer, and K.H. Jamieson. 2008. Schools as incubators of democratic participation: Building long-term efficacy with civic education. *Applied Development Science, 12,* pp. 26–37.

Payne, A.A. 2008. A multilevel analysis of the relationships among communal school organization, student bonding, and school disorder. *Journal of Research in Crime and Delinquency, 45,* pp. 429–455.

Payne, A.A. 2009. Girls, boys, and the school community: Gender differences in the relationships between school-related factors and student deviance. *Criminology, 47,* pp. 1167–1200.

Payne, A.A. 2012. Communal school organization effects on school disorder: Interactions with school structure. *Deviant Behavior, 33,* pp. 507–524.

Payne, A.A., D.C. Gottfredson, and G.D. Gottfredson. 2003. Schools as communities: The relationships among communal school organization, student bonding, and school disorder. *Criminology, 41,* pp. 749–777.

Payne, A.A., D.C. Gottfredson, and C. Kruttschnitt. 2009. Girls, schools, and delinquency. In M. Zahn, ed., *The delinquent girl.* Philadelphia: Temple University Press.

Payne, A.A., and K. Welch. 2010. Racial threat in schools: Modeling the influence of punitive and restorative discipline practices. *Criminology, 48,* pp. 1019–1062.

pbis.org. 2013. What is SWPBIS? Electronic document accessed May 14, 2013, at http://www.pbis.org/school/what_is_swpbs.aspx.

Pepinsky, H.E. 1991a. *The geometry of violence and democracy.* Bloomington: Indiana University Press.

Pepinsky, H.E. 1991b. Peacemaking in criminology and criminal justice. In H.E. Pepinsky and R. Quinney, eds., *Criminology as peacemaking* (pp. 299–327). Bloomington: Indiana University Press.

Pepinsky, H.E. 2000. Educating for peace. *The Annals of the American Academy of Political and Social Science, 567,* pp. 157–169.

Pepinsky, H.E., and R. Quinney. 1991. *Criminology as peacemaking.* Bloomington: Indiana University Press.

Perryman, J. 2006. Panoptic performativity and school inspection regimes: Disciplinary mechanisms and life under special measures. *Journal of Education Policy, 21*(2), pp. 147–161.

Peterson, R.L., J. Larson, and R. Skiba. 2001. School violence prevention: Current status and policy recommendations. *Law and Policy, 23,* pp. 345–371.

Peterson, R.L., and R. Skiba. 2001. Creating school climates that prevent school violence. *The Clearing House, 74,* pp. 155–163.

Petherick, W. 2006. *Serial crime: Theoretical and practical issues in behavioral profiling.* Burlington, MA: Academic Press.

Pew Research Center for the People and the Press. 1999. Columbine shooting biggest news draw of 1999. Accessed on October 3, 2010, from http://people -press.org/report/48/columbine-shooting-biggest-news-draw-of-1999.

Phaneuf, S.W. 2006. School security practices: Investigating their consequences on student fear, bonding, and school climate. Doctoral dissertation, University of Maryland.

Phaneuf, S.W. 2009. *Security in schools: Its effect on students.* El Paso, TX: LFB Scholarly Publishing.

Pinard, M. 2003. From the classroom to the courtroom: Reassessing Fourth Amendment standards in public school searches involving law enforcement authorities. *Arizona Law Review, 45,* p. 1067.

Pinizzotto, A.J., and N.J. Finkel. 1990. Criminal personality profiling: An outcome and process study. *Law and Human Behavior, 14*(3), pp. 215–234.

Polyani, K. 1944. *The great transformation: The political and economic origins of our time.* Boston: Beacon Press.

Posner, R.A. 2004. *Catastrophe, risk, and response.* New York: Oxford University Press.

Pospisil, L.J. 1971. *Anthropology of law: A comparative theory.* New York: Harper and Row.

Public Agenda. 2004. *Teaching interrupted: Do discipline policies in today's public schools foster the common good?* New York: Public Agenda.

Purkey, S.C., and M.S. Smith. 1983. Effective schools—A review. *Elementary School Journal, 83*(4), pp. 427–452.

Putnam, R.D. 2000. *Bowling alone.* New York: Simon and Schuster.

Queensland Department of Education. 1996. *Community accountability conferencing: Trial report.* Brisbane, Australia: Department of Education.

Quinney, R. 2000. *Bearing witness to crime and social justice.* Albany: State University of New York Press.

Quint, J., H.S. Bloom, A.R. Black, L. Stephens, and T.M. Akey. 2005. *The challenge of scaling up educational reform: Findings and lessons from First Things First.* New York: Manpower Demonstration Research Corp.

Rabinowitz, J. 2006. Leaving homeroom in handcuffs: Why an over-reliance on law enforcement to ensure school safety is detrimental to children. *Cardozo Public Law, Policy and Ethics Journal, 4,* p. 153.

Randazzo, M.R., R. Borum, B. Vossekuil, R. Fein, W. Modzeleski, and W. Pollack. 2006. Threat assessment in schools: Empirical support and comparison with other approaches. In S.R. Jimerson and M.J. Furlong, eds., *The handbook of school violence and school safety: From research to practice* (pp. 147–156). Mahwah, NJ: Lawrence Erlbaum.

Rappaport, N., and J.G. Barrett. 2009. Under the gun: Threat assessment in schools. *American Medical Association Journal of Ethics, 11*(2), pp. 149–154.

Rathjen, H., and C. Montpetit. 1999. *December 6th: From Montreal Massacre to gun control.* Toronto: McClelland and Stewart.

Rawlings, K.C., and T.J. Catlaw. 2011. Democracy as a way of life: Rethinking the place and practices of public administration. In C.S. King, ed., *Government is us 2.0.* Rev. ed. Armonk, NY: M.E. Sharpe.

Readiness and Emergency Management for Schools (REMS) Technical Assistance Center. 2011. School and campus emergency management resources. Accessed September 18, 2011, from http://rems.ed.gov/.

Reaves, B.A., and A.L. Goldberg. 2000. *Local police departments, 1997.* Washington, DC: US Bureau of Justice Statistics, Law Enforcement Management and Administrative Statistics.

Reddy, M., R. Borum, J. Berglund, B. Vossekuil, R. Fein, and W. Modzelski. 2001. Evaluating risk for targeted violence in schools: Comparing risk assessment, threat assessment, and other approaches. *Psychology in the Schools, 38*(2), pp. 157–172.

Reese, L.E., E.M. Vera, T.R. Simon, and R.M. Ikeda. 2000. The role of families and care givers as risk and protective factors in preventing youth violence. *Clinical Child and Family Psychology Review, 3*, pp. 61–77.

Reeves, M.A., L.M. Kanan, and A.E. Plog. 2010. *Comprehensive planning for safe learning environments. A school professional's guide to integrating physical and psychological safety—Prevention through recovery.* Abingdon, UK: Routledge.

Reid, J., G. Patterson, and J. Synder. 2002. *Antisocial behavior in children and adolescents: A developmental analysis and model for intervention.* Washington, DC: American Psychological Association.

Reinke, W.M., and K.C. Herman. 2002. Creating school environments that deter antisocial behaviors in youth. *Psychology in the Schools, 39*, pp. 549–559.

Rentschler, C.A. 2003. Designing fear: How environmental security protects property at the expense of people. In J.Z. Bratich, J. Packer, and C. McCarthy, eds., *Foucault, cultural studies, and govermentality* (pp. 243–272). Albany: State University of New York Press.

Reyes, A.H. 2003. Criminalization of student discipline. In Harvard Civil Rights Project, *Reconstructing the school-to-prison pipeline: Charting intervention strategies of prevention and support for minority children.* Accessed from http://www.civilrightsproject.harvard.edu/.

Rhodes, R.A.W. 1994. The hollowing out of the state. *Political Studies, 65*, pp. 138–151.

Rich-Shea, A.M. 2010. Adolescent youth and social control: The changing role of public schools. *Dissertation Abstracts International.* UMI No. 3427444.

Ricketts, M.L. 2007. K–12 teachers' perceptions of school policy and fear of school violence. *Journal of School Violence, 6*(3), pp. 45–67.

Rigakos, G.S., and R.W. Hadden. 2001. Crime, capitalism and the "risk society": Towards the same olde modernity? *Theoretical Criminology, 5*(1), pp. 61–84.

Robers, S., J. Zhang, and J. Truman. 2010. *Indicators of School Crime and Safety: 2010.* NCES 2011-002/NCJ 230812. National Center for Education Statistics, US Department of Education, and Bureau of Justice Statistics, Office of Justice Programs, US Department of Justice. Washington, DC.

Robers, S., J. Zhang, and J. Truman. 2012. *Indicators of school crime and safety: 2011.* NCES 2012-002/NCJ 236021. National Center for Education Statistics, US Department of Education, and Bureau of Justice Statistics, Office of Justice Programs, US Department of Justice. Washington, DC. Accessed July 24, 2012, from http://nces.ed.gov/programs/crimeindicators/crime indicators2011/figures/figure_01_1.asp.

Roberts, S.D., P. Wilcox, D.C. May, and R.R. Clayton. 2007. My school or our school? The effects of individual versus shared school experiences on teacher perceptions of safety. *Journal of School Violence, 6*(4), pp. 33–55.

Robin, C. 2004. *Fear: The history of a political idea.* Oxford: Oxford University Press.

Rodkin, P.C., and E.V. Hodges. 2003. Bullies and victims in the peer ecology: Four questions for psychologists and school professionals. *School Psychology Review, 32*, pp. 384–400.

Romer, D., and T. Heller. 1983. Social adaptation of mentally retarded adults in community settings: A social-ecological approach. *Applied Research in Mental Retardation, 4*, pp. 303–314.

Rose, N. 1997. Governing "advanced" liberal democracies. In A. Barry, T. Osbourne, and N. Rose, eds., *Foucault and political reason: Liberalism, neo-liberalism, and rationalities of government* (pp. 37–64). Chicago: University of Chicago Press.

Rosenbaum, D.P., R.L. Flewelling, S.L. Bailey, C.L. Ringwal, and D.L. Wilkinson. 1994. Cops in the classroom: A longitudinal evaluation of drug abuse resistance education (DARE). *Journal of Research in Crime and Delinquency, 31,* pp. 3–31.

Rowan, B. 1990. Commitment and control: Alternative strategies for the organizational design of schools. *Review of Research in Education, 16,* pp. 353–392.

Ruddick, S. 1989. *Maternal thinking: Towards a politics of peace.* Boston: Beacon Press.

Ruddy, S.A., L. Bauer, S. Neiman, C.A. Hryczaniuk, T.L. Thomas, and R.J. Parmer. 2010. *2007–08 School Survey on Crime and Safety (SSOCS): Survey documentation for restricted-use data file uses.* Washington, DC: US Department of Education.

Rudnick, G.D. 2011. November. Policing in public schools: Beyond the active shooter. *FBI Law Enforcement Bulletin.* Accessed from http://www.fbi.gov/stats-services/publications/law-enforcement-bulletin/november-2011/policing-in-public-schools.

Rutter, M., and B. Maughan. 2002. School effectiveness findings 1979–2002. *Journal of School Psychology, 40,* pp. 451–475.

Rutter, M., B. Maughan, P. Mortimore, and J. Ouston. 1979. *Fifteen thousand hours: Secondary schools and their effects on children.* London: Open Books.

Sachsman, S. September 8, 1997. Prof stalkers beware: MOSAIC is here. *Yale Daily News.*

Salzinger, S., D.S. Ng-Mak, R.S. Feldman, C.M. Kam, and M. Rosario. 2006. Exposure to community violence: Processes that increase the risk for inner-city middle school children. *Journal of Early Adolescence, 26*(2), pp. 232–266.

Sampson, R.J., and J.H. Laub. 1993. *Crime in the making.* Cambridge, MA: Harvard University Press.

Sandu, D.S., and C.B. Aspey. Eds. 2000. *Violence in American schools: A practical guide for counselors.* Washington, DC: American Counseling Association.

Savage, J. 2004. Does viewing violent media really cause criminal violence? A methodological review. *Aggression and Violent Behavior, 10,* pp. 99–128.

Scheffer, M.W. 1987. *Policing from the schoolhouse: police-school liaison and resource officer programs. A case study.* Springfield, IL: Charles C. Thomas.

Schiraldi, V., and J. Zeidenberg, 2001. Schools and suspensions: Self-reported crime and the growing use of suspensions. Washington, DC: Justice Policy Institute.

Schneider, T. 2001. *Safer schools through environmental design.* Eugene, OR: ERIC Clearinghouse on Educational Management, University of Oregon.

Schreck, C.J., and J.M. Miller. 2003. Sources of fear of crime at school. *Journal of School Violence, 2,* pp. 57–79.

Schreck, C.J., J.M. Miller, and C.L. Gibson. 2003. Trouble in the school yard: A study of the risk factors of victimization at school. *Crime and Delinquency, 49*(3), pp. 460–484.

Schur, E.M. 1980. *The politics of deviance: Stigma contests and the uses of power.* Englewood Cliffs, NJ: Prentice-Hall.

Schwartz, G. 1987. *Beyond conformity or rebellion: Youth and authority in America.* Chicago: University of Chicago Press.

Schwarz, E. and J. Kowalski. 1991. Malignant memories: Posttraumatic stress disorder in children and adults following a school shooting. *Journal of the American Academy of Child and Adolescent Psychiatry,* 30, pp. 937–944.

Searight, H.R., and A.L. McLaren. 1998. Attention-deficit hyperactivity disorder: The medicalization of misbehavior. *Journal of Clinical Psychology in Medical Settings 5*(4), pp. 467–495.

Sebring, P.B., E. Allensworth, A.S. Bryk, J.Q. Easton, and S. Luppescu. 2006. *The essential supports for school improvement.* Chicago: University of Chicago, Consortium on Chicago School Research. Accessed from http://ccsr.uchicago.edu/publications/EssentialSupports.pdf.

Sewell, K.W., and M. Mendelsohn. 2000. Profiling potentially violent youth: statistical and conceptual problems. *Children's Services: Social Policy, Research, and Practice,* 3, pp. 147–169.

Shapiro, J.P., and J.A. Stefkovich. 2011. *Ethical leadership and decision making in education.* 3rd ed. New York: Routledge, Taylor and Francis Group.

Shaw, G. 2007. Restorative practices in Australian schools: Changing relationships, changing culture. *Conflict Resolution Quarterly, 25,* pp. 127–135.

Sheldon, S.B., and J.L. Epstein. 2002. Improving student behavior and school discipline with family and community involvement. *Education and Urban Society, 35,* pp. 4–26.

Sheridan, S.M., E.D. Warnes, and S. Dowd. 2004. Home-school collaboration and bullying: An ecological approach to increase social competence in children and youth. In D.L. Espelage and S.M. Swearer, eds., *Bullying in American schools: A social-ecological perspective on prevention and intervention* (pp. 245–267). Mahwah, NJ: Lawrence Erlbaum.

Sherman, L.W. 2003. Reason for emotion: Reinventing justice with theories, innovations, and research: The American Society of Criminology 2002 Presidential Address. *Criminology, 41,* pp. 1–37.

Shibuya, A., A. Sakamoto, N. Ihori, and S. Yukawa. 2008. The effects of the presence and context of video game violence on children: A longitudinal study in Japan. *Simulation and Gaming, 39,* pp. 528–539.

Simon, J. 2007. *Governing through crime: How the war on crime transformed American democracy and created a culture of fear.* Oxford: Oxford University Press.

Simonsen, B.M., G. Sugai, and M. Negron. 2008. School-wide positive behavior support: Primary systems and practices. *Teaching Exceptional Children, Special Issue: Positive Behavior Interventions and Supports, 40,* pp. 32–40.

Skiba, R.J. 2000. Zero tolerance, zero evidence: An analysis of school disciplinary practice. Policy research report SRS2. Bloomington: Indiana Education Policy Center.

Skiba, R.J. 2001. When is disproportionality discrimination? The overrepresentation of black students in school suspension. In W. Ayers, B. Dohrn, and R. Ayers, eds., *Zero tolerance: Resisting the drive for punishment in our schools: A handbook for parents, students, educators, and citizens.* New York: New Press.

Skiba, R.J. 2008. Are zero tolerance policies effective in the schools? An evidentiary review and recommendations. *American Psychologist, 63*(9), pp. 852–862.

Skiba, R.J., R.S. Michael, and A.C. Nardo. 2000. *The color of discipline: Sources of racial and gender disproportionality in school punishment.* Bloomington: Indiana Education Policy Center, Report SRS1.

Skiba, R.J., and R.L. Peterson. 1999. The dark side of zero tolerance: Can punishment lead to safe schools? *Phi Delta Kappan, 80*(5), pp. 372–382.

Skiba, R.J., and R.L. Peterson. 2000. School discipline at a crossroads: From zero tolerance to early response. *Exceptional Children, 66,* pp. 335–346.

Skiba, R.J., and R.L. Peterson. 2003. Teaching the social curriculum: School discipline as instruction. *Preventing School Failure, 47*(2), pp. 66–73.

Skiba, R.J., C.R. Reynolds, S. Graham, P. Sheras, J.C. Conoley, and E. Garcia-Vasquez. 2006. Are zero tolerance policies effective in the schools? An evidentiary review and recommendations. American Psychological Association Zero Tolerance Task Force. Accessed at www.apa.org/ed/cpse/zttfreport.pdf.

Skiba, R.J., S. Ritter, A.B. Simmons, R. Peterson, and C. Miler. 2005. The safe and responsive schools project: A school reform model for implementing best practice in violence prevention. In S.R. Jimerson and M.J. Furlong, eds., *The handbook for school violence and school safety: From research to practice* (pp. 631–650). Mahwah, NJ: Lawrence Erlbaum.

Smith, B.W., and M.D. Holmes. 2003. Community accountability, minority threat, and police brutality: An examination of civil rights criminal complaints. *Criminology, 41,* pp. 1035–1063.

Smith, D.L., and B.J. Smith. 2006. Perceptions of violence: The views of teachers who left urban schools. *High School Journal, 89*(3), pp. 34–42.

Snell, C., C. Bailey, A. Carona, and D. Mebane. 2002. School crime policy changes: The impact of recent highly-publicized school crimes. *American Journal of Criminal Justice, 26,* pp. 269–285.

Solomon, D., V. Battistich, D.I. Kim, and M. Watson. 1997. Teacher practices associated with students' sense of the classroom as a community. *Social Psychology of Education, 1,* pp. 235–267.

Solomon, D., M. Watson, V. Battistich, E. Schaps, and K. Delucchi. 1992. Creating a caring community: Educational practices that promote children's prosocial development. In F.K. Oser, A. Dick, and J.L. Patry, eds., *Effective and responsible teaching: The new synthesis.* San Francisco: Jossey-Bass.

Spencer, J.W. 2005. Ambiguous culpability and ambivalent affect in news representations of violent youth. *Symbolic Interaction, 28*(1), pp. 47–65.

Spencer, J.W. 2011. *The paradox of youth violence.* Boulder, CO: Lynne Rienner.

Spencer, J.W., and G.W. Muschert. 2009. The contested meanings of the crosses at Columbine. *American Behavioral Scientist, 52*(10), pp. 1371–1386.

Sprague, J.R., and A. Golly. 2005. *Best behavior: Building positive behavior supports in schools.* Longmont, CO: Sopris West Educational Services.

Sprague, J.R., and H.M. Walker. 2005. *Safe and healthy schools: Practical prevention strategies.* New York: Guilford Press.

Sprague, J.R., and H. Walker. 2011. Building safe and healthy schools to promote school success: Critical issues, current challenges and promising approaches. In M.D. Shinn and H.M. Walker, eds., *Interventions for achievement and behavior problems in a Three-Tier model Including RTI* (pp. 225–258). Bethesda, MD: National Association of School Psychologists.

Sprague, J.R., H. Walker, S. Sowards, C. Van Bloem, P. Eberhardt, and B. Marshall. 2002. Sources of vulnerability to school violence: Systems-level assessment and strategies to improve safety and climate. In M.R. Shinn, G. Stoner, and H.M. Walker, eds., *Interventions for academic and behavior problems II: Preventive and remedial approaches* (pp. 295–314). Silver Spring, MD: National Association of School Psychologists.

Staderab, D.L. 2006. Zero tolerance: Safe schools or zero sense? *Journal of Forensic Psychology Practice, 6*(2), pp. 65–75.

Staples, W.G. 2000. *Everyday surveillance: Vigilance and visibility in postmodern life*. Lanham, MD: Rowman and Littlefield.

Statistics Canada. 2008. Population and dwelling counts, for Canada and census subdivisions (municipalities), 2006 and 2001 censuses—100% data. Accessed from http://www12.statcan.ca/english/census06/data/popdwell/Table.cfm?T= 301andS=3andO=D.

Statistics Canada. 2010a. Federal electoral district profile of Nepean—Carleton, Ontario (2003 Representation Order), 2006 Census. Accessed from http:// www12.statcan.gc.ca/census-recensement/2006/dp-pd/prof/92-595/P2C .cfm?TPL=RETRandLANG=EandGC=35052.

Statistics Canada. 2010b. Federal electoral district profile of Ottawa West— Nepean, Ontario (2003 Representation Order), 2006 Census. Accessed from http://www12.statcan.gc.ca/census-recensement/2006/dp-pd/prof/92 -595/P2C.cfm?TPL=RETRandLANG=EandGC=35066.

Steiker, C.S. 1998. Forward: The limits of the preventive state. *Journal of Criminal Law and Criminology, 88*(3), pp. 771–808.

Stephen, J.F. 1873. *Liberty, equality, fraternity*. Accessed July 24, 2011, from http://terrenceberres.com/stelib.html.

Stewart, E. 2003. School social bonds, school climate, and school misbehavior: A multilevel analysis. *Justice Quarterly, 20,* pp. 575–604.

Stinchcomb, J.B., G. Bazemore, and N. Riestenberg. 2006. Beyond zero tolerance: Restoring justice in secondary schools. *Youth Violence and Juvenile Justice, 4,* pp. 123–147.

Stokol, D. 1996. Translating social ecological theory into guidelines for community health promotion. *American Journal of Health Promotion, 10*(4), pp. 282–298.

Strong, K., and D. Cornell. 2008. Student threat assessment in Memphis city schools: A descriptive report. *Behavioral Disorders, 34,* pp. 42–54.

"Student suspended after finger gun incident." 2010. Abclocal.go.com. Accessed October 3, 2010, from http://abclocal.go.com/ktrk/story?section=news/local andid=7392273.

Stutzman-Amstutz, L., and J. Mullet. 2005. *The little book of restorative discipline for schools*. Intercourse, PA: Good Books.

Sugai, G., and R. Horner. 2002. The evolution of discipline practices: Schoolwide posiitve behavior support. *Child and Family Behavior Therapy, 24,* pp. 23–50.

Sugai, G., and R. Horner. 2010. School-wide positive behavior support: Establishing a continuum of evidence-based practices. *Journal of Evidence-based Practices for Schools, 11*(1), pp. 62–83.

Sugai, G., J.R. Sprague, R.H. Horner, and H.M. Walker. 2000. Preventing school violence: The use of office discipline referrals to assess and monitor schoolwide discipline interventions. *Journal of Emotional and Behavioral Disorders, 8,* pp. 94–101.

Surowiecki, J. 2004. *The wisdom of crowds: Why the many are smarter than the few and how collective wisdom shapes business, economies, societies and nations*. New York: Doubleday.

Swearer, S.M., and B. Doll. 2001. Bullying in schools: An ecological framework. *Journal of Emotional Abuse, 2,* pp. 7–23.

Syvertsen, A.K., C.A. Flanagan, and M.D. Stout. 2009. Code of silence: Students' perceptions of school climate and willingness to intervene in a peer's dangerous plan. *Journal of Educational Psychology, 101*(1), pp. 219–232.

Tannen, D. 2001. *You just don't understand: Women and men in conversation.* New York: Harper Paperbacks.

Taylor-Butts, A., and A. Bressan. 2009. *Youth crime in Canada, 2006.* Accessed from http://www.statcan.gc.ca/pub/85-002-x/2008003/article/10566-eng.htm.

Teicher, S.A. 2006. How students can break the "code of silence": A number of resources let students anonymously voice their concerns about troubling issues at school. *Christian Science Monitor.* Accessed July 3, 2011, from http://www.csmonitor.com/2006/1019/p15s01-legn.html.

Theriot, M. 2009. School resource officers and the criminalization of student behavior. *Journal of Criminal Justice, 37,* pp. 280–287.

Thompkins, D.E. 2000, January. School violence, gangs, and a culture of fear. *The Annals of the American Academy of Political and Social Science, 567,* pp. 54–71.

Thorsborne, M., and L. Cameron. 2001. Restorative justice and school discipline: Mutually exclusive? In H. Strang and J. Braithwaite, eds., *Restorative justice and civil society,* (pp. 180–194). Cambridge, UK: Cambridge University Press.

Thurau, L., and J. Wald. 2010. Controlling partners: When law enforcement meets discipline in public schools. *New York Law School Law Review, 54,* pp. 977–1020.

Times Wire Reports. 2001. Child suspended for brandishing chicken. *Los Angeles Times.* Accessed September 20, 2010, from http://articles.latimes.com/2001/feb/01/news/mn-19819.

Tittle, C.R. 1995. *Control balance: Toward a general theory of deviance.* Boulder, CO: Westview Press

Tolan, P.H., and N.G. Guerra. 1994. *What works in reducing adolescent violence: An empirical review of the field.* Boulder, CO: University of Colorado, Center of the Study and Prevention of Violence, Institute for Behavioral Sciences.

Tonso, K.L. 2002. Reflecting on Columbine High: Ideologies of privilege in "standardized" schools. *Educational Studies, 33,* pp. 389–403.

Tonso, K.L. 2009. Violent masculinities as tropes for school shooters: The Montréal Massacre, the Columbine attack, and rethinking schools. *American Behavioral Scientist, 52*(9), pp. 1266–1285.

Toronto Star. 2007. Shooting violence in Canadian schools 1975–2007. Accessed from http://www.thestar.com/News/article/217023.

Tredway, L., F. Brill, and J. Hernandez. 2007. Taking off the cape: The stories of novice urban leadership. *Theory into Practice, 46,* pp. 212–221.

Tudor, A. 2003. A (macro) sociology of fear? *Sociological Review, 51*(2), pp. 238–256.

Turvey, B.E. 2008. *Criminal profiling: An introduction to behavioral evidence analysis.* 3rd ed. Burlington, MA: Academic Press.

Tversky, A., and D. Kahneman. 1986. Judgment under uncertainty: Heuristics and biases. In H.R. Hammond and K.R. Arkes, eds., *Judgment and decision making: An interdisciplinary reader* (pp. 38–55). Cambridge: Cambridge University Press.

Twemlow, S.W., and J. Cohen. 2003. Guest editorial: Stopping school violence. *Journal of Applied Psychoanalytic Studies, 5*(2), pp. 117–124.

Twemlow, S.W., P. Fonagy, and F.C. Sacco. 2004. The role of the bystander in the social architecture of bullying and violence in schools and communities. *Annals of the New York Academy of Sciences, 1036,* pp. 215–232.

Twemlow, S.W., P. Fonagy, F.C. Sacco, M.L. Gies, R. Evans, and R. Ewbank. 2001. Creating a peaceful school learning environment: A controlled study of an elementary school intervention to reduce violence. *American Journal of Psychiatry, 158,* pp. 808–810.

Twemlow, S.W., P. Fonagy, F.C. Sacco, M.E. O'Toole, and E. Vernberg. 2002. Premeditated mass shootings in schools: Threat assessment. *Journal of the American Academy of Child and Adolescent Psychiatry, 41*(4), pp. 475–477.

Tyack, D. 1974. *The one best system: A history of American urban education.* Cambridge, MA: Harvard University Press.

Upreti, G., C. Liaupsin, and D. Koonce. 2010. Stakeholder utility: Perspectives on school-wide data for measurement, feedback, and evaluation. *Education and Treatment of Children, 33*(4), pp. 497–511.

Urbina, I. 2009. It's a fork, it's a spoon, it's a . . . weapon. *New York Times.* Accessed October 3, 2010, from http://www.nytimes.com/2009/10/12/education/12discipline.html?_r=2.

US Census Bureau. 2011. American Community Survey Main. Washington, DC: US Census Bureau. Accessed at http://www.census.gov/acs/www/.

US Department of Education. 2003. *2000 School Survey on Crime and Safety: Detailed data documentation.* Washington, DC: US Department of Education.

US Department of Health and Human Services 2001. *Youth violence: A report to the Surgeon General.* Rockville, MD: US Department of Health and Human Services, Center for Disease Control and Prevention, National Center for Injury Prevention and Control, Substance Abuse and Mental Health Services Administration, Center for Mental Health Services, and National Institutes of Health, National Institute of Mental Health.

US Department of Justice, Bureau of Justice Statistics, 2010. *Prisoners in 2009.* Data file. Accessed from http://bjs.ojp.usdoj.gov/index.cfm?ty=pbdetail andiid=2316.

US Federal Trade Commission. 2000. Marketing violent entertainment to children: A review of self-regulation and industry practices in the motion picture, music recording & electronic game industries. Washington, DC: Federal Trade Commission.

US Institute of Medicine (IOM). 2009. Preventing mental, emotional, and behavioral disorders among young people: progress and possibilities. Committee on Prevention of Mental Disorders and Substance Abuse Among Children, Youth, and Young Adults: Research Advances and Promising Interventions. Washington, DC: National Research Council and Institute of Medicine.

US National Institute of Education. 1978. *Violent schools—Safe schools: The safe school study report to Congress.* Washington, DC: US Department of Health, Education and Welfare.

US Secret Service and US Department of Education. 2002. *The final report and findings of the Safe School Initiative: Implications for the prevention of school attacks in the United States.* Accessed November 12, 2007, from http://www.secretservice.gov/ntac/ssi_final_report.pdf.

Valenzuela, A. Ed. 2005. *Leaving children behind: How "Texas-style" accountability fails Latino youth.* Albany: State University of New York Press.

van Dijk, J., J. van Kesteren, and P. Smit. 2007. *Criminal victimization in international perspective.* The Hague, Netherlands: United Nations Office on Drug and Crime.

Vavrus, F., and K.M. Cole. 2002. "I didn't do nothin'": The discursive construction of school suspension. *Urban Review, 34,* pp. 87–111.

Vera Institute of Justice. 1999. Approaches to school safety in America's largest cities. Accessed March 14, 2011, from http://www.vera.org/publication_pdf/apprchs_school_safety.pdf.

Verdugo, R. 2002. Race-ethnicity, social class, and zero-tolerance policies: The cultural and structural wars. *Education and Urban Society, 35,* pp. 50–76.

Verlinden, S., M. Hersen, and J. Thomas. 2000. Risk factors in school shootings. *Clinical Psychology Review, 20*(1), pp. 3–56.

Vincent, G.M., A.M. Terry, and S.M. Maney. 2009. Risk/needs tools for antisocial behavior and violence among youthful populations. In J.T. Andrade, ed., *Handbook of violence risk assessment and treatment: New approaches for mental health professionals* (pp. 377–424). New York: Springer.

Virginia Tech Review Panel. 2007. *Report of the Virginia Tech Review Panel.* Accessed November 11, 2010, from http://www.governor.virginia.gov/TempContent/techPanelReport.cfm.

Vossekuil, B., R. Fein, M. Reddy, R. Borum, and W. Modzeleski. 2002. The final report and findings of the safe school initiative: Implications for the prevention of school attacks in the United States. Washington, DC: US Secret Service and US Department of Education.

Wachtel, T. 1999. *Restorative justice in everyday life: Beyond the formal ritual.* Paper presented at the Reshaping Australian Institutions Conference: Restorative Justice and Civil Society. Canberra: Australian National University.

Wachtel, T. 2001. SaferSanerSchools: Restoring community in a disconnected world. Accessed from http://www.safersanerschools.org/Pages/restorative practices.html.

Wachtel, T., and P. McCold. 2001. Restorative justice in everyday life: Beyond the formal ritual. In H. Strang and J. Braithwaite, eds., *Restorative justice and civil society.* Cambridge: Cambridge University Press.

Wacquant, L. 2001. Deadly symbiosis: When ghetto and prison meet and mesh. In D. Garland, ed., *Mass imprisonment: Social causes and consequences.* London: Sage.

Wacquant, L. 2009. *Punishing the poor: The neoliberal government of social insecurity.* Durham, NC: Duke University Press.

Wald, J., and D.J. Losen. 2003. Defining and redirecting the school-to-prison pipeline. In J. Wald and D.J. Losen, eds., *New directions for youth development, No. 99: Deconstructing the school-to-prison pipeline* (pp. 9–15). San Francisco: Jossey-Bass.

Walker, H.M., R.H. Horner, G. Sugai, M. Bullis, J.R. Sprague, D. Bricker, and M.J. Kaufman. 1996. Integrated approaches to preventing anti-social behavior patterns among school-age children and youth. *Journal of Emotional and Behavioral Disorders, 4*(4), pp. 194–209.

Walker, H.M., E. Ramsey, and F. Gresham. 2004. *Antisocial behavior in school: Evidenced-based practices.* Florence, KY: Cengage.

Warren, K.J., and D.L. Cady. 1996. Feminism and peace: Seeing connections. In K.J. Warren and D.L. Cady, eds., *Bringing peace home: Feminism, violence, and nature* (pp. 1–15). Bloomington: Indiana University Press.

Watts, I.E., and N. Erevelles. 2004. These deadly times: Reconceptualizing school violence by using critical race theory and disability studies. *American Educational Research Journal, 41*(2), pp. 271–299.

Wearmouth, J., R. McKinney, and T. Glynn. 2007. Restorative justice: Two examples from New Zealand Schools. *British Journal of Special Education, 34*, pp. 196–203.

Weisbrot, D.M. 2008. Prelude to a school shooting? Assessing threatening behaviors in childhood and adolescence. *Journal of the American Academy of the Child and Adolescent Psychiatry, 47*, pp. 847–852.

Weiss, J. 2010. Scan this: Examining student resistance to school surveillance. In T. Monahan and R.D. Torres, eds., *Schools under surveillance: Cultures of control in public education* (pp. 213–229). New Brunswick, NJ: Routledge.

Welch, K. 2007. Black criminal stereotypes and racial profiling. *Journal of Contemporary Criminal Justice, 23*, pp. 276–288.

Welch, K., and A.A. Payne. 2010. Racial threat and punitive school discipline. *Social Problems, 57*, pp. 25–48.

Welch, M., E.A. Price, and N. Yankey. 2002. Moral panic over youth violence: Wilding and the manufacture of menace in the media. *Youth and Society, 34*(1), pp. 3–30.

Welsh, W.N. 2000. The effects of school climate on school disorder. *The Annals of the American Academy of Political and Social Science, 567*, pp. 88–107.

Welsh, W.N., J.R. Greene, and P.H. Jenkins. 1999. School disorder: The influence of individual, institutional, and community factors. *Criminology, 37*, pp. 73–115.

Werner, E.E., and R.S. Smith. 1992. *Overcoming the odds: High risk children from birth to adulthood.* Ithaca, NY: Cornell University Press.

Whitehead, J.T., W. Gillespie, and M. Braswell. 2008. The future of the peacemaking perspective. In J.F. Wozniak, M.C. Braswell, R.E. Vogel, K.R. Blevins, eds., *Transformative justice* (pp. 231–250). Lanham, MD: Lexington Books.

Whitehead, J.W. 2011. Zero tolerance policies: Are the schools becoming police states? Accessed July 24, 2011 from http://www.lewrockwell.com/white head/whitehead26.1.html.

Whitlock, J.L. 2006. Youth perceptions of life at school: Contextual correlates of school connectedness in adolescence. *Applied Developmental Science, 10*, pp. 13–29.

Wike, T.L., and M.W. Fraser. 2009. School shootings: Making sense of the senseless. *Aggression and Violent Behavior, 14*, pp. 162–169.

Williams, K.M. 2005. *Socially constructed school violence: Lessons from the field.* New York: Peter Lang.

Williams, K.M., and K. Corvo, 2005. "That I'll be killed": Pre-service and in-service teachers' greatest fears and beliefs about school violence. *Journal of School Violence, 4*(1), pp. 47–69.

Willis, P. 1977. *Learning to labor: How working class kids get working class jobs.* New York: Columbia University Press.

Willower, D.J. 1978. Inquiry on school organizations: Some hunting stories. *Studies in educational administration and organization, 79*, pp. 34–55.

Willower, D.J., T.J. Eidell, and W.K. Hoy. 1967. *The school and pupil control ideology.* University Park: Pennsylvania State University.

Willower, D.J., T.J. Eidell, and W.K. Hoy. 1973. *The school and pupil control ideology.* 2nd ed. University Park: Pennsylvania State University.

Wilson, D. 2004. The interface of school climate and school connectedness and relationships with aggression and victimization. *Journal of School Health, 74*, pp. 293–299.

Winkler, A. 2011. *Gunfight: The battle over the right to bear arms in America.* New York: W.W. Norton.

Winslade, J., and M. Williams. 2011. *Safe and Peaceful Schools: Addressing Conflict and Eliminating Violence.* Thousand Oaks, CA: Corwin Press.

Wozniak, J.F. 2008a. Introduction to transformative justice: Critical and peace-making themes influenced by Richard Quinney. In J.F. Wozniak, M.C. Braswell, R.E. Vogel, and K.R. Blevins, eds., *Transformative justice* (pp. 1–30). Lanham, MD: Lexington Books.

Wozniak, J.F. 2008b. The relevance of Richard Quinney's writings on peace-making criminology: Toward personal and social transformation. In J.F. Wozniak, M.C. Braswell, R.E. Vogel, and K.R. Blevins, eds., *Transformative justice* (pp. 167–190). Lanham, MD: Lexington Books.

Wozniak, J.F. 2008c. Toward a theoretical model of peacemaking: An essay in honor of Richard Quinney. In J.F. Wozniak, M.C. Braswell, R.E. Vogel, and K.R. Blevins, eds., *Transformative justice* (pp. 141–161). Lanham, MD: Lexington Books.

Ybarra, M., M. Diener-West, D. Markow, P. Leaf, M. Hamburger, and P. Boxer. 2008. Linkages between internet and other media violence with seriously violent behavior by youth. *Pediatrics, 122*, pp. 929–937.

Yogan, L.J., and S. Henry. 2000. Masculine thinking and school violence: Issues of race and gender. In D.S. Sandhu and C.B. Aspey, eds., *Violence in American schools: A practical guide for counselors* (pp. 89–108). Alexandria, VA: American Counseling Association.

Young, J. 1994. Incessant chatter: Recent paradigms in criminology. In M. Maquire, R. Morgan, and R. Reiner, eds., *The Oxford handbook of criminology* (pp. 69–124). Oxford: Oxford University Press.

Young, J. 2007a. Slipping away: Moral panics each side of "The golden age." In D.M. Downes, ed., *Crime, social control and human rights: From moral panics to states of denial—Essays in honour of Stanley Cohen* (pp. 53–65). New York: Taylor and Francis.

Young, J. 2007b. *The vertigo of late modernity.* London: Sage.

Young, M.D., and C. Brewer. 2008. Fear and the preparation of school leaders: The role of ambiguity, anxiety, and power in meaning making. *Educational Policy, 22*(1), pp. 106–129.

Youth Justice Board. 2005. National evaluation of the restorative justice in schools program. Accessed from http://www.youth-justice-board.gov.uk.

Zaff, J.F., K.A. Moore, A.R. Papillo, and S. Williams. 2003. Implications of extra-curricular activity participation during adolescence on positive outcomes. *Journal of Adolescent Research, 18*, pp. 599–630.

Zimmerman, A.L., M.L. McDermott, and C.M. Gould. 2009. The local is global: Third wave feminism, peace, and social justice. *Contemporary Justice Review, 12*(1), pp. 77–90.

Zimmerman, M.A., and R. Arunkumar. 1994. Resiliency research: Implications for schools and policy. *Social Policy Report, 8*(4), 1–18.

Zins, J.E., and C.R. Ponte. 1990. Best practices in school-based consultation. In A. Thomas and J. Grimes, eds., *Best practices in school psychology, Vol. 2* (pp. 673–694). Washington, DC: National Association of School Psychologists.

Zins, J.E., R.P. Weissberg, M.C. Wang, and H.J. Walberg. 2004. *Building academic success on social and emotional learning: What does the research say?* New York: Teachers College Press.

Zorn, D., and M. Boler. 2007. Rethinking emotions and educational leadership. *International Journal of Leadership in Education, 10*(2), pp. 137–151.

The Contributors

Lynn A. Addington is associate professor in the Department of Justice, Law and Society at American University, Washington, DC. Her research focuses on violent victimization and has examined the short- and long-term consequences of Columbine. Her recent work has appeared in the *Journal of Quantitative Criminology, Justice Quarterly,* and *Homicide Studies.* She is the coeditor of *Understanding Crime Statistics: Revisiting the Divergence of the NCVS and UCR* (2007). She has also published articles on school violence in *American Behavioral Scientist* and the *Journal of American Education.* Email: adding@american.edu

Paula Allen-Meares is chancellor and John Corbally Presidential Professor at the University of Illinois at Chicago. She is a member of the Institute of Medicine of the National Academies, the Royal Academy of Medicine; a trustee of the New York Academy of Medicine; a board member of the Civic Consulting Alliance; a member of the American Council on Education's Commission on Racial and Ethnic Equity; and a board member of the Coalition of Urban Serving Universities. She is currently the principal investigator of the Skillman Good Neighborhoods Grant. Dr. Allen-Meares has over 140 publications and several books including the recently released *Cross Cultural Research.* Email: pameares@uic.edu

Nicole L. Bracy is research associate at Harder+CompanyCommunity Research in San Diego. She also holds a research appointment at the University of California, San Diego, in the Department of Family and Preventive Medicine and is a lecturer at San Diego State University in the School of Public Affairs. She has published multiple articles and book chapters related to school security and discipline and is particularly interested in the implications of school security policies and practices for students' legal rights. Nicole is currently managing editor of *Western Criminology Review.* Email: nbracy@ harderco.com

Curtis A. Brewer is assistant professor in the Department of Educational Leadership and Policy Studies at the University of Texas at San Antonio. He was the 2009 recipient of the Distinguished Dissertation Award from Division G, Social Context of Education, one of twelve divisions within the American Educational Research Association. His research focuses on the unexplored political role of school principals. He has published articles in *Peabody Journal of Education, Discourse,* and *Educational Policy.* Email: brewer4@clemson.edu

Thomas J. Catlaw is associate professor in the School of Public Affairs at Arizona State University in Phoenix. He is the author of *Fabricating the People: Politics and Administration in the Biopolitical State.* Dr. Catlaw is the current editor of *Administrative Theory and Praxis,* an international journal dedicated to the theoretical analysis of governmental practice. He has published numerous articles in *Administration and Society, Administrative Theory and Praxis,* and *Public Administration Quarterly.* Email: Thomas.Catlaw @asu.edu

Daniel W. Close is associate professor and director of the Family and Human Services Program in the College of Education at the University of Oregon. Email: dclose@uoregon.edu

Dorothy L. Espelage is professor of child development and associate chair in the Department of Educational Psychology at the University of Illinois, Urbana-Champaign. She has fellow status in Division 17 (counseling psychology) of the American Psychological Association. She presents regularly at national conferences and is author of over a hundred professional publications and coeditor of four books, including *Bullying in North American Schools: A Social-Ecological Perspective on Prevention and Intervention* and *International Handbook of Bullying.* She is also associate editor of the *Journal of Counseling Psychology.* Email: espelage@illinois.edu

Christopher J. Ferguson is a clinical psychologist and associate professor at Stetson University. He recently guest-edited the American Psychological Association journal *Review of General Psychology* special issue on video games. He has written extensively on youth violence, school shootings, and media effects. He is editor of *Violent Crime: Clinical and Social Implications* and has published articles in professional journals including *Aggression and Violent Behavior, Journal of Social Psychology, and Journal of Forensic Psychology Practice.* Email: CJFerguson1111@aol.com

James Alan Fox is the Lipman Family Professor of Criminology, Law and Public Policy at Northeastern University. He has written eighteen books, including *Violence and Security on Campus: From Preschool Through College,* and has published hundreds of articles for both academic and popular audiences. Fox often gives invited lectures and expert testimony, including fifteen appearances before Congress, and presentations to former president Bill Clinton, attorneys general Janet Reno and Eric Holder, and Princess Anne of Great Britain. Finally, he served on White House advisory committees on school shootings and youth violence and a U.S. Department of Education advisory panel on Safe, Disciplined and Drug Free Schools. Email: j.fox@neu.edu

Stuart Henry is professor of criminal justice and director of the School of Public Affairs at San Diego State University. He is the author or editor of twenty-eight books and over one hundred professional journal articles on the topics of criminological theory, deviant behavior, law and society, and occupational crime. His books include: The *Hidden Economy, Criminological Theory, Constitutive Criminology, What Is Crime? Essential Criminology, The Politics of Interdisciplinary Studies,* and *Social Deviance.* He is currently coeditor of *Western Criminology Review.* Email: shenry2@mail.sdsu.edu

Daniel Hillyard is associate professor in the Department of Criminology and Criminal Justice at Southern Illinois University Carbondale. He writes on the intersections of law, morality, social change, and social control, emphasizing the history, politics, ethics, and legal aspects of race, class, gender, and sexuality. His current focus is on overuse of the criminal sanction and administrative systems of punishment as means of social control. Email: hillyard@siu.edu

Jun Sung Hong is assistant professor in the School of Social Work at Wayne State University. He is also currently a Council on Social Work Education (CSWE) Minority Fellow and a former Fulbright fellow. His research interests include school violence, school-based intervention, juvenile delinquency, child welfare, and cultural competency in social work practice. Email: junsung-hong@hotmail.com.

Douglas Kellner is George Kneller Chair in the Philosophy of Education at the University of California at Los Angeles and is author of many books on social theory, politics, history, and culture, including works in cultural studies such as *Media Culture* and *Media Spectacle.* *Guys and Guns Amok: Domestic Terrorism and School Shootings from the Oklahoma City Bombings to the Virginia Tech Massacre* won the 2008 Association of Educational Service Agencies (AESA) award as the best book on education. In 2010 he published *Cinema Wars: Hollywood Film and Politics in the Bush/Cheney Era,* and he has a forthcoming book titled *Media Spectacle and Insurrection, 2011: From the Arab Uprisings to Occupy Everywhere!* Email: kellner@ucla.edu

Aaron Kupchik is professor in the Department of Sociology and Criminal Justice at the University of Delaware. He is author of *Judging Juveniles: Prosecuting Adolescents in Adult and Juvenile Courts* and *Homeroom Security: School Discipline in an Age of Fear,* as well as numerous articles in journals including *Punishment and Society, Justice Quarterly, Crime and Delinquency,* and *Youth and Society.* Email: akupchik@udel.edu

Jane Clark Lindle is Eugene T. Moore Professor of Educational Leadership, Counselor Education, Human and Organizational Development, E.T. Moore School of Education, Clemson University. Professor Lindle's research includes grants, contracts, and publications focused on the interactions of leadership, teaching, learning, and accountability policies. She is author, coauthor, or editor of five books and over forty research and professional articles on topics including school-based governance and micropolitics examining the untoward effects of centralized policy on school communities and relationships among students, teachers, and families. She is also the past editor of *Educational Administration Quarterly.* Email: jlindle @clemson.edu

Eric Madfis is assistant professor of criminal justice at the University of Washington, Tacoma. He has published numerous articles and book chapters on school rampage shootings, theoretical criminology, and crime in the media, and his most current work explores how school and police officials perceive, assess, and prevent threats of school rampage. Email: emadfis@u.washington.edu

Gary T. Marx is Professor Emeritus of Sociology at Massachusetts Institute of Technology. He is the author of *Undercover: Police Surveillance in America; Undercover: Police Surveillance in Comparative Perspective* (with C. Fijnaut); and *Protest and Prejudice: A Study of Belief in the Black Community.* Email: gtmarx@mit.edu

M. Joan McDermott is Emeritus Associate Professor in the Department of Criminology and Criminal Justice, and former director of women's studies, Southern Illinois University Carbondale. She has written in the areas of school crime and fear of crime, the victimization of women, peacemaking, and feminist criminology. Email: joanmcd@siu.edu

Glenn W. Muschert is a sociologist of social problems who serves as criminology program coordinator and associate professor in the Department of Sociology and Gerontology at Miami University in Oxford, Ohio. His research focuses on school shootings, mass media coverage of crime, and social control through surveillance, and his publications have appeared in a variety of sociology, criminology, and media studies venues. Email: muschegw@MiamiOH.edu

Allison Ann Payne is associate director of the University Honors Program and associate professor in the Department of Sociology and Criminology at Villanova University. Her research interests include crime and delinquency prevention, criminological theory, juvenile delinquency, and school-based delinquency prevention. She has published articles in *Social Problems, Criminology, Journal of Research in Crime and Delinquency, Prevention Science,* and *Deviant Behavior.* Email: allison.payne@villanova.edu

Anthony A. Peguero is assistant professor of sociology at Virginia Polytechnic and State University. His research interests include youth and adolescence; violence and victimization; race, ethnicity, and immigration; schools; and education. Anthony has published over thirty articles as book chapters or in journals, including *Journal of School Violence, Youth and Society, Journal of Interpersonal Violence, Crime and Delinquency,* and *Punishment and Society.* Email: anthony.peguero@vt.edu

Aviva M. Rich-Shea is associate professor of criminal justice at Massasoit Community College. She was formerly research project manager with the Shannon Anti-Gang Initiative, member of the Massachusetts School to Prison Pipeline Task Force, and fellow at Suffolk University's Center for Restorative Justice. She has recently completed a study looking at the role of the school resource officer in the disciplinary process in Massachusetts high schools. Email: arich-shea@massasoit.mass.edu

Jeffrey R. Sprague is professor of special education and director of the University of Oregon Institute on Violence and Destructive Behavior. He directs federal, state, and local research and demonstration projects related to positive behavior interventions and supports, response to intervention, youth violence prevention, alternative education, juvenile delinquency prevention and treatment, and school safety. Email: jeffs@uoregon.edu

Valerie Steeves is associate professor, Department of Criminology, University of Ottawa. Her research interests include social construction of crime, privacy and surveillance, human rights and technology, media stereotyping, online hate propaganda, and pornography. She is the editor of *Privacy, Identity and Anonymity in a Network World: Lessons from the Identity Trail* and author of articles in the *Canadian Journal of Criminology and Criminal Justice, Surveillances and Society* and numerous chapters in books. Email: Valerie.Steeves@ uottawa.ca

Hill M. Walker is professor of special education and codirector of the Institute on Violence and Destructive Behavior in the College of Education, University of Oregon and senior research scientist at the Oregon Research Institute in Eugene, Oregon. He has a longstanding interest in behavioral assessment and in the development of effective intervention procedures for use in school settings with a range of behavior disorders. He has been engaged in applied research during his entire career, dating from 1966. His research interests include social skills assessment, curriculum development and intervention, longitudinal studies of aggression and antisocial behavior, and the development of early screening procedures for detecting students who are at-risk for social-behavioral adjustment problems or later school dropout. Email: hwalker@oregon.uoregon.edu

Kelly Welch is associate professor in the Department of Sociology and Criminology at Villanova University. Her primary research interests include the sociology of punishment, racial and ethnic justice, school discipline, criminological theory, and social justice. She has published articles related to these issues in *Criminology, Social Problems, Crime and Delinquency, Youth Violence and Juvenile Justice,* and *Social Science Research.* Email: kelly.welch@villanova.edu

Index

About the Book

Why do so many school antiviolence programs backfire? And why do policymakers keep making the same mistakes? The authors of Responding to School Violence examine the pervasive rise of school security measures since the Columbine shootings, highlighting the unintended consequences of policymaking too often shaped by fear and sensationalism.

Probing an array of now ubiquitous tactics and programs—metal detectors, police patrols, zero tolerance policies, and more—the authors show how increasingly punitive schoolhouse dynamics negatively affect student safety and even educational experiences. They also share lessons from past mistakes and identify workable, comprehensive approaches for addressing a recurrent social problem.

Glenn W. Muschert is associate professor of sociology at Miami University. **Stuart Henry** is professor of criminal justice at San Diego State University. **Nicole L. Bracy** is adjunct professor of criminal justice at San Diego State University. **Anthony A. Peguero** is assistant professor of sociology at Virginia Polytechnic Institute and State University.